Madness, Murder and Si
in the Deep

D0795383

Yonder Stands Your Orphan
BARRY HANNAH

The first novel in a decade from
'the maddest writer in the USA' (Truman Capote)

'A literary event . . . The welcome return of a brilliant writer'
New York Times

'Brilliant... Hannah lights fireworks on every page'
Boston Globe

Atlantic Books • British publication: September 2001 • £9.99

GRANTA

GRANTA 75, AUTUMN 2001
www.granta.com

EDITOR *Ian Jack*
DEPUTY EDITORS *Liz Jobey, Sophie Harrison*
US EDITOR *Kerry Fried*
EDITORIAL ASSISTANT *Fatema Ahmed*

CONTRIBUTING EDITORS *Neil Belton, Pete de Bolla, Ursula Doyle,*
Will Hobson, Gail Lynch, Blake Morrison, Andrew O'Hagan, Lucretia Stewart

ASSOCIATE PUBLISHER *Sally Lewis*
FINANCE *Geoffrey Gordon*
SALES *Frances Hollingdale*
PUBLICITY *Louise Campbell*
SUBSCRIPTIONS *John Kirkby, Darryl Wilks, Chris Bennett*
PUBLISHING ASSISTANT *Mark Williams*
ADVERTISING MANAGER *Kate Rochester*

PUBLISHER *Rea S. Hederman*

Granta, 2-3 Hanover Yard, Noel Road, London N1 8BE
Tel 020 7704 9776 Fax 020 7704 0474
e-mail for editorial: editorial@granta.com

Granta US, 1755 Broadway, 5th Floor, New York, NY 10019-3780, USA

TO SUBSCRIBE call 020 7704 0470 or e-mail subs@granta.com
A one-year subscription (four issues) costs £26.95 (UK), £34.95 (rest of Europe) and £41.95 (rest
of the world).

Printed in Italy by Legoprint.

Design: Random Design.
Front cover photographs: top: J. R. Ackerley by Howard Coster/National Portrait Gallery; middle:
Anthony Burgess by Mark Gerson; bottom: W. H. Auden by Mark Gerson
Back cover photographs: top: Norman Lewis; bottom: Theodore Roethke

ISBN 0 90 314146 9

ROYAL COURT

"The most important theatre in Europe"
New York Times

JERWOOD THEATRE DOWNSTAIRS

6 September - 6 October
REDUNDANT by Leo Butler
Supported by JERWOOD NEW PLAYWRIGHTS

1 November - 15 December
BOY GETS GIRL by Rebecca Gilman
Sponsored by AMERADA HESS
Also supported by the American Friends of the Royal Court Theatre

JERWOOD THEATRE UPSTAIRS

30 August - 22 September
THE ROYAL COURT THEATRE AND OUT OF JOINT PRESENT
SLIDING WITH SUZANNE by Judy Upton

28 September - 27 October
NIGHTINGALE AND CHASE by Zinnie Harris
Supported by JERWOOD NEW PLAYWRIGHTS

8 November - 8 December
F*ING GAMES** by Grae Cleugh
Supported by JERWOOD NEW PLAYWRIGHTS

Tel: +44 (0)20 7565 5000

BOOK ONLINE AT www.royalcourttheatre.com
BAR AND FOOD open 11am - 11pm Monday to Saturday
SLOANE SQUARE, LONDON SW1
TUBE Sloane Square on District and Circle Lines

LONDON ARTS

GRANTA 75

Brief Encounters

A cool, cruel and calculating dissection of a French affair

Marta Morazzoni
The Alphonse Courrier Affair

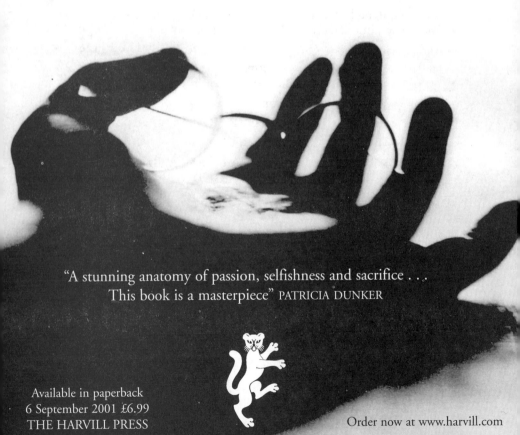

"A stunning anatomy of passion, selfishness and sacrifice . . .
This book is a masterpiece" PATRICIA DUNKER

Available in paperback
6 September 2001 £6.99
THE HARVILL PRESS

Order now at www.harvill.com

GRANTA

BRIEF ENCOUNTERS
Richard Murphy

Richard Murphy, 1968

When did I first want to write poetry? My memory is that the ambition caught me in the turmoil of adolescence, when I was learning some Shakespeare sonnets by heart at Wellington College, a boarding school founded to commemorate the Iron Duke, the victor at Waterloo, and to train boys to become army officers. The year was 1944. The Germans had started to rain their first flying bombs on England. As long as you could hear the puttering jet engines of these unpiloted 'doodlebugs', which sounded like a motorbike in the sky, you were safe. When the plane ran out of fuel, the engine would cut; the flying bomb was on its way to earth. Then you'd wait in an awesome silence, wondering when and where it would explode.

I'd fallen in unrequited love with a college athlete of my own age, who was destined for the Royal Navy. Scared of bombs, excoriated by my housemaster—a survivor of the Somme—I took refuge in the renaissance conceit that a poem, if well made, could last longer than its maker, giving life after death to himself and his loved ones in the minds of his readers. Rather than in church, I began to seek redemption through poetry. I wrote sonnets to my mother, who lived across the U-boat-patrolled Atlantic in Bermuda; to my sister Mary, who had given birth to her first child—the father was a Dunkirk hero—and lived away in the West Country; and to the inaccessible, beautiful athlete who trained on the college playing fields.

A year or so later, as a seventeen-year-old Oxford student starved of sex, I drugged myself on the idea of being a poet. I believed inspiration would descend on me like the Holy Spirit granting the poem in a vision. I would cycle on my own ten miles out of town, the roads empty of traffic, to a little medieval church where I knelt staring for hours at a mural of St Christopher, praying that the poem would enter my mind without being soiled by any effort on my part. No words came. The ecstasy of feeling on the verge of a revelation turned into a hollow lump of loneliness. Naturally I failed my first exam.

Once I went to a meeting where Stephen Spender spoke. If he read his poems I've forgotten. I remember only his big luminous eyes, and my feeling that if those were the eyes of a true poet, I must be an impostor. How could you tell if you were a born poet or not? I'd been reading the novels of Charles Williams, lent to me, one by one, by my tutor C. S. Lewis: metaphysical thrillers in which characters descended into hell or were blessed with beatific vision. I was sitting on the floor looking up at Spender, who stood with his back to the fireplace, his eyes, moist with emotion, focused on things above our heads. He looked as I imagined poets to be. Anyone could see by the dimness of my spectacled eyes, as my mother would confirm, that poetry was not my birthright. To me poetry would never come naturally, as a gift. It would have to be made.

A decade later, in 1954, I was a student again and living in a room with chocolate-brown furniture in the male section of the Collège Franco-Britannique in Paris. I was poor, obscure and miserable enough to qualify as a promising poet. I was also, again, sexually starved. I kept my spirits high and low by trying to fulfil two deviously related desires: to write poetry that might be accepted by T. S. Eliot at Faber, and to meet among strangers on the Left Bank a young soldier, sailor or gypsy who might give my poetry the passion and inspiration it lacked.

One day, with both forlorn missions in mind, I entered the vast Papeterie Joseph Gibert on the Boulevard St Michel, looking for a blank notebook to fill the deep pocket of my old Donegal tweed jacket. I wanted it to contain the scraps of verse, elusive images, dreams, desires and revelations that would otherwise be forgotten if they cropped up in bed or on the metro or during a boring seminar at the Sorbonne or in a noisy, steamy student restaurant.

Instead, I discovered and bought, from a pile of black, orange and green *cahiers*, a small notebook for mathematicians, the pages lined with little squares, bound in green boards, quite cheap. I imagined that as numbers underlie music, and a score is essential for composition, so the page might hold in its net the music of poetry, and prevent words from swimming into measureless prolixity.

As a symbol of perfection, the mesh of vertical and horizontal lines, which every word written by hand with a fountain pen would overlay, might exert day after day a subtle influence not to lie. So from the start I knew the notebook would have to be kept secret, under guard like a salmon river, in which I alone could fish in the future for poems that might be lured to the surface from the stream of my past.

But these books also became something else: my diaries of everyday encounters and events. They are the source of the following narratives.

J. R. Ackerley

My friendship with J. R. Ackerley began with his kindly worded, handwritten rejection of poems that I submitted to the *Listener* at the age of twenty-four. He got to my heart by mixing approval—'I enjoyed reading "Snow", which has much of interest and feeling in it...'—with fingering of faults—'but suffers, to my mind, from too many adjectives, especially hyphenated ones. And "pelvised", is there such a word?'—as if he were trying to help the poem, wilfully obscure, to emerge from its raw material.

No reader could have guessed that it was inspired by a single, solitary act of rolling naked in snow on a patch of level ground outside my cottage in Connemara, beside a waterfall at the foot of a mountain on the edge of a lake, where I'd gone, over Christmas 1950, from reviewing poetry for the *Spectator* in London, to try to write it myself. I was without a companion, a car, a telephone or electric light, living a mile across a moor from the nearest house.

What made me decide to strip off my clothes and go out in a bitter cold wind and lie on the snow and turn over and over was a rumour I had heard at the Choir School before the war, that the Red Dean of Canterbury, who always appeared impressively garbed in immaculate white or black or scarlet robes of office, sometimes took off all his clothes and wallowed in snow baths on the lawn of the Deanery. In the tingling flow of blood to the top of my head and the tips of my fingers, as I warmed myself at a turf fire after the burning pain of the snow all over my body, a poem began to form in my mind around the image of a boar staining the snow with peaty soil, uprooted by its tusks, as if with the blood of Adonis or Diarmuid.

Back in London, fortified by Ackerley's note, I dared to ring him up, never having spoken to him before, and ask him whether he would look at the poem again if I could manage to improve it. He agreed, and I set to work at once.

This was in February 1951, when my sister was giving me the leisure to write, while she toiled around London for a small weekly wage, trying with elegance and charm to persuade executives to place advertisements in *Queen* magazine. She let me have a room of my own in a tiny flat, where she slept on a couch in the sitting room, while her two small children of her wartime marriage shared the only other room. As our bath was in the kitchen, it was covered by a board when not in use.

My view was of a lane so narrow that when Lord Beaverbrook called to see where Mary was living, his green Rolls-Royce filled it from wall to wall. Her view from the sitting room was of huge extractor fans in a towering brick side wall of the Royal Cancer Hospital on Fulham Road. To enter or leave our rundown four-storey block, you had to step over a lazy old spaniel lying with its rotting bone on the red tiles.

The few guineas earned by my reviews contributed little to our budget, but I helped by babysitting, decorating the flat, and neither smoking nor drinking. Instead, I craved to see my name in print, especially for the first time with a poem in one of the London literary weeklies. Opening a BBC envelope addressed by Ackerley, and finding the poem in proof, was a moment of great joy.

This led to our meeting in the basement of a tavern near Victoria Station at the tail end of an evening rush hour. Ackerley's reputation as a misanthrope who lived with a dog had not prepared me for the tall, affable, ageing man who entered, wearing a navy-blue beret and casual clothes without a tie. He looked deliberately déclassé, no slave to his office, in that place and time, carrying a satchel of books and papers on one shoulder. Though his face when he was reflecting could seem grim, it glowed with warmth when he smiled or spoke.

After bringing two pints of bitter to a round table, he sat down facing me, and said, in a voice loud enough for anyone in the crowd who might have been an off-duty policeman to hear, 'I'm homosexual.' My pulse raced, and I tried not to blush.

His candour caught me between not wanting to tell a lie, and being too scared to tell the truth. It brought back the horror of being accused of a homosexual offence by a blackmailer who claimed to be a police officer in the Piccadilly Underground the previous year. I had never admitted to myself that I was queer, let alone to anybody else, and felt morally bruised by his naked honesty. So I smiled with noncommittal complicity, and raised my glass, pretending I was neither frightened nor shocked. Though alarmed, I was glad to meet a man who could freely admit to another that he was queer. But what pleased me more was that a literary editor of his importance was accepting me as a friend. As all his lovers had been working class, and mine never older than myself, our friendship involved sex only as conversation.

Over the next eight years, his fingering of faults in my poems continued to annoy me and improve my poetry, while giving it an audience that was better than it usually deserved. Sometimes he gave my poems short shrift, while inviting me to dinner, with a note like this in 1953:

Dear Richard
No I shan't take these from you & ought not to keep them longer
in case you can place them elsewhere. I look forward to seeing you
Thursday: The Shaftesbury again, at 6.45 p.m.
Joe

He rejected in 1953 my poem about Wittgenstein at Rosroe, where the philosopher tamed the birds so well that when he left they were eaten by the village cats. Ackerley thought there were 'too many birds in the poem', and 'it looks as though you are blaming the cats, who I'm sure are full of philosophical retorts'. The retort of Isaiah Berlin on reading the poem at All Souls was, 'When the great man is gone, the disciples get gobbled up, gobbled up!'

The most considerate, and honest, of his rejections, dated June 29, 1963, went like this: 'I am sorry, but I simply don't enjoy them: they seem so awkward, the assembly of words and phrases, but without poetic release. I want to like them, because I like you, but I cannot, & so I cannot publish them... Heaven bless & protect you, Joe.' Other poems written after that in Crete he found 'so cerebral & over-worked...one simply notices the overload of carefully considered adjectives...something else, and more important slips away while they are being forged... I fancy one should never notice the workmanship of a thing in its various parts; one should get it instantly as a whole.' Another poem was 'far too muscle-bound for my liking. But the *New Statesman* will like it, no doubt.'

He was more generous to my work than I was to his; and his lessons in style culminated in a detailed critique of *The Woman of the House*, before he published a much improved version in the *Listener* ahead of its broadcast on the Third Programme in 1959. Looking back, I can see that the clear style and wit of his letters taught me as much as their content.

My affection for him was sharpened by fear of his power as moralist, critic, editor and friend. His belief in the value of friendship was absolute, and extended to the animal kingdom. This meant that I had to allow his Alsatian bitch Queenie to nip my ankles as I entered his flat to dine on the top floor of Star and Garter Mansions overlooking the Thames in Putney. In checking her, his voice gave more encouragement to the dog than correction. He seemed proud of her assault, and greatly amused by my discomfiture. I hated this, and Queenie's continual barking, which he permitted on the very English moral ground of kindness to an animal. It meant that for ten or twelve years he was perversely cruel to his neighbours by allowing her to bark.

Our friendship survived and increased during my marriage, as he accepted Patricia as 'one of us', wrote her many letters, published her poems in the *Listener*, and came to stay with us in Ireland more than once. He was cross with her when she wanted a divorce, but remained in touch. In June 1966, a year before he died, he stayed at my cottage in Cleggan, County Galway. Feeling isolated by his deafness, he would sit in a deckchair on the tiny lawn, taking ticks out of the ears of a friend's sheepdog called Nero. After giving Nero a worm powder, he followed her around until he could see that she had passed all her worms.

He bought his own gin, and drank rather a lot, but never lost his courtesy, poise and intelligence. John McGahern once remarked that Joe's trouble was that he had spent most of his life dealing with people less intelligent than himself. At the *Listener* he was the servant of writers who were his inferiors, and sexually he chose working class men for his friends. 'A writer is a servant of the muse,' John added clinchingly.

Late one evening, when the long summer twilight off the ocean continued to filter into my cottage, I returned from the Pier Bar, and thought I heard Joe talking to somebody in his bedroom, with the door ajar. Then I realized he was talking to himself, and this is the gist of what he was saying:

'What a rotten thing to do! To cast the devils out of a wretched human being, and make them drive a herd of poor unfortunate pigs over a cliff to their death. I think Jesus Christ was a most unpleasant person. I am glad we never met, because I would not have liked him.'

I felt guilty about eavesdropping on my guest, so I confessed to Joe in the morning what I had heard. Exonerating me, he replied, 'That's exactly how I feel.'

Theodore Roethke

In 1960, I was living in the only hotel on the island of Inishbofin off the Galway coast and finding it hard to make ends meet. I had a boat, and to make money took tourists on trips. When I heard that the American poet Theodore Roethke was coming to Ireland, I decided to try to entice him from the literary pub life of Dublin and invite him across to the west coast. Ambition prompted me: aged fifty-two, Roethke was then at the height of his fame. I thought he might help me to find a publisher in America if he were to stay on Inishbofin for a few weeks and sail on my boat. We had never met, but I had introduced and praised three of his poems on the BBC Third Programme in 1955. I wrote on notepaper headed with a silly address that seemed to link ideas of prostitution and the Virgin Mary:

Hooker 'AVE MARIA'
INISHBOFIN nr. CLEGGAN CO. GALWAY

His reply came from France, suggesting that he and his 'one wife, aged thirty-four, part Irish' should arrive on July 25. Phone calls followed, and I sailed the *Ave Maria* alone from Inishbofin to meet them at Cleggan in the late evening.

The sky was dark with a drizzly mist, requiring me often to wipe my spectacles while controlling the tiller with my chest and arm. Preoccupied with lowering sail at precisely the moment that would allow the boat to reach the pier almost without touching it, I saw two glossy blue suitcases designed for American air travel. There was no sign of their owners. The luggage looked surreal, set down beside broken lobster pots, torn fishing nets and empty wooden Guinness barrels.

When a man and a woman emerged from where they were sheltering, I wondered if I'd done wrong in luring them from Dublin. There they were: Ted and Beatrice. A touching sadness seemed to connect her fragile elegance to his hunky dishevelment, as they stood at the top of slippery steps, unprotected from the drizzle, waiting to be transported. Her nylon stockings and dainty shoes seemed designed for cocktails at their journey's end, not cups of tea from a metal pot stewing in the ashes of a peat fire. The whiteness of her face glowed like porcelain through a veil of mist. She regarded the roughness of my boat with unconcealed disdain.

Beside her, Roethke was like a defeated old prizefighter, growing bald, groggy and fat, clumsy on his feet, wrapped in silence, which he kept for the hour it took us to reach the island. He wore a grey city suit smart enough for lunch with T. S. Eliot at the Athenaeum, but the ragged poet and his neat clothes were at loggerheads. I helped him climb down into the cabin of the *Ave Maria*, where he sat brooding, his high forehead creased with anxiety, sweating alcohol. He groaned a little now and then, hummed a tune to himself, and grunted in answer to trivial questions such as 'Are you comfortable?'

They were planning to leave for the Ring of Kerry after one or two days. I argued that they might get to know Ireland better by remaining on the island for longer. More persuasive was the copious hospitality of the island's hotelier, Margaret Day, mother of five, and also Inishbofin's midwife and district nurse. Her hotel was an old ramshackle two-storey building with ten rooms, all facing the inner harbour. The view of stone and water, grass and rocks, fishing boats and rotting hulks, shore birds, gulls and an occasional heron, in weather that was always getting worse, had the makings of an inspired poem by Roethke. The island was his place before I placed him on the island.

Margaret remembered later, 'It was pitch-dark when Richard brought in this great big heavy man, and he had a limp. It took him ten minutes to get upstairs. I wondered what Richard had inflicted on me now, but I persuaded him to stay for a month or two.'

Our rooms were divided by narrow partitions that allowed

pillow talk to be overheard. Theirs at the end of the upstairs corridor overlooking the inner harbour was two doors from mine. The hotel was still furnished with iron and brass-knobbed bedsteads, horsehair mattresses, hand-woven blankets smelling of mountainy sheep, and other relics of a Victorian landlord who had left everything behind including a grand piano which had not been tuned since his departure in 1922.

Another attraction for Roethke was the island's one and only pub, on the ground floor of a dilapidated building fifty yards from the hotel, next to a roofless ruin that served as a toilet. Dark mildewed walls imprisoned in a sense of damnation its entirely male customers, who never took off their caps and overcoats as they sat in a dank odour of stout, tobacco and turf smoke. The poet appeared in their midst as a big-mouthed Yank flush with dollars and bravado. Silent on the boat, he ranted in the bar. It was run by Margaret's husband Miko, a handsome tall witty man who found Roethke a godsend in dispelling the boredom of listening to the same old men of the sea repeating their stories night after night.

Meanwhile, the weather being fine and the sea calm, I continued to take tourists from hotels on the mainland sailing and fishing on the *Ave Maria*. Often I landed them on the island for a lobster or crayfish lunch at Margaret's. Some nights I slept on the boat at the quay in Cleggan, to be ready for more tourists the next day. One such night, after two or three pints in the Pier Bar, I was involved in a row that drew an astonishing reaction from Roethke when he heard the story.

A small trawler that fished out of Cleggan that summer was owned by an islander who wanted no crew but his son. He had red hair and a fiery temper. Only his son dared go near him when he was drunk, to try to stop him punching the mast, and to carry him below to bed.

Raising an argument with me, knowing that my Galway hooker and her passengers were fully covered by insurance, he said in a voice that everyone could hear: 'No man would insure a boat, Murphy, unless he meant to sink her!'

He kept provoking me, and when I asked him to stop, he swung back his fists, and seemed about to hit me in the face. Foolishly I pulled out a yachting knife, not to attack him, but to show I could defend myself. Matthew, the old publican, whose back was curved like the bows of a curragh upturned on a beach, intervened at once, mercifully taking the knife from my hand.

When I told Roethke in Miko's at noon the next day that I had been provoked into drawing a knife on a man who was about to strike me, he got wildly excited, and began to tremble with anger on my behalf. There and then he insisted on giving me a lesson about knives he had learned from a hood in a Chicago speakeasy during Prohibition.

'How did you hold the knife?' he began. 'Show me!'

I took it out, opened the long blade, and held the hilt against my chest.

'No good! He could have killed you if that's how you held it. Let me show you how to fight with a knife! Look!'

He seized the knife, made of stainless steel, and examined it with the disdain of someone who had used better knives in places where his life had hung on their quality. Then he said:

'You gotta have two of these. First, you hold one in your mouth, with the sharp side out, and you clench your teeth on the blade, like this'—he demonstrated, with a savage grunt that rumbled from the pit of his bloated belly—'while the other,' he said, taking the knife from his mouth and lowering it to his groin, 'you hold down low, low, low like this, and then you rip up and up till his guts are wide open and spill on the ground.'

Once I saw him coming from the pub to our table at the window of the dining room, carrying a pint of Guinness in one unsteady hand, and a large notebook in the other. As soon as he sat down, he ordered a bottle of wine. Now and then as we spoke he would make a few notes, disconcerting me. What had we said that was worth recording, and why was I not recording it myself, instead of wasting my energy in action on a boat and unrecorded chatter with tourists and fishermen? I admired his devotion to his craft, even in his cups. It was my first encounter with a poet who made a profession of teaching students to write poetry, in the optimistic American belief that this was possible. He sipped alternately the wine and the stout. When these were finished he took a noggin of Irish from a pocket of his coat, and put it to his lips. I never saw him collapse.

But more than for alcohol he thirsted for praise. He envied the wealth as well as the poetic fame of Wallace Stevens. When I mentioned a poem by Robert Lowell favourably, he banged the counter in the pub with two fists and snarled, 'Why are you always praising Lowell? I'm as mad as he is!' Then he roared with laughter, making me feel that perhaps he was deploying madness, which caused him terrible suffering when he plunged from a manic high into deep depression, as part of a grand strategy to win fame as the greatest poet on earth—America's answer to William Blake. He gave me an offprint of the poem he was proudest of having written about his madness, called *In a Dark Time*. Insanity was the stinking wound that went with his talent. In *Life Studies* (1959) Lowell had obliquely praised himself as 'nobly mad' and as a drunkard who 'outdrank the Rahvs'. Roethke acted as if the famous lines of Theseus in *A Midsummer Night's Dream*:

The lunatic, the lover and the poet
Are of imagination all compact,

licensed him to be what his wife once called 'a nut, a drunk and a lecher', because he could write poetry. After keeping her awake half the night with brutal raving, he would redeem himself by writing at dawn a contrite lyric celebrating her beauty and his love. The woman he worshipped as 'My lizard, my lively writher' managed to protect herself from his tirades with the cool detachment she had gained as a model in New York.

Whether his mania drove him to drink or drink aggravated his mania, both got worse after eight of my family from England and Rhodesia arrived to stay in the hotel in mid-August, followed by an ardently republican priest called Mairtin Lang, and the actor John Molloy. Molloy gave what my father described in his diary as 'a brilliant series of impersonations ending with a Picasso and an El Greco', after which Roethke went around collecting for the actor with a hat.

Roethke got on well with the priest, whose recollections I recorded in Galway in 1992. 'He used to come in to breakfast each morning, and he'd sit opposite me, and he'd throw a manuscript across the table to me, and he'd say, "Gee, Father, you be my Roman Catholic censor," and it was a poem he'd have written the night before under the moon, he was very much in love with this woman, Beatrice. So I'd read the poem, and I'd say, "There's nothing against faith and morals in that."'

Sunday, August 21, 1960, was a miserably wet day in the priest's memory. There was an entertainment followed by a dance in the hall late that night, which my parents and I didn't attend, but my sister Mary and her husband Gerald Cookson went with her two children, John, aged sixteen, and Grania, thirteen. When the fiddle and piano accordion struck up for the dance, according to the priest, Roethke 'came in and started dancing around the hall on his own...he was the first on the floor'. Later, Father Lang said a drunk fisherman approached Grania, and demanded that she go dancing, which she refused. Then there was a scuffle, in which Mary thought the man was going to murder Gerry, but instead he fell on the floor on his back, and was carried out by Father Lang and the Bofin priest.

At six o'clock the next morning, my father, in swimming togs and bare feet, stepped out of the hotel to dive off the quay into the harbour, as he and his brother in their teens used to dive off a rock into the sea near Clifden before breakfast at the Rectory. He was not expecting to meet a soul at that hour, when Roethke beckoned to him across the lawn in front of the hotel, and drawing a half pint of whiskey from a pocket of his dressing gown, said in a husky conspiratorial whisper: 'Hey! Sir William! Care for a snifter?' My father thanked him, but refused. In his classical opinion, Roethke's trouble came from lack of moderation.

An hour later Margaret saw him sitting on the sea wall in the garden with a glass of wine in his hand. The morning was cool, and she urged him to come into the kitchen and warm up. He followed her inside, and while she was making porridge, he came up behind her, put his right arm around her neck, and held a carving knife with a nine-inch blade pointed at her heart, saying, 'If that man had touched Richard Murphy or any of his relations last night in the hall, I'd have sunk this knife to the heart in him.'

My father wrote in his diary, 'Mr Theodore Roethke the poet in a frenzy today!' And my mother asked Beatrice, 'Don't you think it's time you did something about your husband?' So Beatrice sent for the doctor, who signed a certificate of insanity committing him as a voluntary patient to the County Mental Hospital at Ballinasloe, halfway across Ireland. But we were weatherbound on the island. No boat could leave the harbour until the sea calmed down the following day.

When Beatrice was packing, Ted wandered into my room, trembling and hesitant, wanting to borrow some books, carrying a Harvard book bag. Naturally he chose the greatest—Wordsworth, Hardy and Yeats. He had just pulled the cord that closed the bag on their collected poems when Beatrice came in to see what he was doing. She opened the bag, looked inside, and said with the venom of revenge, 'You won't need those where you're going.'

Roethke was in tears as he stumbled down the slippery pebbled shore, past the anchor of an Armada galleon dredged up in a trawl, to the wooden punt that was waiting with a man to row him out to the mailboat on its harbour moorings; a poet on his way to an asylum escorted by a priest. It was the saddest sight of my years at Inishbofin.

Margaret Day remembered 'the extreme peace in Bofin after he'd gone'.

As Roethke had been certified, the law in Ireland required that he be brought to the asylum by the police. But when the boat reached Cleggan, according to Father Lang, Beatrice was worried.

'She said, "He'll go round the bend entirely if the police arrive," and she told me what happened in the Waldorf Astoria Hotel in New York, the time he was presented with his Pulitzer Prize for poetry. He had got a turn, and a policeman was sent for, two policemen arrived, and he took the two of them up, one in either arm, and carried them to the door and threw them out. They had to send for reinforcements. So she says, "Have you a car there?" "Well," I said, "I have a small car, a Volkswagen Beetle." "Will you bring us to Ballinasloe?" she says. "Certainly," I said. I was an awful chancer really, looking back on it, I took a big chance...

'So we put him into the back of my Volkswagen Beetle, sitting across the seat, and his feet were up against the window. He was a tall man, and I was afraid he'd push the window out with his feet, but fortunately the window stood. Beatrice gave him a bottle of wine, red wine, to soothe him. Anyway, as we were pulling out of the quayside, just going up the hill from the quayside, the squad car comes down, and I just wave to the guards and continue on the journey.' Priests in Ireland in 1960 could exercise spiritual—and other—authority over the police.

About six weeks later he returned, without Beatrice. 'He was as quiet as could be,' according to Margaret. All my relations had gone, and my boat was laid up for the winter. Roethke and I were the only visitors on the island, with enough time, space and loneliness to observe, remember and write. He was drinking less and writing more. He praised the treatment at Ballinasloe as better than his previous experience at the most expensive private clinics in America. His psychiatrist had allowed him to wander into the town and drink in a pub frequented by male nurses who kept him out of harm.

His great ambition at this time was to acquire an Irish reputation, rivalling Yeats. I suggested that he should offer his next collection of poems to the Dolmen Press, and I spoke to Liam Miller, who seemed to welcome the idea. Roethke happily agreed, but Miller vacilated and in the end rejected two books that were later published by Doubleday. One of these contained 'nonsense' poems which Roethke performed for the children in Bofin. Margaret told me, 'When he read his poems to the kids in the school, they were like dormice...they were thrilled listening to him.'

Without Beatrice, he needed me to type his new poems for mailing to the *New Yorker* and other magazines. One had only six short lines, five of them quoting 'what they say on the quay'. He was disheartened by my failure to perceive the value of this trinket, and cheered himself up by saying, 'You're a mean grouch, Murphy, but what do I care? The *Ladies' Home Journal* will love it, and pay me ten dollars a line.'

When I had finished typing 'The Shy Man', inspired by Beatrice on Bofin, he asked: 'Don't you think I've got Yeats licked?' I was embarrassed, and withheld the praise he may have needed to avoid depression. Pointing to the line 'And I lie here thinking in bleak Bofin town', I said there was no town in Bofin, and he argued that I was being pedantic. 'Town' had no function in the poem except to rhyme with 'down'.

When I asked him for introductions in America, he gave me addresses of people to whom I could write, mentioning his name. It helped in getting a poem accepted by the *Yale Review*, and polite letters of rejection from Howard Moss at the *New Yorker*, always asking to see more, but crushing my ambition. To Yale I sent a Cretan poem that Roethke had redeemed from opaque obscurity with good workshop advice one afternoon. He read the poem aloud, praising passages that he liked, exposing the hollowness of turgid, vague sonorities.

As the nights grew longer and darker, with storms cutting off the island for several gloomy days, the longing came upon him to feel celebrated by talking to a celebrity. One evening he asked me to put through a call to Dame Edith Sitwell, once we had found her number through Directory Enquiries.

To place a call from Inishbofin in 1960, you had to lift the receiver off a box on the wall in the lobby of the hotel, where everyone in the building could hear what you were saying, then twist a handle on the box, and wait a few minutes, and twist it again, and wait another few minutes, until an old woman, taking her time, clicked a switch and said 'Number, please!' in a faraway voice that sounded a little vexed at being disturbed out of a fireside reverie. Then you had to hang up and wait an hour or two until the call was connected. Having gone out in the slanting rain to the pub to beg Miko to spare a lot of coins from his till, you had to be ready to insert these in the box when told to do so, and press button A before you could speak, and shout in order to be heard.

At the end of all this we learned that her number was ex-directory. So he gave me the number of Princess Caetani in Rome, an American married to an Italian prince. She had published many of his poems in *Botteghe Oscure*, and paid him well. Eventually he spoke to the Princess, or rather shouted so that she could hear his voice above the maddening interference on the line. At least he was connected to an old friend and admirer.

One evening he showed all of us in the pub a sheaf of Seattle newspaper cuttings about the discovery of a beautiful Irish island by the Pulitzer Prize-winning poet, Theodore Roethke, who was writing poems there. He had supplied the news himself from what he called 'the Bughouse', the mental hospital, which he kept out of the story. Treatment had not curbed his mania for self-promotion.

We parted at the end of a journey in a hired van from Cleggan to Galway. I was catching a train to Dublin, and he was going to stay with John Huston's beautiful young wife, who was living alone at St Cleran's, the Hustons' big house in east Galway, while her husband was filming abroad. Meeting Ricki Huston was a prize he refused to share. She was to meet him at the Great Southern Hotel next to the railway station. Before I'd even got out of the van, he'd said goodbye, giving me a dismissive hug, to make sure I wouldn't linger in his company and spoil his meeting with Ricki.

Three years after this he died of a heart attack in a swimming pool on an island in Puget Sound. Robert Lowell concluded that 'Roethke fevered to be the best poet, and perhaps strained for the gift.' Lowell fevered as much, but his gift was greater. Roethke's ambition seemed deplorable because he displayed it so stridently. Without ambition I might never have written poetry, but many years later I came across a sentence by Henri Michaux that left me chastened and subdued: 'The mere ambition to write a poem is enough to kill it.'

W. H. Auden

Barbara Epstein, my editor at the *New York Review of Books*, gave me dinner at her apartment in New York on November 22, 1975. The only other guest was W. H. Auden. It was several years since I had met him in Stratford-upon-Avon, where his poetry reading impressed me because he knew his poems by heart. When his memory lapsed in the middle of a longish poem, he didn't fuss and fumble for the book, but closed his eyes and raised his face up to heaven as if he were asking God to remind him of what he had wanted to say when writing the poem. Then, recovering his speech, he seemed to be inspired with thoughts he was just now putting into words. It made the poem all the more interesting to hear.

Barbara told me that once when he was coming to dine, he got out of the elevator on the wrong floor, rang the bell, was admitted by a couple, who did not protest when he came in, and, seating himself in an armchair, asked for a vodka martini. With this in hand, he kept up a monologue that amazed and silenced the couple until his glass was empty. Then noticing the rather strange absence of the Epsteins, Auden asked where they were. 'Barbara and Jason live in the apartment above us,' he was told.

Auden was there when I arrived. He was sixty-four years old, looking rather scruffy and neglected, slouching on a Chesterfield, his hair 'all over the place', his nails dirty, slippers for shoes. Conversation with him was daunting, because he interrupted everything Barbara or I said. He seemed to have made up his brilliant mind about every possible topic, and condensed his conclusions into unanswerable aphorisms. The great crusted oyster of his mouth would open, an artificial pearl of polished thought would pop out, and the mouth would clam shut again. The voice was that of an English prep school swot who could answer every question, pronouncing the letter r with a hint of the sound of a w.

While Barbara was cooking the dinner, I tried to coax him down off the platform from which he seemed to be addressing an anonymous representative of an audience whom he had no wish to meet socially. So I mentioned J. R. Ackerley, knowing that Auden had liked him enough to invite him to stay in Ischia. I plunged into a topic that was very close to Joe's heart, hoping to touch Auden's. I told him that when Joe came back from a visit to Athens in the mid-Fifties, where he was a guest of the young novelist Francis King, a charming epicurean host, he told me he was shocked at being given a choice of a sailor, airman or royal guardsman for dinner in a taverna night after night. The promiscuity of his host seemed immoral. I suggested to Joe that age had altered his judgement. Hadn't he pursued guardsmen and sailors when he was young enough to enjoy the pursuit?

'You don't seem to understand,' Joe corrected me, 'I was never promiscuous: I was always looking for an ideal friend.' Then Auden opened his mouth and out popped this pearl: 'All promiscuity is a search for the ideal friend.'

During dinner he said, 'I hope God will let me die at seventy. I don't want to live longer than my natural span.' He wanted all his letters burned at his death, as he burned without reading his father's letters when he died; and he wanted his friends to burn his letters to them; he was asking for this in his will. By destroying all his papers, he hoped to make it impossible for anyone to write his life. Like the doctors of long ago, whose medical discoveries were kept secret, he expected his secrets to die with him.

In spite of his face's celebrated corrugations of age, he looked strong. He said he was disturbed by not being able to communicate with the students who attended his seminars at Columbia. They had no knowledge of the past, or of form, and no interest in either, which made it impossible for them to understand what poetry, his kind of poetry, was about. Barbara had once told me that she felt he wasn't aware of her as a person, and probably gave his students the same feeling. He had refused to give the Charles Eliot Norton lectures at Harvard, for which he was offered $29,000, on the grounds that he had nothing to say. 'Of course I could have dug something up that I've said before, but that would be bad.' Barbara had told me that he really needed the money.

How did we get on to the subject of witches? 'My mother-in-law was a witch,' he said, referring to the mother of Erika Mann, Thomas Mann's daughter, whom Auden had married in 1935, purely to make her a British subject. Then he said, 'And Louis's first wife is a witch,' referring to MacNeice. 'I'll drink a bottle of champagne the day I hear she's dead.' He was glad that Louis in his last years had found in Mary Wimbush 'the first non-violent woman in his life.' Barbara said she thought my mother was a witch, adding that she liked witches and liked my mother. I agreed that my mother had the power of bewitching people.

Auden also talked of Vietnam, and other politics. He thought 'we' must take over the north of Ireland. Of the carnage in East Pakistan, soon to become Bangladesh, he remarked: 'I ought not to say this, but I'm sure it would never have happened if Britain had still been ruling India. The Greeks,' he continued, 'were better off under the Turks, as they can never govern themselves. They alternate between anarchy and despotism, you've only to read Thucydides.'

Then he denounced the camera as one of the two most abominable inventions—the internal combustion engine was the other—on the ground that it told lies, and reduced human suffering, as in Auschwitz or Hiroshima, to a cheap thrill. At twenty past nine he got up from the table, put on purple shades, and we walked with him to a taxi. On the way he informed us that he always made sure he had twenty dollars to satisfy a mugger, and so avoid being murdered. But he had not allowed for inflation since the day he decided ten or fifteen years ago that twenty dollars would be enough to save his life. His opinions, once formed, became rigid.

After he'd gone, Barbara mentioned that his friend, Chester Kallman, had returned to New York this winter for the first time in many years since he'd been arrested by a detective acting as an agent provocateur. Chester invited all his friends to a party at Auden's apartment in Greenwich Village, and at half past eight, when the party was in full swing, Auden went round saying to the guests, 'I'm afraid you'll have to go now because it's my bedtime.'

Barbara said that before I arrived at her apartment she had told Auden that Edmund Wilson, an old friend whom they both admired, was dying at his house on Cape Cod, and had asked about him. Barbara was struck by the stoicism of Auden's answer: 'He should die.'

□

cheltenham festival of
literature

12-21 OCTOBER 2001

In the year of a General Election, and the centenary of Marconi's first broadcast across the Atlantic, the Festival pulls no punches investigating ideas of power and literature. Over two hundred events are set to showcase the best in current writing, as poets, novelists and biographers descend upon Cheltenham for a ten-day literary feast.

For younger readers the **Book It!** programme offers activities and storytelling for children of all ages. Venues across the town will be echoing to the sound of performing poets and spirited storytellers, appearing in distinctive and unusual venues as part of the **Voices Off** programme. And there are more opportunities than ever to hone your creative writing and book craft skills in our expanded series of **Write Away** workshops.

Write to: **Festival Box Office, Town Hall, Imperial Square, Cheltenham GL50 1QA.**

24-hour Brochure Hotline **01242 237377**

Box Office Hotline **01242 227979**

www.cheltenhamfestivals.co.uk

Media Sponsor ✦ THE INDEPENDENT

Douglas Coupland

Kate Atkinson

Paddy Ashdown

Joan Plowright

Irvine Welsh

Iain Sinclair

Ruth Rendell

V S Naipaul

Benjamin Zephaniah

U A Fanthorpe

Roy Hattersley

Louis de Bernières

Sebastian Faulks

Fay Weldon

George Alagiah

Martin Amis

Mary Warnock

Roy Jenkins

are just some of the three hundred writers appearing at this year's Literature Festival.

GRANTA

DO I OWE YOU SOMETHING?

Michael Mewshaw

Anthony Burgess, 1980   MARK GERSON

Do I Owe You Something?

In the fall of 1971, Rome enjoyed an unbroken skein of bright crisp mornings and balmy afternoons that stretched on into November. During days when the wind blew out of the south, the air was heavy with African heat and crackling with static electricity. Housewives watered down the cobblestones in front of their houses, flung carpets over their window sills and walloped away the sand of the Sahara.

We were Americans and new to the city. The smell of fall in Italy seemed much the same as in America—roasting chestnuts, wood smoke and burning leaves. But there was also the aroma of spices, pizza crust and sizzling meat as Romans rushed to eat a last meal alfresco. At a restaurant on the Piazza del Popolo I saw a party of eight pass around a truffle the size of a man's fist. Each diner sniffed it, eyes shut in ecstasy, then handed it to the waiter and had him shave microscopic slices on to the pasta.

Smelling, touching, looking, tasting—during that season everybody appeared to be storing up sensations as a defence against the catastrophe they recognized was coming. Finally the weather broke with the abrupt emphasis of a slamming door and cold rain soaked the city. If, as Eleanor Clark has written, the streets are the real home of Romans, then during those first wet, winter days the town had the haunted look of a house abandoned. Weeds sprouted in the mortar between bricks, white marble slabs became veined with green moss, and the metal flanges that bolted ancient buildings together bled rust. As a vast loneliness settled over the piazzas, nothing looked more forlorn than those empty cafes outside of which tables and chairs were stacked haphazardly like flotsam washed up by high tide.

When the sun reappeared, it was too feeble to provide warmth, too wan to burnish the city's colours. My wife Linda and I had begun packing for a trip to Israel when Albert Erskine forwarded a letter from Anthony Burgess. Having read the galleys of my second novel, *Waking Slow*, Burgess wrote: 'A poignant piece of invention... It's essentially a true picture of America today, and its talent is very formidable. Such solid construction, such fluency, such totally credible characterization make this a very memorable novel.'

Since Burgess had written from Rome—his address and phone number were at the top of the page—my editor suggested I thank him in person.

Michael Mewshaw

At this remove in time it may be difficult to remember the multifaceted role Anthony Burgess once played in the cultural world on both sides of the Atlantic. A tax exile from England, he raced around the globe, touching down in the Far East, on the island of Malta and at various American colleges, all the while bringing out novels, biographies, books of criticism, film scripts, plays and libretti. He had kick-started his career, according to legend, when doctors informed him he was dying of a brain tumour. To build a financial cushion for his wife's imminent widowhood, he wrote four novels in the space of a year.

When predictions of his death proved to be decades premature, Burgess continued working at the same breakneck pace. He taught, reviewed books and tossed off lively copy for newspapers; he appeared on TV talk shows as a commentator on a polymathic range of subjects; he played the piano and sang; wrote musical scores and operas; he was reputed to have acquired fluency in a dozen languages. He described his best known novel, *A Clockwork Orange*, published in 1962, as partly a philosophical examination of free will, partly a Russian lesson. Since his cast of delinquent characters spoke an argot loosely derived from Russian, Burgess promised that readers would finish the book having learned, if nothing else, several hundred words of the language. Subsequently, in a film script for *The Quest for Fire*, he invented an entire vocabulary of grunts and groans and crude locutions for Neanderthals. Then, after adapting the Bible for a TV miniseries called *Jesus of Nazareth*, he translated the poetry of Giuseppe Gioachino Belli, rendering the spectacularly obscene Italian dialect into demotic English.

With so many more interesting and profitable ways to occupy himself, Burgess hardly seemed the sort to bother blurbing books. But he had become the Blurb King, and as new novelists charged out of the starting blocks, he read them all and took the time to say something nice about each. Some cynics groused that he was simply promoting himself by attaching his name like a franchise logo to every book. But while it was doubtful how many copies his endorsement sold, any author who didn't get a quote from Anthony Burgess had to suspect that he was starting off with two strikes against him.

So I was relieved, and called to thank him. His wife answered the phone. Not the wife whose widowhood he had worried about and rushed to provide for. That wife had died long ago, and Burgess married an Italian translator named Liana. Speaking flavourful English, Liana asked if I was a friend to Anthony. And could I come right over? Some badness had happened and she needed help.

'I'm not a friend. Mr Burgess wrote kindly about my new novel and I wanted him to know I'm grateful.'

'But if he read your book, you must be friends. Come quick.' Though her voice throbbed with urgency, I had already lived long enough in Rome to realize that I might be mistaken. Many Italians had a histrionic style that charged even commonplace exchanges of information with high drama.

'I don't want to interrupt Mr Burgess's work,' I said.

'Anthony is not here. He is in Mini-soda, in Mini-apples making an opera.'

'Please tell him thanks the next time you speak to him.'

'But he would want you to come today, this minute,' she declared. 'I have been *sciapatta*—robbed in the street. Two boys on a motorbike stole my handbag. They took my money, my cards, my keys, everything! I am obliged to change the locks on the apartment, but I can't get to the locksmith because I have a baby and the *sciapattori* might break in while I am gone. *Per piacere*, help me.'

Why she couldn't call the locksmith to her apartment or leave her baby with a neighbour, Liana didn't say and I didn't ask. Together Linda and I hurried across the Tiber to Trastevere. Guidebooks referred to the area as a workers' quarter, a rough and tumble neighbourhood where authentic Romans lived. In fact it contained rows of boutiques that specialized in scented candles, hand-made jewellery, cowboy boots and pirated blue jeans. One barbershop hung out a sign advertising Hippy Hairstyles. Amid the folkloric trattorias and loud discos something called a Brazilian supper club had opened for business.

The Burgesses' apartment was regally located on Piazza Santa Cecilia in a restored building of high-ceilinged rooms. In the front hall, in a position of prominence, stood what appeared to be a marble bust of a Roman emperor. On closer inspection, it proved to be a bust of Anthony Burgess, his Hibernian head crowned by curls as artfully sculpted as acanthus leaves. To my eyes, Anthony's hair in life never looked any realer than those stone tresses. Worn long and combed over a bald spot, his hair sometimes resembled a raccoon, sometimes a carelessly flung frisbee, sometimes a straw hat on a horse with the brim drooping over its eyes.

By contrast, Liana, although frothing with worry, had not a single strand of her coiffure out of place. She wore hip-hugging slacks and knee-high boots. Fulminating about Rome, its filth, its crime, its corruption, she herded us into the kitchen to meet the 'baby' who turned out to be a boy of six or seven. Unlike his mother, who spoke English with a Sicilian accent, and his father, who had the plummy voice of a BBC newsreader, Andrea talked in the jaunty tones of a Cockney street urchin.

Barely pausing for introductions, Liana made for the door and promised that she wouldn't be gone long. 'Just a few minutes. There is food to eat, mineral water for drinking. Andrea is sometimes hungry. You too maybe.' She stopped at the door, drew a deep breath and struggled to get a grip on herself. 'This all makes me so fastidious,' she shouted, then scurried out.

'Fastidious?' I looked blankly at my wife.

'She means bothered, flustered. Bugged.'

It shouldn't have puzzled me that the word's Italian connotation was the opposite of its English meaning. This was, after all, a country where a popular cigarette bore the brand name of Stop, apparently on the assumption that smokers would see it and think, Go!

With his mother away, Andrea ran around the kitchen, climbing up on the table, jumping off chairs, sitting on the drainboard beside the sink and playing with the taps. There was something too excitable about the boy. Or so it seemed to us. But then that was back before we had children and other people's kids all seemed peculiar. Linda did her best, telling him stories, asking him his favourite movies, favourite colours and flavours and singers. Andrea mocked her questions. 'I'm bored,' he announced.

Soon we were all bored. An hour limped by, and then another. Where was the locksmith? Liana could have had the whole door replaced by now. When Andrea complained that he was hungry, Linda asked what he'd like to eat, and the little guy canted his head and gave her a leer. 'How about your bum?'

'That's not nice,' I said.

'Oh, isn't it?' he taunted me. 'Have you tried it?'

Linda fixed sandwiches of prosciutto and mozzarella. Andrea gobbled his down and then grabbed mine and bit off half. When he said he was going to his room, our hearts soared. But minutes later he bounded back into the kitchen dressed in a martial arts tunic. Flailing his tiny fists, kicking his feet, he accentuated each lunge with an ear-piercing, oriental cry.

'It's time for karate,' he said.

'Why don't you go practise in your room?' Linda suggested.

'No, it's time for my class. The *palestra* is across the piazza.'

'Your mother will take you when she gets back.'

'That'll be too late.'

'She'll be home in a few minutes.'

'No, she won't,' Andrea squawked. 'You're going to make me miss it. The maestro will be mad.' He began punching the air, screaming and kicking.

'Take him,' I told Linda. 'Take him before I start kicking him back. I'll stay and guard the house.'

'What if his mother comes?'

'What if she doesn't? That's what worries me.'

'If she shows up,' Linda said, 'come and get me right away.'

I swore I would.

'You don't suppose this is what it's like to have kids?' she whispered.

'Of course not. He's upset that his mother had her purse snatched.'

But when Linda left with little Kung Fu, I surrendered to the suspicion that this was exactly what it meant to be a parent. It meant being desperate to escape, desperate to the point of parking your kid with anybody naive enough to buy your story.

By now it was late afternoon and the December light was failing. More than five hours had passed since Liana left for the locksmith's. When Linda returned with Andrea from karate practice, the boy continued to punch and kick and bellow. He was thirsty. When Linda poured him a glass of milk, he gulped it down and wiped his mouth on her sweater.

And now he was once again demanding food. We fixed him dinner. As for our own, we were due to join friends at a restaurant. I called and pushed back the reservation. Then I phoned our friends and confessed I couldn't guess when we would get away from the Burgess apartment. At this rate, we might have to spend the night.

Three more hours went by before Liana breezed in. She offered no apology and no explanation beyond a repeated litany of laments about Rome, its inefficiency, the insanity of the narrow streets clotted with cars, the sloth of bureaucrats, the Byzantine closing hours. 'It all makes me so fastidious,' she said. 'Now, if you don't mind, I am too tired to entertain tonight. When Anthony returns, we will invite you for dinner. I must rest and you must go.'

We made for the door without a goodbye to Andrea or a backward glance at Burgess's imperial bust.

The following spring, we were house-sitting a villa eight miles from Cannes when the annual film festival took place. Among the movies that year, none generated more controversy than Stanley Kubrick's production of *A Clockwork Orange*. Early reviews raved about its visual excitement, Malcolm McDowell's wonderful performance as a music-loving sociopath, and the black comedy of the choreographed scene of rape and savage assault, but a second round of articles called the film an incitement to violence and accused Kubrick of exploiting a fine novel for commercial purposes.

Then Burgess chimed in, adding intellectual weight to the argument that his literate meditation on good and evil and free will had been trivialized. What's more, he felt ripped off. Kubrick had bought the film rights cheaply years ago, when Burgess was strapped for cash and eagerly accepted a pittance as full payment.

To capitalize on the publicity, Penguin rushed a paperback of *A Clockwork Orange* into print and lined up a series of interviews and TV appearances for the affronted author. During the Cannes Film Festival, Burgess called a press conference at the Carlton Hotel. Linda and I decided to attend, and if the opportunity presented itself, thank him in person for his blurb and enquire whether new locks had been installed yet at his apartment.

The event attracted several hundred reporters and photographers.

Despite a dishevelled suit and dishevelled hair—today it appeared that a pair of lobster claws lay draped across his forehead—Burgess was eloquent in his defence of the primacy of fiction, convincing in his Jesuitical exegesis of the necessary correlation between free will and salvation, and puckish in his comments about the absurdity of a multimillion-dollar screen version of his book. Then, lighting a cigar, he opened the floor for questions.

As at all film festival press conferences, there were professionals on hand to translate the proceedings. But Burgess, the eminent polyglot, assured them their expertise wouldn't be required except in the extraordinary circumstance that a Magyar or Mayan wished to speak to him.

To the audience's embarrassment, however, Burgess had trouble with French and performed no better in Italian and Spanish. Not only did he misconstrue the questions, he couldn't string together coherent answers. Perhaps he was nervous, perhaps hard of hearing, but as his famous fluency deserted him, reporters began to grumble.

An obsequious moderator suggested that translators might save time and allow Anthony to respond to more questions. But Burgess wouldn't hear of it, even though several people were already on the way to the door. The moderator was about to impose a translator on Burgess whether he wanted one or not, when a woman sprang to her feet, clambered on top of a chair, and shouted, 'Let him speak! Let him speak! Why must there be censorship? Why are you afraid to hear what he has to say?'

Anthony alone appeared unperturbed by this outburst. Puffing the cigar and patting the lobster-claw curls on his forehead, he stood impassively at the microphone while photographers whirled around and snapped shots of the distraught woman. Her reaction to the flashbulbs was to crouch down on the chair and pull her coat-tails over her head. But we had recognized her: Liana.

Burgess murmured into the mike that if it would expedite matters, he would be happy to have a translator. After that, the Q and A proceeded smoothly, and once the press extracted the quotes it came for, the moderator announced that copies of *A Clockwork Orange* were on sale. Mr Burgess had graciously agreed to sign books for anybody who cared to line up.

Linda had had enough and left. I suspect she meant to put distance between Liana and herself. But I stayed and got in line, and when my turn came, I introduced myself to Burgess and told him how much I appreciated his blurb for *Waking Slow*.

At the mention of my name and novel, a dim flicker of recognition focused his close-set eyes. 'Why yes, what a pleasure to meet you.' He shook my hand. 'Refresh my memory. Do I owe you something? A letter? A recommendation? Money?'

I swore the debt was all mine. Linda and I had spent a delightful eight hours in Rome getting acquainted with his son Andrea.

'Yes, yes, Liana said you were a godsend. And your marvellous novel, is it out now? Is it doing well?'

I confessed that three months after publication, it was about to be remaindered.

Anthony scowled. 'Terrible business, publishing. I'd like to switch to music. Writing songs and musical comedies and operas, that's the way to make money. Here, let me sign that.'

On the inside cover of my copy of his novel, he scrawled his name, then sketched a line drawing of a hybrid orange with a clock face and numerals and bolts and springs flying off it. 'As soon as I look after these other good people, Michael, why don't you and I go down to the terrace and have a deserved drink.'

I stepped aside and waited. The next person in line didn't have a book to be signed, but he had a reporter's spiral notepad. After talking to Burgess for a minute or two, he moved over beside me. Sun-pinkened, he wore white socks under open-toed sandals. 'Are you a friend of Anthony's?' he asked.

'Just met him,' I admitted.

'He talked to you for a long time. He must be a very generous man, don't you think?' He had an accent that might have been Scottish or Welsh.

I agreed that Burgess was generous.

'He promised me an interview. He told me you're a writer too and invited me to have a drink on the terrace with you.'

Although disappointed that I wouldn't have Burgess to myself, I smiled and said, 'Great.'

'I see you and Nigel have become friends,' Anthony said once he finished signing paperbacks. 'Michael has just published a smashing novel,' he told Nigel.

'Brilliant! I'll look for it on the best-seller list.'

'I expect you're in Cannes to explore the film possibilities,' Burgess said as we made our way on to the terrace. 'Your writing is so visual, Michael, your dialogue so spot on, they should let you have a crack at the script.'

'So you've got a movie deal?' Nigel said to me.

'Nothing solid. Just a couple of lukewarm nibbles.' Even this equivocation was an absolute lie. To date, *Waking Slow* had prompted no enthusiasm, in fact no interest at all, from Hollywood.

'You're too modest,' Burgess said. 'Michael's novel is set in Los Angeles. That automatically gives it a leg-up. Some studio will grab it.'

Seated on wire-harp chairs far from the power tables overlooking La Croisette, the three of us must have seemed a sorry lot to the Carlton's waiters. They marched back and forth ignoring Nigel's '*Garçon!*' and Burgess's gesticulating cigar. Only after they had served the stars and some tobacco-brown old men with young women in tow did they get around to us. Since cocktails cost as much as I usually paid for a meal, I ordered a citron pressé. Nigel and Anthony each had a glass of champagne. Burgess proposed a toast to literature.

'Actually,' Nigel announced, 'I'm more than just a journalist. I do a bit of creative stuff on the side.'

'I had a hunch that might be true.' Burgess concentrated on the chains of bubbles in his champagne. 'You struck me as the creative sort.'

'That's why it's such a thrill to meet you and get a chance to trade ideas. And of course interview you.'

Like Burgess, I fixed my eyes on my glass. Queasy with recognition, I knew what was coming and so did he. I, too, had pursued famous authors. Had I sounded this awful in my pursuit? Was I as smarmily humble as Nigel as he inched up to the big question— will you read my work? I prayed that I hadn't been and prayed, too, that this moment would pass painlessly. How had I ever put myself— how had I put so many novelists—in this hellish position?

But Anthony was affably relaxed. Signalling for the waiter to

Michael Mewshaw

pour him a refill, he said, 'If you gentlemen will excuse me for a second, I have to find a loo.'

At first it didn't hit Nigel. He believed Burgess would come back. All he had to do was wait. But I knew better. As the author of the Enderby novels about a besieged poet who habitually hides in the bathroom, Burgess was undoubtedly an expert at escape. We could wait eight hours, as Linda and I had done for Liana. We could cool our heels until closing time, we could take up permanent residence on the Carlton terrace, and, I bet, Anthony still wouldn't return. Nigel's was one book the Blurb King wouldn't be reading or praising.

At a different time, I might have resented getting stuck here with Nigel and stiffed for the drinks—one of which, Burgess's second champagne, remained untouched. Instead, I admired the deftness with which he had shifted the burden from his shoulders. Like a ju-jitsu artist, he had absorbed our energy, our need, and turned it against us. Whatever the extortionate price of three champagnes and a glass of lemon juice, the lesson was worth it.

After half an hour, I told Nigel to finish off Anthony's bubbly before it lost its effervescence. By now he knew the score. I picked up the bill, wished him the best of luck and headed off in a direction where I wasn't likely to cross paths with Burgess.

Years later, at the American Academy in Rome, I ran into Burgess at a dinner party on the night he gave a reading from his translations of Belli. Again the foxy flicker of recognition brightened his eyes. Again, as if in a recorded announcement, Anthony asked, 'Do I owe you something? A letter? A recommendation? Money?'

'Not a thing. You've already given me so much.' □

GRANTA

AT THE VILLA MORO

Paul Theroux

This is my only story. Now that I am sixty I can tell it.

Years ago, when Taormina was a village most travellers avoided in the summer, because of the heat, I sought it out, to feel the heat. Heat was everything in the poem 'Snake', that D. H. Lawrence wrote in Taormina. Great names and associations also mattered to me, which was another reason, lingering in the steep town of old stone and fresh flowers, I stopped by the Villa Moro, loving that name too. Beyond the black cast-iron faces on the spiked gateway to the terrace, I saw a handsome couple dressed in loose white clothes enjoying a big Italian lunch. I imagined being seated at that table. I thought, I want your life—the sort of envious wish I was too young to know was like asking for my undoing.

I always excused my waywardness by saying that I was poor and so was forced into this or that course of action. The truth was that I enjoyed taking risks. I should have been ashamed. It was not that I behaved badly, rather that I was secretive and seldom straight. I was creative in my lies. Saying I was poor was one of them.

I was a boy of twenty-one in the hot summer of 1962 when I found myself in Sicily, outside the gate of the Villa Moro. In those days I travelled with one change of clothes. I wore a seersucker jacket over a T-shirt, and a pair of jeans. My bag was so small I didn't look like a traveller but rather like a student on his way from school, with books and papers. In addition I carried a small sketch pad which allowed me to stop whenever I felt like it and make a quick pencil drawing of the scene. With so little to carry it was easy for me to explore and make sudden decisions: to stay, to move on, to kill time at the beach, to hitch-hike, or to sleep third class on the night train to save money. Usually I wouldn't decide where to stay until nightfall, and now it was hardly mid-morning in Taormina. Of course, I couldn't afford the Villa Moro. All I had money for was one of those very dirty places on the road below the town, between the public beach and the railroad track which had taken me south from Messina a few hours before. Still, I lingered in front of the villa's walls. I imagined writing someone a letter on the hotel's headed notepaper. I saw a sheet of it on a menu posted near the gate—two black faces, and palm trees, a glimpse of Africa in Sicily. Eventually I went in, crossed the hot terrace, and ordered a cup of coffee and a glass of water, pretending to be poised. There was an awning near the pool—few people sunbathed in Sicily then—and under it the couple sat like lovers, wearing identical panama hats, the woman in white, and wearing lovely lacy gloves, intent in conversation, no one else around.

From a distance—and I had been a little bleary-eyed from my sleepless night—the woman looked young and attractive—mid-thirties, maybe; and the man seemed more attentive than a husband. I took them to be lovers, for the way he beseeched her, imploring her, looking helpless. The meal set up in front of them looked delicious—the sort of salads and antipasti served at lunch in the Italian summer, yellow tomatoes, red lettuce, sliced meat, lobster tails, prawns, olives and pickles, artichokes and palm hearts, fruit drinks in tall glasses—and this lovely day, the blue sea in the distance, a rising trickle of grey smoke from Etna, and the squat thick-walled villa. The two people looked magical in their white hats under the big green awning.

Thinking again, I want your life, I envied them with an envy I could taste on the roof of my mouth, something unfamiliar and corrosive. They had no idea how lucky they were, and I tried to imagine displacing them, being at their table myself this fine Sicilian noon, eating lunch, with nothing else to do, with a room in this elegant hotel. My curiosity made me bolder. I got up and strolled nearer to them, as I made sketches of the glazed plates and the flower vines on the wall and the beautiful blue sea beyond the tops of the poplars and cypresses. Often bystanders said to me, Let's see, asking to look at my sketches.

The couple said nothing. Closer to them, I realized that the sun's glare had been kind to the woman, had smoothed and simplified her features. I could see from her lips that she was older than I had guessed, a tight white fish face and bleached hair, a very skinny figure—a girl's stick figure, somewhat starved. But I was still intrigued by her hat and her sunglasses and her strawlike hair and her gloves of lace. The man was scribbling on a pad, the meal was untouched.

I was on the point of walking back to my table when the man said hello and beckoned. The way he crooked his finger, and his intonation, told me he was not Italian.

'We want to see your sketches,' he said.

Just as I had guessed, yet I hesitated.

'You'll have to show us, you know,' he said, with the sort of confidence I associated with wealthy people. 'There is no one else here.'

In the moment of saying OK I was betrayed by my first feeling, my sense of I want your life. I had seen these people as lovers enjoying a romantic lunch. I could not have been more mistaken. I knew at once that I was wrong and it seemed to me that I would have to pay for this envious feeling of finding them attractive and wishing to displace them and wanting what they had. I approached their table feeling disappointed and yet I was compelled to follow through, for I had nowhere else to go.

'Have you just come to Taormina?'

'I've been here awhile,' I said, being evasive. 'In town doing some drawings and a little literary research. D. H. Lawrence lived up the road in the Via Fontana Vecchia in the 1920s.'

Ten minutes at Lawrence's house, looking for a water trough to sketch. I could not tell them the truth, or give anything away: the hard seats of third class, the long walk up the hill, the stink of cigarettes called Stop—these were just too awful.

'His wife was German,' the woman said in a correcting tone. 'Thomas Mann was also here.'

The statement, and her accent, told me she was German, but she said nothing else. The man, who was swarthy and yet fine featured, with a thin face and a beaky nose, did the rest of the talking, complimenting my sketches and asking questions. I answered him untruthfully to put myself in a good light.

I had been wrong about their age. A twenty-one-year-old knows nothing of time and cannot assign anyone an age—thirty-eight is old, forty is hopeless, fifty is ancient, and anyone older than that is invisible. Desirable and ugly are the only criteria. The German woman was not ugly but in attempting to appear young she seemed faintly doll-like and trifled with.

Yet they were obviously rich and the rich to me then were like a race of giants, powerful in every way, even physically superior, protected, able to buy anything, confident, speaking a special language and from their towering position regarding only each other. It was painful for me to think about the couple in this way. I tried to forget how limited my choices were.

The woman seemed to be smiling to herself and presenting her profile to me, her chin slightly lifted on a lacy finger of her gloved hand.

'We were just talking about opera, what a shame it is that the Teatro Greco here has no production,' the man said.

This was a helpful cue. I had no material resources but I was well read, I spoke Italian, and in my determined self-educating mission I had tried to know as much as possible about opera.

I said, 'I've just seen a new production of *Hamlet* in Urbino. *Amletto*.'

This seemed to perplex them, which pleased and emboldened me.

'By Orsini. He just wrote it. It was the premiere. Lots of swordplay.'

'French opera is more to my taste,' the man said.

'I wish Bizet had succeeded with *Salammbô*,' I said.

'There is no *Salammbô*,' the woman said, a querulous tone of literal-minded contradiction pinching her face.

'He never finished it. Flaubert wouldn't let him.'

Was what I was saying true? Anyway they believed it. They were listening closely to my cleverness. Instead of dealing with Wagner or Verdi, whom they would have known well, I made myself seem intelligent by mentioning obscure works. We would take the others for granted—though I knew very little, just the records not the performances. Removing the great works from the discussion deflected their scrutiny. I was young but rich in ruses.

'I get tickets for Glyndebourne every year.'

Saying this, 'I' rather than 'we', the woman revealed that the man was neither husband nor lover. The man was a flunkey or a friend.

'We have very good opera where I come from. In Boston. And in Tanglewood, in Lenox.'

'I have heard so,' the man said.

We talked some more—trivialities about the heat, the blinding brightness of noon, the wild flowers, the emptiness, the absence of visitors.

'It is why I come,' the woman said.

Again that 'I' told me she was in charge and the man a mere accessory.

'Have you had lunch?' the man said, with a gesture that took in all the plates of food. 'You are welcome to help yourself.'

I was ravenous yet I said, 'No, thank you.' I was too proud to accept, and anyway, by my seeming restrained and polite they would be reassured and would respect me more.

'You will forgive us?' the man said, and picked at some salad. The woman, still with her gloves on, and using a silver tool, pierced olives from a dish of antipasto and nibbled them.

'Such a pleasure to talk with you,' I said, and excused myself. I went back to my table, my empty coffee cup, and opened my sketchbook again and indulged myself in shading a sketch I had done.

The couple conferred some more. Then the woman got up slowly and in a stately way, for her white dress was long and lovely, she left the terrace. The man paid the bill—the Italian business, the saucer, the folded bill, the back and forth, and more talk with the waiter. When the waiter left, saucer of money in hand, the man came to my table.

He looked at me intently and then smiled in a familiar way as though he knew me well.

'I have arranged for you to stay here,' he said. 'I was once a student'—I had started a polite protest—'No, no. It will be pleasant to have you as a neighbour. We will talk.'

He had read me perfectly.

So, within an hour of happening across the Villa Moro, I was installed in a room with a view of the sea, seated on my own balcony in a monogrammed bathrobe, eating a chicken sandwich, clinking the ice in my Campari and soda, the breeze on my face. I had been transformed: magic.

'This is my guest,' the man had said—I still did not know his name—and he asked for my passport, which he glanced at. 'Mr Mariner requires a double room with a view of *il vulcano*. Put it on my bill.'

A moment later he gave me his name but in an offhand way: 'You can call me Harry'—as though the name was fictitious; and it was. His name was Haroun.

When I tried to thank him he put a fingertip to his lips and then wagged the finger sternly. There was no mistaking this gesture. He made this admonishing finger seem a very serious instrument if not a weapon.

'This can be our secret,' he said. 'Not a word to the Gräfin.'

That gave me pause yet I had no choice but to agree, for I had accepted the free room. To ease my conscience I told myself that if I wished I could leave at any time, as impulsively as I had come; could skip out and be gone. Even so, I felt that in acquiring the room I had been triumphant, it was a windfall, and there was a hint of mystery about Haroun that I liked, a conspiratorial tone that was comic and pleasing. And the Gräfin? I supposed the Gräfin was the woman.

'Not a word to anyone,' I said.

'The Gräfin is not my Gräfin, as you probably think, but she is a very dear friend. I have known her for years—we have been absolutely everywhere together.'

This was in my room—he had followed me there with the room boy, a square-shouldered Sicilian boy, and Haroun was sort of eyeing the boy as he spoke to me, sizing him up as the boy bent and stretched, putting my bag on a small table and adjusting the fastenings of the shutters.

'Look at the skin these people have!'

He pinched the boy's cheek and arm, like someone choosing cloth for a suit. The boy, preoccupied with the shutters, smirked and allowed it.

'Never touch their women,' Haroun said. 'That is the iron rule in Sicily. They will kill you. But their boys—look what skin!'

Now it seemed to me that the boy knew he was being admired, and he stepped away from Haroun and said, *'Bacio la mano'*—I kiss your hand—and somewhat giddy with this byplay Haroun snatched the boy's hand and pressed some folded money into it.

'Ciao, bello,' Haroun said to the boy, smiling as he watched him leave my room and shut the door.

Alone with Haroun I felt more uncomfortable than I had when the boy was there—the compromising sense that it was not my room, that in accepting it I had accepted this small dark smiling man who I felt was about to importune me. But from what he said next I realized that his smile meant he was remembering something with pleasure. Sometimes people smile to show you they are remembering something happy in their past.

'The Gräfin is such a dear friend,' he said. 'And we have our secrets too.'

Something in the way he spoke made me think the woman was giving him money.

'She is a fantastic person,' he said. 'Wonderful. Generous.'

Then I was sure of it.

'And she is very sensitive.' The way he stood in the room, lingering and looking around, conveyed the impression that the room was his—and of course it was. 'All her noble qualities have given her a great soul and a fantastic capacity for friendship. I think somehow you guessed that about her.'

I had guessed that she was a rich difficult woman who was not interested in anyone but herself, yet I smiled at Haroun and agreed that she was a sensitive person with a great soul. In this room I felt I had to agree, but agreeing was easy—this was small talk, or so I thought.

'I can see that you understand things quickly,' he said. 'I admire you Americans, just showing up in a strange place with your passport in your pocket, and a little valise. Fantastic.'

He saw everything. He made me shy.

'Probably you want to rest,' he said. 'We usually have a drink on the terrace at seven. This is a lovely place. I think you will enjoy it. *Ciao* for now.'

Was that an invitation? I didn't know, but it did seem to me that I was part of a larger arrangement that at the moment I could only guess at. After he left I ordered the sandwich and the Campari and soda and tried not to ponder what the larger arrangement was. I told myself: I can leave tomorrow, just as I came, on the train to Messina. Being hard up in Italy didn't frighten me—people were friendly, strangers could be hospitable, I spoke Italian, I was personable—well, this hotel room was proof of that.

I guessed that something was expected of me, I did not know what, but something.

Because I had not been specifically invited I did not appear on the terrace until nearly eight o'clock. The woman Haroun called Gräfin was holding a glass of wine and looking at the lights on the distant sea—fishing boats—and Haroun raised his hand in an effortless beckoning gesture that had a definite meaning; the languid summons of a person who is used to being obeyed. The woman herself, her head turned to the bobbing lights, seemed uninterested in me.

'Look, Gräfin, our friend the American.'

I joined them. Gräfin—a name I first heard as 'Griffin'—still showed no interest in me. She sipped her wine. She might have been a little drunk—the way drunks can seem to concentrate hard when they are just tipsy and slow, with a glazed furrow-browed stare. I studied her smooth cheeks. She was German, he was not. She looked like a ruined and resurrected queen—someone who had suffered an illness that had left a mark on her beauty, not disfiguring it but somehow fixing it, ageing it.

We talked. Haroun asked me questions which, I felt sure, were intended to impress Gräfin, or any listener—sort of interviewed me in a friendly appreciative way, to show me at my best, to establish that I had been an art teacher at the selective school inside the Ducal Palace at Urbino, that I was travelling alone through Sicily, that I was never without my sketchbook, which was a sort of visual diary of my trip; that I was knowledgeable about artists and books—'Rafael was born in Urbino, he says.'

'I know that,' Gräfin said. She always spoke with a lifted chin, into the distance, never faced the listener, never faced the speaker for that matter. 'I prefer Tiziano.'

'Would that be Titian?'

She didn't answer. 'I have one, like so, not large'—but her slender measuring hands made it seem large—'however, yes, it is a Tiziano.'

'You bought it yourself?'

'It has been in my family.'

'And your Dürer,' Haroun said.

'Many Dürer,' Gräfin said.

'I'd hate to think what those would have cost,' I said, and as soon as the words were out of my mouth I regretted them for their vulgarity.

'Not much,' Gräfin said. She was addressing a large glazed salver hooked to the brick wall of the terrace. 'Very little in fact. Just pennies.'

'How is that possible?'

'We bought them from the artist.'

I saw Albrecht Dürer putting some dark tarnished pfennigs into a leather coin purse and touching his forelock in gratitude, as he handed over a sheaf of etchings to one of the Gräfin's big patronizing ancestors.

Gräfin had a brusque uninterested way of speaking—but saying something like *We bought them from the artist* was a put-down she seemed to relish. She never asked questions. She seemed impossible, spoiled, egotistical, yet strong; in a word, she was the embodiment of my notion of wealth. I did not dislike her, I was fascinated by her pale skin and soft flesh in this sunny place, by her full breasts and pinched doll's face and bleached hair and plump disapproving lips, even by her posture—always facing away from me. I saw her as indifferent to me and something of a challenge.

'I am hungry,' she said to Haroun. 'Will you call the boy?' This was also interesting, the fact that she spoke to him in English when I was present. When they were alone, I was sure they spoke German. The English was for my benefit—I didn't speak a word of German. But why this unusual politeness, or at least deference to me? Haroun snapped his fingers. The waiter appeared with two menus. Gräfin opened hers and studied it.

Holding his menu open but looking at me, Haroun said, 'Have you seen the olive groves?'

I said no, feeling that it was expected of me, to give him a chance to describe them.

'They are quite magnificent,' he said, as I had expected. 'We are driving out tomorrow to look at one near Sperlinga. You know Sperlinga? No? Perhaps you would like to accompany us?'

'Morning or afternoon?' I didn't care one way or the other but I did not want to seem tame.

'It must be morning. Afternoons here are for the siesta,' he said.

'I'd love to go with you.'

'We leave at eight.'

'I want the fish,' Gräfin said. 'Grilled. Tell them no sauce. Small salad. No dressing.' She snapped her menu shut. So, in that way, I was informed that I was not a dinner guest. But once again I saw how, in the manner of trying to appear casual, Haroun was manipulating the situation. Gräfin was indifferent, though, or at least made a show of indifference. She did not look up as I excused myself and left. My audience was over. I had been summoned, I had been dismissed.

Haroun was in the lobby the next day before eight. Gräfin was already in the car. These people were prompt. I imagined that their wealth would have made them more casual. Haroun greeted me and directed me to the front seat, where I would sit next to the driver. This made me feel like an employee—one of Gräfin's staff. But Haroun, too, seemed like an employee.

We drove through Taormina and down the hill, took a right on the main road, and then another right after a short time, heading inland and upward on a narrow road, heading into the island.

'Bustano,' Haroun said. Then he conversed with the driver in a language that was not Italian—and not any language I recognized.

Haroun laughed in an explosive way, obviously delighted by something the driver had said.

'He said it will take more than one hour,' Haroun said. 'Because, he says, this is a *macchina* and not a flying carpet.'

'What is that language?'

'Arabic. He is originally from Tunisia.'

'The Moro of the Villa Moro.'

'Exactly.'

'How do you know Arabic?'

Gräfin said, 'Harry knows everything. I am lost without this man.'

'I can speak English. I can write English,' Haroun said. 'I can write on a "piss" of paper. I can write on a "shit" of paper.' He made a child's impish face, tightening his cheeks to give himself dimples. He tapped his head. *"Ho imparato Italiano in un settimane. Tutto qui in mio culo."*

'Now he is being silly.'

'Where did you learn Arabic?'

'Baghdad,' he said. 'But we didn't speak it at home. We spoke English, of course.'

'You're Iraqi?'

He sort of winced at my abrupt way of nailing him down and rather defensively he said, 'Chaldean. Very old faith. Nestorian. Even my name, you see. And my people.'

'He is German,' Gräfin said, and patted his knee as though soothing a child. 'He is now one of us. A wicked German.'

We drove along the mountain road past clusters of cracked farmhouses, their walls daubed with political slogans—some from Mussolini's time.

'Where is the olives?' Gräfin asked.

'Just ahead, beyond Sperlinga.' There was something anxious in Haroun's helpfulness that suggested he was afraid of her. He said, 'Bustano—that is not Italian. It is from Arabic. *Bustan* is garden. Caltanissetta, near here, has a place called Gibil Habib. From Arabic, *Gebel Gabib*, because it is a hill.'

'But where is the olives?' Gräfin asked again, in the impatient and unreasonable tone of a child.

Bustano, when we got there, turned out not to be a village, but an estate, a whole valley of neat symmetrical rows of ancient olive trees and at the end of a long driveway a magnificent villa, three storeys of yellow stucco with a red tiled roof, and balconies, and an enormous portico roof under which we drove and parked.

A man appeared—not a squat Sicilian farmer but a tall elegant-looking man in a soft yellow sweater and light-coloured slacks and sunglasses. He greeted us, and Gräfin and Haroun spoke to him in French. I smiled and nodded and stepped aside.

I said in Italian, 'I need to walk a little after that long ride.'

'Yes, you are welcome,' the man said in English, which disconcerted me. 'Over there is a little pond, with ducks. And many flowers for you. *Bellina*.'

Haroun said he would come with me. We walked to the ornamental lily pond. Haroun picked a flower and held it to his nose.

I said, 'He's right. It is *bellina*.'

Haroun shrugged. 'The flowers, yes. But the trees. The *frantoio*. The storage and cellars.' He crumpled his face, which meant I am not impressed.

'It is not great quality. Toscano is better. But this villa is charming—very comfortable. And Gräfin wants it. She likes the business.' He made a gesture of uncorking a bottle and pouring. '"This is my olive oil. I grow it. I press it. You eat it"—she is a romantic, you see?'

He had a way, in speaking of Gräfin, of being able to turn his criticism into a compliment, which made me admire him for his loyalty.

I plucked the petals from the flower I was holding and said in a stilted way—I had been practising the speech: 'This is nice—very pleasant. And you have been very kind to me. But—forgive me if I'm wrong—I feel you expect something from me. That you are arranging something. That you want me for some purpose. Tell me.'

I was glad we were outside, alone. I would never have been able to say this back in Taormina at the villa where he had made me a guest.

Haroun looked away. 'See how they dig and scratch the roots to fertilize the tree. Some of these trees are hundreds of years old. Maybe here in Norman times.' And he walked ahead of me, and he glanced back at the villa in which Gräfin had vanished with the elegant olive man.

'What is it?' I asked.

'You are very intelligent,' he said. 'I like that. Very quick. Bold, too, I can say.'

Two things struck me about this speech. The first was that he wasn't telling me what he really felt—that my intelligence made him uneasy. And that, even then I knew that when someone complimented me in that way they were about to ask a favour.

As a way of defying him and taking a gratuitous risk I told him this.

'You are my guest, so you should be a little more polite to me,' he said, laughing in a peculiar mirthless way to show me he was offended.

So I knew then that what I had said was true and that his reply was a reprimand. Given the fact that I had accepted his hospitality I should have felt put in my place, but I resisted, wishing to feel free to say anything I liked.

He said, 'What do you think of Gräfin?'

'I don't know anything about her.'

'Exactly. You are right,' he said. 'She is a great mystery. That is why I love her.' He came closer to me. I seldom noticed anything more about Haroun than his beaky nose, but his nose was so big and expressive it was all I needed to notice.

'But when you see Gräfin what do you feel?'

What did this man want? I said, 'I feel curious. I feel she is very nice.'

'She is fantastic,' he said, another reprimand. 'She has everything. But do you believe me when I say to you she is lonely?'

'I believe you.'

'Because you are intelligent. You can see.'

'But you're her friend. So how can she be lonely?'

'That's the mystery, you see,' Haroun said. 'I am her friend, yes. I am also her doctor. I qualified in Baghdad, I studied more in Beirut. I went to Germany for further study. I did my residence in Freiburg. And I stayed there. Gräfin became my patient.'

We had begun to kick through the avenues between the rows of olive trees. Men were trimming the trees, lopping branches, fussing with ladders and buckets.

'A doctor can be friendly with a patient, but not intimate,' he said. 'So we travel, and I take care of her. But it ends there.'

'What a shame,' I said, hoping for more.

'But you see even if I were not her doctor I could not help her,' he said. He was looking away. 'I am of a different disposition.' His gaze fell upon a strapping bare-chested man with a pruning hook, and Haroun glanced back as we walked on, seeming to hold a conversation with his eyes alone, the man too responding with a subtly animated and replying gaze.

'What a shame.'

'It is how God made me.'

'I think you want me to be her friend.'

'More than friend maybe.'

'I see.'

As though he too had been practising sentences he said, 'I desire you to woo her.'

The expression made me smile.

'Do you find her attractive?'

I had to admit that I did. She was pretty in a brittle old-fashioned way. She was chic, she was demanding. Yes, she was much older than me—I could not tell how much, thirty-five, perhaps—and I was twenty-one. But strangely her age did not prejudice me against her. I was attracted to her for it, for the oddness of it. She was certainly unlike any woman I had ever met—in fact she was a woman; I did not know any women. I had only slept with girls, pretty, pleading, marriage-minded girls. What did a woman want? Not marriage. Perhaps a woman of such experience as Gräfin wanted everything but marriage, and that included debauchery and that I craved.

'But she's not interested in me.'

'Because she doesn't know you,' Haroun said, and I hated him for agreeing with me.

We walked some more, Haroun steering our course towards more young men trimming the thick twisted olive trees.

'Another question,' he said. 'Do you find Taormina to your taste?'

'Oh, yes.'

The prompt way I answered showed that I had been a little reluctant in replying to his first question—the one about her. My sudden eagerness about Taormina made him laugh.

'You ask me what I want,' he said. 'I want you to be content in Taormina. I want my friend to be content. I think you can find contentment together.'

I saw exactly what he meant: he was, in a word, pimping for Gräfin. Well, I was not shocked. I was pleased. I was even flattered. I liked the obliqueness that had characterized the beginning—his getting me a room at the Villa Moro. And I liked the fact that he was petitioning me, soliciting my help, asking me to do him a favour; for all these things gave me some power.

'You will be my guest,' he said. 'And the guest of Gräfin too.'

'What a funny name,' I said.

He half smiled, with a distinct alertness, as though divining through a slip I had made that I was not so bright as I appeared.

'Not a name. Her name is Sabine, but I would never call her that.'

'Why not?'

He looked a little shocked, and he stiffened and said, 'Because she is Gräfin. It is her title. You would say countess.'

'From her family?'

'From her husband. The Gräf.'

With that revelation I was dazzled. But before I could reply there was a scurrying sound on the road—a boy summoning us to the house.

'If the answer is no, you must leave tomorrow,' Haroun said, in a very businesslike way, as though trying to conclude a difficult sale, and he started towards the house where the olive man and the Gräfin stood waiting for us.

The day dawned fine and clear, another Sicilian day of blazing heat, and I loved everything I saw and smelled—the prickly aroma of pine needles and hot bricks, the whiff of salt water from the blue sea, my freshly laundered clothes, the new espadrilles I had bought in town, my breakfast of fruit and coffee, my body outstretched on the chaise lounge. On that early morning, I loved my life. After breakfast I walked downstairs to the terrace, where I knew the two of them would be.

'Good morning,' Haroun said.

'Hello,' I said, with as much friendliness as I could muster, trying to look at Gräfin's face, which of course was turned aside. She was idly examining her gloves, twisting the lacy fingers to give them a tight fit.

'You mentioned something about leaving Taormina,' Haroun said.

'I changed my mind. I think I will stay awhile.'

Haroun smiled, exhaled, and looked away. Gräfin turned her big blue eyes on me with curiosity, but again peering as though she hardly knew me.

'Contessa,' I said.

She shrugged and lifted her gloved hand again, a fan of fingers that held her attention. And while she was preoccupied I imagined kissing her, holding her head, sucking slowly on her lips, slipping my hands beneath her dress and stroking her body.

Yes, I was staying. I told myself that I was poor; not ruthless but desperate. This excuse made me untruthful, it made me willing. To succeed with the Gräfin I had to convince myself that I desired her. I had to make her desire me. I did desire her, yet I could see that she was not particularly interested in me. She was vain, she seemed shallow, even her most offhand remarks sounded boastful, she was certainly aloof—now I knew why: not just money, she was an aristocrat.

There is wealth that makes people restless and impatient and showy—American wealth, on the whole. But Gräfin was European. Her wealth had made her passive and presumptuous and oblique, indolent, just a spender, and as a countess she seemed to me regal now.

I found it hard to get her attention. That morning, pleased by my announcing that I would be staying, Haroun began to devise ways of giving me access to Gräfin. To me, his ruses were transparent; but she was so bored and inattentive she did not seem to suspect a thing. He developed a stomach upset, and later that morning disclosed his infirmity in a solemn self-mocking way.

'Africa is taking its revenge upon my entrails.'

'What are you talking about?' Gräfin demanded, without seeming to care about Haroun's reply.

Another obvious trait of very rich European aristocrats was their literal-mindedness, I felt: you didn't become wealthy by being witty and alliterative, or hyperbolic like Haroun. He was the Gräfin's retainer, a sort of lapdog and flunkey, roles I was rehearsing for myself.

'Africa?' I said.

'*Africa commincia a Napoli,*' he said.

'What revenge?' Gräfin said.

'The Visigoths came here, as you know, and they engaged in systematic plunder, raping and pillaging. And I am being blamed for these misfortunes.'

'How can that be so? You are Arab.'

Haroun's toothy smile was a keen expression of pain. But gallantly he said, 'Not an Arab, my dear, but a Christian. Chaldean. From Baghdad. We spoke English at home. My father was a distinguished merchant. He had powerful friends.'

'You are not white. You are Semitische. Arab-speaking.'

'You are speaking English, dear Gräfin, but are you an Englishwoman?'

She said to me, 'He makes me tired with his arguments, but he is my doctor, so I must listen.'

'I am a witch doctor,' Haroun said.

'Idiot!' Gräfin said. She hated this sort of facetiousness.

Haroun said sadly, 'I am not well.'

Gräfin gave him a querying stare, as though he was a clock face showing the wrong time.

'What will I do now?' she said, twisting her gloved hands in impatience. 'How can the doctor be sick?'

Tapping his tummy through his shirt buttons, Haroun said, 'I shall take some medicine. I shall improve very soon.'

'What about today?'

Still, she clung to him. Hearing this exchange I got a distinct sense of witnessing a father and daughter at odds—an indulgent father, a spoilt daughter. This did not put me off or intimidate me, nor did it diminish the desire I had for her. If she had been highly intelligent and subtle I would have been more wary, but her diabolical girlishness was something I felt I could deal with. Besides, her air of spiteful superiority was like a goad to me; I found something stimulating in it.

'I must go to my room,' Haroun said.

'You cannot leave me alone.'

'Gräfin, you are not alone.'

All this time they were speaking English for my benefit in this stilted way, yet Gräfin refused to acknowledge my presence.

'Would you be so kind?' Haroun said to me. 'Gräfin will need some things from the town. A particular shop near the station.'

'Mazzaro?'

'Yes, down there.'

'What things?'

Gräfin behaved as though the question was inappropriate. She pouted and looked annoyed. In her role of little girl she refused to help by naming the things she wanted.

'Cosmetics, newspapers, some chocolate, a certain kind of fruit drink, bottled.'

'Maybe the hotel could send someone.'

'You see? He does not want to help.'

'I do want to help,' I said.

'The boys at the hotel are careless. They hold the chocolate all wrong. It melts in their hot hands. How can I eat it?'

Whatever else I did I would not bring the countess melted chocolate.

Haroun said, 'You will assist?'

'Of course,' I said. 'I'll go right away.'

Haroun took out a prescription pad and wrote a shopping list on it, while Gräfin looked away, seemingly preoccupied—with what? I could not imagine what was in this woman's mind. She was like another species: I did not discern a single thing we had in common. The paradox was that this sense of difference made me desire her but not in a way I had ever felt towards a woman. Though I did not fully formulate the thought at the time I wanted to dominate her, and I saw that our difference gave me an advantage. It was true that I knew nothing of aristocracy, while she was a countess; but I was astute enough to understand that she knew absolutely nothing of me or my background. I also guessed that her wealth had made her complacent and unsuspicious—Haroun ran all her errands, like this one he was foisting on to me.

The shopping list was very specific: mascara, a copy of *Bild Zeitung*, a large bar of Lindt Swiss chocolate ('no nuts'), and Orangina—three small bottles. She believed that the Orangina served at the Villa Moro was adulterated: her general belief was that Italians were cheats and dolts. She said that she liked Taormina because it was not popular with Italians.

I was given a string bag and directions to the lower town, Mazzaro, at the seaside—twenty minutes down, forty minutes up.

'This should cover it,' Haroun said, handing me a sheaf of new inky 10,000 lire notes. Gräfin turned away as she always did when someone produced money—or a bill to pay.

I walked down the Via Pirandello towards the sea. Mazzaro was hardly more than a village and still inhabited by many fishermen. I drank an espresso at the local cafe, caught the eye of the pretty girl wiping the tables, and then set off to do Gräfin's shopping, a task so simple as to seem unnecessary—but perhaps I was being tested? I didn't care. The weather was perfect, late August, and the life I had begun to live there was a variation of much of what I had seen in Italian movies.

In those black-and-white movies, a solitary fellow, bright but hard up, encounters some bored wealthy people on the shores of the Mediterranean and is ambiguously adopted—the hitch-hiker, the chance meeting, the stranger at the party, the wanderer. What seemed like random and apparently meaningless events were full of tension and complexity and were part of a larger design which, as the movie advanced, became apparent. The arrangement was not American—it was European, dissolute, heavily textured, unmistakably vicious, with shocking plot twists—Fellini, Antonioni, Pasolini. The films were of hot days, long nights, strangers, whispers, risks, excesses, and they were all tantalizingly vague. Even then I thought of these years as the era of the chance encounter. The foreign hitch-hiker was picked up by the wealthy jaded Italians and from that moment his life was changed.

I had been rehearsing this sort of meeting ever since I'd got to Italy. I told myself: Sometimes life is like that—you fantasize so intensely that when the opportunity presents itself you know exactly what to do, repeating moves you have practised in your head. Haroun had given me more money than I had needed for the items on Gräfin's shopping list. Obviously he meant me to keep the change—and there was so much of it that I felt secure: money in my pocket, a lovely place to stay, all my meals paid for, and a mission—the easiest part of all, so I thought—becoming the Gräfin's lover.

Pleased with myself—I had never been happier; then, such happiness was my sense of being a man—I walked up the hill to Taormina and the villa. Gräfin was at her usual place on the terrace, staring at the sea. Her big black sunglasses made her seem not just mysterious but unknowable. Without turning, but she must have heard me place the string bag beside her chair, she spoke—the bug-eyed glasses seemed to give her an insect's voice.

'You are late.'

I smirked at the back of her head and murmured, hoping that she would interpret this ambiguous noise as an apology, though it was intended as nothing of the kind. Then she turned and the collar of her loose dress slipped sideways and exposed a smooth plump breast with a dark nipple. She cupped it with her black gloved hand, but did not tuck it away and caressed it with a kind of admiration.

'I will take an Orangina.'

I lifted out a bottle and gripping it by its pot belly I held it out to her.

'How can I drink it unless it is opened?'

I had been struck dumb by the sight of her breast and the nipple between her lacy fingers. Her dense sunglasses meant that I could not read her expression. Now a waiter had to be found, a bottle opener, a glass, a napkin: then her breast was back beneath her dress. She muttered that the glass should be served on a saucer. She took

61

the glass without thanking me.

'Let me feel the chocolate.'

I had made a point of keeping the chocolate beside the cold Orangina and out of the sun. She slipped it out of its wrapper and poked it with her finger. Satisfied that it was not soft, she grunted. Then she took the newspaper and glanced at it.

'All bad news,' she said with relish, and began to read.

'If there is anything else I can do for you,'—and here I stepped in front of her and looked into her dark glasses, seeking her eyes— 'just let me know.'

Her handbag, a Sicilian raffia handbag, was in her lap. She rummaged in it, making its weave lisp and creak, and took out some serious-looking German banknotes. Without paying much attention to them, not counting them, just crumpling them and pinching them as she had the chocolate, she handed them over. Her hand returned to her dress, to her loose collar, and she stroked her throat, and kept stroking to where her breast bulged, a gesture of languid autoeroticism.

Putting the money in my pocket, I said, 'Anything you like?'

She said, 'Yes,' and made me alert, and then, 'Tell Harry to get well.'

Later, walking down the corridor near her room, I thought I heard her laughing. No, she was sobbing. Hold on, she was laughing. God, I had no idea. That was my first day of wooing her.

The next three days were the same—the same shopping, the same waiting, the same snubs, even the same startling glimpses of her body. Her aloofness became more erotic to me, because it made me a voyeur. The shame was mine.

I imagined licking and nibbling her body, saw myself cupping her bare breasts, each one filling my hand, and sucking on them and holding her spongy nipples lightly in my teeth. But I did nothing; I watched her, I was polite—too polite for her. Once she let the paper slip and when I grabbed at it I brushed her arm and she recoiled and said, 'Please'—meaning 'Don't touch me!'

She would sit, with one finger in her mouth, looking cross, and although her sucking on this gloved finger was also erotic to me, it was just another way for her to express her impatience.

'He is a doctor! How can a doctor be sick?'

Haroun remained in his room all this time. I told Gräfin that he was probably improving and that we would see him any day now.

'He doesn't care about me,' she said.

'He does,' I said. 'And I do too.'

She frowned, looking insulted and intruded upon.

'How do you feel?'

'Not well,' she said, still sounding insulted. As though it was none of my business. She was eating chocolate, kissing dabs of it from her lacy fingertips—and it all looked like fellating foreplay to my eager eyes.

'Maybe I can help.'

She raised her head and looked at me as though I had just dropped from the sky. She said, 'What could you do?'

Even though she was wearing sunglasses I could tell from the curl of her lips that she was scowling.

'Anything you suggest.'

She went a bit limp just then, indicating a pause with her whole body. She looked away and said in a little-girl voice, 'Haroun brings me presents. You don't bring me presents. You don't care.'

I was not insulted. I was fascinated: I fantasized that she was a small girl urging me to corrupt her. I was willing, the thought would not leave me, and I was now pretty sure that she knew what she was doing to me. The next day, dipping into the stash of money she had given me, I bought her a bunch of flowers from the flower seller at the stall on the Corso.

'They will die unless they are put into water,' Gräfin said.

But she was pleased, I could tell, the little girl's satisfaction was as expressive as the little girl's tyranny. In the following days I brought her a pot of honey, a lump of dense amber, a chunk of lapis lazuli, a length of lace—the black intricate sort that matched her gloves; a small nervous bird in a wicker cage the shape of an onion. I used the money she had given me, for there was always a wad of lire left over, but so twisted from the way she crumpled and handled it the notes had taken on the appearance of a leafy vegetable—wilted kale, dying lettuce.

By now Haroun had emerged from his seclusion, frowning and

clutching his stomach. 'This is bad—when I have such an illness of the bowels it is like giving birth'—he made a face and grunted with pain—'to monsters.' Then he seemed to forget his ailment and he said, 'You are succeeding?'

'Of course.'

The higher pitch in my voice was my inability to disguise my forcing a reply. I felt I was getting nowhere.

Haroun vanished again, groaning, and on the night of his disappearance, Gräfin said she was hungry, which was her oblique way of telling me that I would be joining her at dinner. We drank wine together in silence on the terrace. As usual, I sat fantasizing, imagining myself licking her cleavage, fondling her. I was tipsy when the food was served and I flirted with her, none of it verbal, but rather a sort of overfamiliar manner of gesturing and facial expressions, behaving like a much-loved and trusted waiter, which seemed the only relationship that worked with her.

She was wearing the dress I liked the most, a white crocheted one, loose on her slender figure, her shoulder bare, her long collar affording glimpses of her breasts which slipped against her dress as she leaned and moved. She wore her reddest lipstick, with a gleaming redness that made her lips swell, and in the candlelight of the Villa Moro she was beautiful to me. I desired her, I ravished her with my eyes, but even as I was staring at her in this way, she began complaining about Haroun, and a hard and ugly expression surfaced on her features, defined by shadows.

I said, to divert her, 'How about joining the natives in the *passeggiata*?'

On Saturday nights, the Italians in Taormina paraded, chattering, along the Corso, from the church of Santa Caterina down to the Duomo: men with men, women with women, children playing, groups of boys eyeing groups of girls. It was like a tribal rite, and there were always foreign visitors like us, couples usually, who tagged along for the fun, for it was a noisy pleasurable parade.

'What a vulgar idea,' Gräfin said. 'I would never do that.'

'But I would protect you.' I was still a little drunk.

She sniffed, she touched her fingers to her nose. She said, 'I will go to my room.'

This to me sounded like an invitation. I walked with her to the second floor, loving each step, following slightly behind her, anticipating what was to come, wishing with all my heart that I could cup her buttocks in my hands. I imagined that I could feel the heat of her body, the warmth of her bare skin, through the perforations in her crocheted dress.

At her room, she opened the door—in a distant second room I saw her bed, a frilly coverlet, some fur slippers—she turned briefly and said, 'Goodnight.'

I leaned and put my face near hers, to kiss her. Swiftly, she pushed me with her hands and made as if to bat me on my head.

'What do you think you are doing?' she said, through gritted teeth.

Although she had only grazed me, I reacted as though I had been slapped in the face. I was so embarrassed I was off balance. I tried to explain. She rejected me, she rejected my explanation. She entered her room—fled into it, and shut the door hard.

A foot-shuffle down the hall told me that someone had heard, and that bothered me more than anything.

The next day she was at breakfast as usual, looking composed, even refreshed: no sign of distress.

I said, 'I am very sorry about last night.'

Just a slight flash of her eyebrows indicated she had heard me, but there was nothing else, and not a word.

I said, 'I'm afraid I was a little drunk.'

For a moment I thought she was going to cry, her skin wrinkled around her eyes, her mouth quivered, and she struggled with it, the effort showing on the thin pale skin of her face, and as she fought it her eyes glistened.

Finally the emotion passed and though she did not say anything I knew she was angry—because of what I had tried to do, or because of my lame apology? I did not know, but I saw that afterwards she turned to stone. Except for our chewing, breakfast was silent, and it was all so painful I finally crept away, feeling like the dog I was.

Haroun recovered that day. He looked brighter, he offered to run the errands, taking a taxi to the shops below in Mazzaro. He spent the day with Gräfin and by the afternoon he looked harassed and impatient. I began to surmise that in his absence he had been enjoying a dalliance with one of the Italian boys on the staff, that he resented having to reappear for duty with the Gräfin. They spoke German that day. I was excluded and it seemed to me that not I but Haroun was being given an ultimatum.

That night, exactly a week after I had arrived in Taormina, Haroun said, 'Gräfin is very unhappy. You must go.'

'I did my best,' I said.

He shook his head. He said, 'No. I have failed.'

It amazed me that he did not offer me any blame. He reproached himself. He sucked on his cigarette and spat out the smoke, looking rueful, hardly taking any notice of me, and not mentioning the fact that he had been paying my hotel room and all my expenses for a week, enriching me. 'She does not think she is beautiful,' Haroun said.

That was not at all the impression I had. Gräfin seemed impossibly vain about her beauty, and I knew that from the casual way she moved her body and exposed herself, utterly unselfconscious, which was the ultimate sexuality.

'She is lovely,' I said.

'You think so?' He looked into my face, as though testing it for truthfulness.

'Yes, I do.'

'She doesn't agree. She is not convinced.' Haroun stared in silence at the stars and dropped his gaze to where they sparkled on the sea.

'A lovely face,' I said. 'Like a Madonna.'

This was a bit excessive, but what did it matter? I was on my way out. Why not leave them smiling? But Haroun liked what I said, and nodded heavily, looking moved.

'If you truly think so, you must find a way of convincing her. I will give you some days. Otherwise you must go.'

That was my challenge: like the strange task assigned to a wanderer in a folk tale, the young man who comes to a palace and is bidden to woo the princess. I saw myself in a complex full-page woodcut from a book of such stories. I stood perplexed on the parapet while the countess sat in her tower, facing her looking glass— and in my version of this scene she had a mirrored glimpse of the young man on the balcony above her, as well as of her pretty face.

I had to succeed or else I would be banished. That was the narrative. But there was something beneath it. I had not been lying to Haroun in praising Gräfin. I thought she was beautiful, I knew she was wealthy, she seemed like a sorceress, I desired her. I wanted badly to make love to this seemingly unattainable woman, who did nothing but insult me and reject my advances.

I did not want to think that I was in a trap. But a week in that great hotel, a week of luxury, had spoiled me—'corrupted' is too big a word; I was softened. I had become accustomed to the sweet life that, up to then, I had known only in Italian films. I was habituated to luxury, the easiest habit to acquire, like a taste for candy or for lying in a hammock; like being on a fine yacht and saying, 'I don't want to get off—sail on!'

I had begun to love waking to each hot day in the comfort of the villa; I had even begun to enjoy the challenge of the Gräfin, seeing myself as the youth being tested by the lovely countess and her riddling adviser in the palace. I was enacting the struggle in the folk story; an evocative figure, black and pivotal, wearing a half smile and looking jaunty, poised between success and failure.

I did not take her rejection personally. It was for me to solve the riddle—to find a way to make love to her. The Gräfin's obstinacy did not turn me off—it made me calculating and desirous.

Haroun, confused by my lack of progress, was by turns abusive and encouraging.

Abusive: 'How can you take my money and do nothing? You are selfish, in love with yourself. You pretend to be one of the elite, but I know you to be a poor American student. Oh, yes, maybe intelligent and you will amount to something, or maybe you will be like this always—taking money to look pretty, and lying to people and misleading them.'

He went on in this vein but I just stared at him. He had a very strong Iraqi accent overlaid by certain German mispronunciations. I found it hard to take any abuse seriously when it was spoken in such a heavy unconvincing accent, since it all sounded faked or approximated.

'I could cut you off today and you would have to depart on a train travelling in the Third Class carriage with all those dirty people, those stinking men and thieving boys, and you wouldn't think so much of yourself then!'

Stinking men and thieving boys were the object of his desire and so this was rather an ambiguous threat.

I could bring you down, he was saying. But he was wrong, for I had arrived in Taormina with nothing and it made no difference to me if I left the same way. I could not be reduced, for I came from nowhere. I was strengthened by that thought. Having nothing to lose I felt indestructible. Seeing this, Haroun would tack in a different direction. On one of these occasions we were at the Teatro Greco, the dramatic amphitheatre, the ancient setting, the sight of Etna and the sea. Clapping his hands he said, 'You say she is beautiful. I did not command you to say that, correct? You say her face is like a Madonna—your own word. I am happy! This is very positive. It means you believe it. I did not tell you what to say.'

I liked him in this encouraging mood, because he was so lively and joyous himself—inexplicable to me, but pleasant to hear someone so attached to his friend that he glowed when she was praised.

'You thought these thoughts yourself, from your own heart and brain. It is what I always hope—that people will make up their own minds and go forward.'

I thanked him for understanding me.

'But the Gräfin does not understand,' he said. 'You are not so convincing to this wise woman.'

'I'll try again.'

He said, 'People's lives are much the same. The rich envy the poor. The poor envy the rich. People with great riches are afraid of losing what they have. Famous people fear falling into obscurity. Beautiful woman are fearful. Everyone in the world has the same fears.'

Was it the setting, this Greek theatre, that inspired this speech? Certainly he was strutting on the cracked marble of the ancient stage and striking poses. What he said made no sense to me and I was on the point of arguing with him when he spoke again.

'Of growing old and ugly. Of dying.'

I almost laughed at this, because I saw those fears as so distant for me here in Taormina, where I seemed just born and almost immortal. I wondered if he and the Gräfin had returned to Taormina to ease their fears.

Gräfin was inert. Did she know that she was the subject of our strolls around the town, our whispered discussions among the ancient ruins of Taormina? But why should she care? She was above all of this, she was powerful, she was resisting. Someone with little or no desire seemed very strong to me. It was so hard to influence such a person. The Gräfin's rejection of me was a sign of her strength.

In this second week I saw this wooing of the Gräfin, this ritual courtship, as a battle of wills. I also believed that I was strong, at least wanted to believe it: Haroun had said what I felt deep in my heart. And for all their power, wealthy people always, I felt, had an inner weakness, which was their need to be wealthy, their fear of poverty. I had no such fear. What confused me was that I felt them to be undeserving—lucky rather than accomplished. That luck had given them privileges, but left them with a fear of losing their luck. They were no better than me, but they were on top. I knew I was anyone's equal, even Gräfin's. But I told myself that I lacked funds.

Even then, dazzled as I was, I felt an element of resentment in myself, for the people of power who had not created their own wealth. They were children of privilege. I consoled myself with the belief that privilege made them weak, and I had proof of it, for my short time in Taormina had weakened me.

Gräfin was a countess by an accident of fate. She was someone's daughter, someone's lover, someone's ex-wife, just a lucky sperm. She had done nothing in her life except be decorative: her life was devoted to her appearance—being beautiful, nothing else. Yet what seemed shallow, her impossible vanity—her wish to be pretty, nothing else— attracted me. She was completely self-regarding, she existed to be looked at. She was utterly selfish: her narcissism made me desire her.

I wanted, in my passion for her, to discover her weakness, and to awaken passion and desire in her. I feared that there might be none, that she was too powerful in other ways for these emotions. So far, I had failed to awaken even mild interest; so far, she had not asked me a single question—did not know who I was, where I came from; did not care.

I made no active attempt to woo her now. My one pass at her

had been a humiliation for us both. But neither was I submissive. I continued to buy the German newspaper and the other trivial items from Mazzaro, I flunkeyed for her, watching her closely. I did not volunteer any information, did not allude to anything in my own life, nor did I ask her any questions. I imitated her; I put on a mask of indifference.

My coolness worked, or seemed to. I sometimes found her staring at me, silently quizzing me. But when I turned to meet her gaze she glanced away, pretending not to care.

Late one afternoon in the large crowded Piazza Nove Aprile some street urchins, gypsy children perhaps, began pestering, asking for money, tugging our clothes—Gräfin hated to be touched. When I told them to go away, they began making obscene remarks, really vulgar ones, variations of 'Go fuck your mother'. I took this to be commonplace obscenity but then it struck me that they might be commenting on our ages, Gräfin's and mine. That angered me and I chased them away, kicking one of the boys so hard he shouted in pain and called out, saying that I assaulted him.

'Di chi e la colpa?' a shopkeeper jeered—So whose fault is that?

'Haroun never treats them that way,' Gräfin said. 'I think he's a bit afraid of them.'

That sounded like praise. We walked some more. Still she was inscrutable behind her dark glasses.

'Or maybe he likes them too much.'

Recalling their obscenities, I said, 'I hate them.'

She gasped in agreement, a kind of wicked thrill. 'Yes.'

So that was a point in my favour, my harrying the ragged children. I earned more points not long after that. Gräfin was confounded and angered by anything mechanical. She saw such objects as enemies, they made her fearful. Breakdowns, even the chance of one, horrified her. She was very timid in the real world of delays and reverses—things she had no control over, which produced anxiety and discomfort.

We had gone back to Bustano, the olive estate, one day. She said, 'Harry says he cannot accompany me—so you must come'—one of her usual graceless invitations. As she had hired a driver I sat next to him, Gräfin having the entire back seat to herself. We travelled in silence and I missed Haroun now. I looked for anything familiar, a village, the signs of old earthquake damage, the Mussolini slogans.

At Bustano, we were greeted by the owner and some servants. I was not invited into the villa, though the owner (yellow shirt, pale slacks, sunglasses), with gestures of helplessness and fatalism, indicated that if it had been up to him I would have been welcome. I trembled to think what he made of me, in my white slacks and white espadrilles, my striped jersey, my new blue yachting cap. She had bought me the cap the day of the pestering children.

'The cap now, the yacht later,' she said, and what she intended as humour sounded like mockery to me.

On the way back to Taormina, at dusk, nowhere near any village, on a mountain road way beyond Troina, the car stalled at a stop sign—just faltered, chugged and coughed to a stop, like a death from black lung.

'This is impossible!' Gräfin was angry. She repeated the sentence, sounding uncertain. She said it again, sounding fearful.

The driver fiddled with the ignition key and stamped on the gas, and hit the steering wheel with the flat of his hand. He knew absolutely nothing. He was a villager, he had grown up among animals not machines. He treated the car as though it were an ox, dawdling in its yoke, or a wilful shivering dray-horse. His Sicilian instinct was to whip and punch the car.

I told Gräfin this, hoping to impress her, but she was too fearful to listen.

The car had faltered before this. Even when we had set out from Taormina it had been slow in starting up, and sometimes died while idling. I suspected the battery, perhaps a bad connection on the terminal. The engine was good enough. The car was an Alfa-Romeo TI.

'What is your name?'

'Fulvio, sir.'

'Open the hood, Fulvio.'

'Yes, sir.'

Gräfin said, 'What do you know about these things?'

'It's a good car, an Alfa, TI. You know what that stands for?'

'Of course not.'

'*Tritolo Incluso*. Bomb included. *Tritolo* is TNT.'

That was the joke in Palermo that year, where the Mafiosi were blowing each other up in touring cars exactly like this. Gräfin did not find this in the least bit funny, in fact she was annoyed by it.

'What can you possibly do?' she said, a sort of belittling challenge.

I said, 'It's almost dark. We're not going anywhere. The only other living things here are goats'—I could hear their clinking bells— 'What do you think I should do?'

This little speech, so theatrical in its rhetoric and unnecessary detail, served to make her more afraid, which was my intention. But fear also made her nervously bossy and she began to bully the driver Fulvio in German-accented Italian.

'*C'era d'aspettarsela*,' he said, meaning: We should have expected this.

I said to Gräfin, 'He doesn't seem to care very much.'

'We must go now to the villa,' Gräfin said. 'I have had so much to drink. I must pass water.'

The idea of relieving herself anywhere except in her suite at the villa being out of the question made me smile.

'I have pain here,' she said, touching herself unambiguously, and I stopped smiling. 'Maybe we need *benzina*.'

'We've got *benzina*.'

I looked under the hood in the last of the daylight. Although the Alfa was fairly new, the engine was greasy and looked uncared-for. The battery appeared serviceable yet the terminals were gummed up with that bluey-green mould as lovely and delicate as coral froth that accumulates on copper wires. I could see that the clamps were loose and sticky with the same froth. This bad connection could have accounted for the faltering start. I easily twisted one terminal and lifted it off and I guessed that the terminal was overlaid with scum, a sort of metallic spittle.

Flicking the wire on to the terminal produced a strong audible spark: it might be just this simple, I thought. I had dealt with enough cheap old cars to reach this conclusion. A more expensive car would have baffled me, but this was Sicily, and although this was an Alfa-Romeo it had the same battery as a Fiat or an old Ford.

Gräfin got out and from her stamping and hand wringing I

could tell that she was bursting for a pee. She berated the driver. I took pleasure in showing her the large greasy engine, of which she knew nothing. I made an elaborate business of pretending to fuss and fix it, tweaking wires, testing wing nuts, tapping the caps on the spark plugs, all the while hoping it was just the battery. Fulvio stood just behind me, sighing, muttering *'Mannaggia'*—Dammit!

With a broken knife-blade I found in a tool box in the trunk— Fulvio seemed surprised there was a tool box at all—I scraped the terminals clean, shaving the lead to rid it of scum. I did the same to the clamps.

Fulvio looked hopeful, though it was now fully dark, the goat bells clanking in the deep gully beside the road, the hoofs scrabbling on the stony hillside.

Gräfin said, 'What shall we do? It's all his fault.'

'This guy is useless,' I said.

'This guy is useless,' she repeated, using my words approvingly. But she was still twitching, clutching her sunglasses as though to ease her need.

'Don't worry. I'll get you back there. You'll be fine, Gräfin.'

For the first time, I used her title. She looked at me with a kind of promise, a kind of pleading.

She was now a small girl. I was her father. I scraped away at the terminal for a while longer. Then I tightened the nuts on the clamp—just fuss and delay, for at last I was in control.

'Get out,' I said to Fulvio, a little louder than I should have, but I wanted Gräfin to hear.

I ostentatiously took the ignition key and sat in the driver's seat. Seeing Gräfin beating her feet beside the car, I said, 'Sit here,' and indicated the passenger seat. Getting in awkwardly, she looked more than ever like a little girl.

I turned the key, pumped the gas, got the engine to chug, and then it roared.

'Ai!' Gräfin clapped. 'Hurry.'

'Get in the back seat, Fulvio,' I said. So we drove back to Taormina, sitting side by side, Gräfin and me; Fulvio muttering *'Mannaggia'* in the back seat.

Gräfin said, 'I can hold it. I need to pass water but I like the feeling. The pressure makes a nice feeling.'

She giggled. She was five or six again, with her daddy in the car on the road, heading home; but I was still thinking, What?

'I don't want to make an accident!'

We were heading up the steep hairpin curves of the Via Pirandello to the town. She had never seemed so frail and small and helpless; so lost in the world. Gratitude did not come naturally to her, yet I could sense something like an admission of her dependency on me in her respectful way of addressing me.

She said, 'I give you the key. You run and open the door to my suite—you are faster than me. Also, I think I can't open the door.'

She was a bit breathless and almost hysterical in the same girlish way.

'This is so funny. The chauffeur is sitting in the back!'

At the hotel, she pressed the key into my hand. I hurried through the villa and into her suite, racing ahead of her, opened the door and switched on the lights. The suite was beautiful, smelling of floor wax and fresh flowers.

I was in the hall, turning on the light in the toilet stall when she pushed past me, flung the door open and ducked into the toilet, lifted her skirt and pissed loudly into the shallow ceramic basin, sighing, her face shining with pleasure, while I stood gaping, too fascinated to move. And I thought that if I ducked aside and hid my face she would be embarrassed. As it was she seemed triumphant, like a sudden spattering fountain.

I had heard of people so used to having servants that they walked around naked in front of them; got servants to dress them; treated them as though they were blind, obedient, without emotion. But this was different. Gräfin was engaged in an intimate, deeply satisfying act, groaning with satisfaction. Then she straightened and slowly, fastidiously wiped herself with tissue, pulled the chain, rearranged her dress, and stepped into the hall where I stood.

'That was great,' she said in a hearty way, and kissed me. 'Now, you go,' and she flicked the dampness from her fingers at me, but playfully.

I was not disgusted. I thought, Germans! The breakdown, this simple inconvenience was our adventure. I told her that I liked her courage. I used this trivial event to apostrophize her. And she saw the day as a triumph with a terrific ending, the pay-off that farce in her suite.

She told Haroun: 'We were left by the side of the road. The driver was an idiot. I had to pass water. We could have died!'

As a result of this successful day, we spent more time together, and on better terms than before. She seemed much happier and more trusting. I began to dislike her, first in an irritated way, and then felt a kind of loathing.

Haroun said to me confidentially, 'Yet you have not succeeded.'

I wondered whether I would. I wondered now whether I wanted to. I still saw her in the bright light of the narrow stall of her toilet, smiling, pissing, utterly human and helpless and happy, less like a countess on her throne than a small girl on her potty, crying, Look at me! Look what I'm doing!

Then, a few days after Yet you have not succeeded, we were sitting on the terrace.

Haroun said, 'Now I go.'

Gräfin said nothing. Last week she would have said, What about me? Or, Why so early?

I said, 'That smell, is it jasmine?'

'Gelsomino,' she said, teaching me the word.

I used the perfume to lead her into the garden, where the fragrance was stronger. She picked a blossom, sniffed it, inhaled the aroma. I sidled up to her and touched her. She was so slender, and there was so little of her—small bones and tender muscles that were wisps of warm flesh—she seemed brittle and insubstantial. I always thought of the Gräfin as breakable. I tried to hold her.

'Nein,' she said, startled into her own language.

I was thinking: If this doesn't work I am done for. I did not want to leave Taormina, yet leaving was the only alternative, the consequence of my failure. This was my last hope, and I truly hated her for making me do this.

I said, 'The first time I saw you I wanted to kiss you.'

'You're drunk,' she said.

'No. Listen. You have the face of a Madonna. Kissing it is

wrong. I want to worship it.'

'How stupid,' she said, but even saying that she was thinking—I knew her well—not about my words but about her face.

'Please let me,' I said, grappling with her a little, and also glancing around the garden to make sure that we were alone, that we were not being observed.

She did not say anything yet she was definitely resisting; she had a body like a sapling, skinny but strong. I got my mouth close to her ear. I breathed a little and my breath was hot as it returned to me from the closeness of her head. I was at the edge, I knew that; I had to fling myself off.

I said, 'I love you,' and as I said it the wind left me, and I went weak, as though I had said something wicked, or worse, uttered a curse—as though I had stabbed her in the heart and then stabbed myself. And that was how she reacted, too, for she began to cry, and she held me, and sobbed, and was a little girl again.

'Help me,' she said. Her small voice in the twilight.

With that lie I became her lover. I stayed on at the Villa Moro, Haroun paying the bill with the Gräfin's money. After two weeks I left, took the train to Palermo, and the ship home.

And then I had my life, forty years more, the ones that matter most, the years of family and struggle, of love and popular acclaim, my illustrated travels.

When I am disparaged by critics for painting 'accessible' pictures I say that my strength is storytelling. What I have never said is that the most resourceful storytellers are the ones who avoid a particular story, the only story the teller has; the very avoidance of it is the reason for the other wilder tales. The source of fantastic narratives is often this secret, the fantasist using a concealment to hint at the truth, but always skirting the fundamental story. This is one ritual of creation. As I say, this is my only story. ☐

Royal Festival Hall
Queen Elizabeth Hall
Purcell Room
Literature Talks

Monday 24 September
Queen Elizabeth Hall 7.30pm

Fiction International
W G Sebald in conversation with Maya Jaggi
W G Sebald makes his only London appearance this year. 'One of the most exciting, and most mysteriously sublime, of contemporary European writers' *Guardian*.
This is the 2001 St Jerome event, organised by the British Centre for Literary Translation and held annually to celebrate the work of literary translators.
Tickets £8 (concessions £5.50)

Tuesday 2 October
Queen Elizabeth Hall 7.30pm

Fiction International
V S Naipaul with Patrick French
An unmissable rare appearance. 'In the canon of postwar British fiction Naipaul is without peer.' Jason Cowley, *Times*.
Tickets £8 (concessions £5.50)

Wednesday 10 October
Chelsfield Room 7.30pm

My Last Book: Trieste and the Meaning of Nowhere
Jan Morris
Jan Morris' final book is about Trieste, and is a meditation on 'nostalgia, sweet melancholy, the ageing process, the loss of friends, the scrapping of great ships, the decline of empires and all that kind of stuff.' (Jan Morris).
Tickets £6 (concessions £3.50)

Thursday 18 October
Purcell Room 7.30pm

Black History Month Event
Stuart Hall with Lola Young
Stuart Hall, leading social commentator and thinker, gives a lecture to mark Black History Month. The event will be chaired by Lola Young.
In association with the Archives and Museum of Black Heritage.
Tickets £7.50 (concessions £5)

20 - 27 October 2001
Imagine: Writers and Writing for Children
Events for children with writers Jacqueline Wilson, Malorie Blackman, John Agard and many others, a storytelling day, the transformation of the RFH Ballroom Floor into a space for children to read, write and enjoy multimedia displays and much more!
For full details call 020 7960 4242.

Tuesday 23 October
Purcell Room 7.30pm

Alice in Wonderland
Will Self and Fabian Peake
Will Self and illustrator Mervyn Peake's son Fabian Peake talk about the alchemy of text and image in *Alice*, and the other sources of its eternal fascination.
Tickets £7.50 (concessions £5)

Join the ebulletin list, email: Literature & Talks@rfh.org.uk
Box Office 020 7960 4242   www.rfh.org.uk
NO BOOKING FEE

GRANTA

THE WAR OF
THE WORDS
Alexander Stille

Alexander Stille

In Hargeisa, the capital of the self-proclaimed Republic of Somaliland, in the north of what used to be called Somalia, there are audio and videotape shops on nearly every street corner. Cassettes of recordings by Somali oral poets are displayed alongside videos of the latest Hollywood films starring Sylvester Stallone and Jean-Claude Van Damme. Poetry is broadcast regularly on the radio and television programmes featuring poets are beamed in by satellite from neighbouring Djibouti. One of the hottest new videos when I arrived in Hargeisa last summer was a film of the wedding of Mohammed Ibrahim Warsame, a leading Somali poet, universally known by his nickname, 'Hadrawi'. Even the Somali immigration officials brightened when I mentioned his name and proceeded to tell me about the recent marriage in detail, a traditional nomad ceremony with camel's milk and dates at the reception.

Somaliland declared its independence from the rest of Somalia in May 1991, four months after the fall of President Said Barre, who had ruled Somalia since 1969. The civil war that followed reduced Somalia to famine and chaos. What most people in the West recall are the images of United States marines being dragged through the streets of the capital, Mogadishu, in 1993 and the withdrawal of United Nations troops two years later. Somalia no longer has a seat at the UN, nor does it have an internationally recognized government. But that doesn't mean it plays no part in the global media. There are five different phone companies competing ferociously for business and a cellular phone system that offers the lowest rates in Africa. Satellite dishes are fixed to many houses and to shops where people watch European soccer and CNN. With about a million refugees scattered around the globe, the Somalis have formed a kind of virtual nation, knitted together by a strange combination of electronic signals and traditional kinship.

Almost all their media are audio-visual. Somalis belong to what is still principally an oral society. The majority are non-literate nomads who move around the country tending flocks of camels, sheep and goats. There are no publishing houses and the one daily newspaper in Somaliland, *Jamhuriya,* sells only 2,000 copies. There are hardly any written slogans on billboards and most shops illustrate their goods and services on elaborately painted storefronts rather than with written signs. One advertisement for a cell phone company, for example, shows a camel with a transmitting tower on its back. But though many of Hargeisa's 250,000 people live in makeshift huts in squatters' camps, most of them have tape recorders and radios. One Somali told me that if they had to choose between a tape recorder and a sack of rice, they'd take the tape recorder.

Until thirty years ago, when Siad Barre introduced an official Somali script in an attempt to impose state control on the population, the Somali language had no written form. Unluckily for Barre, the portable tape recorder arrived at the same time and was far better suited to Somalia's oral culture. When opposition to the Barre regime began to grow, poems dictated on to cassettes and circulated among the people became one of the chief forms of dissent. Barre had the poets arrested, but their recordings still changed hands. Many Somalis believe that it was a specific poetic duel (a chain of poems, a popular form in Somalia) between Hadrawi and another prominent poet in 1979 that marked the beginning of the end for Barre. Most of these poems criticized the government and they sparked off a national debate. Barre was powerless to stop the underground traffic in recordings. It was a clear sign that he had lost his popular mandate.

Hadrawi belongs to the first generation of poets to have used a whole array of technologies—writing, audio tape cassettes, radio, satellite television, video and international air travel—to disseminate his work. I first met him in the United States where he was representing Somalia at a millennium celebration in Chicago. Now, after a few days in Hargeisa, I travelled to visit him with an interpreter at his family home in Burao, about 200 kilometres away. When we arrived, he was standing in front of the nomad hut which had been built in celebration of his wedding. He is a distinguished looking man of fifty-seven with muttonchop sideburns and a light, stubbly beard. His straight nose and features, more Arab than African, reflect the long-standing contacts between Somalia and the Middle East. He was dressed in a brightly coloured *shaal*, which Somali men traditionally wrap around their waists, and a Western shirt.

Among Somalis, Hadrawi enjoys the combined status of prophet, intellectual and rock star. Many of his poems are put to music and performed by popular singers. I was told by several Somalis—those living in the West, as well as in Somalia—that lines Hadrawi had written twenty years ago had, as one of them put it, 'come true exactly'. Hadrawi says that all he did was describe what seemed obvious at the time: that the corruption and repression of the Barre dictatorship would eventually bring about its own downfall.

We talked about his wedding and the thousands of guests, invited and uninvited, who had joined the procession. The president of Somaliland had donated $10,000 towards the costs (which Hadrawi insisted he would give away to worthwhile causes); he had also sent a large number of government agents to observe the event. 'There were rumours that it was not a wedding but a camouflage for a big political meeting, so there were a lot of security people present,' Hadrawi explained with some amusement. 'Poets in Somalia are not just admired, they are feared,' added my interpreter, Saeed.

Hadrawi is not associated with any particular political faction but his return to live in Somaliland after years of exile was seen as an important confirmation of the legitimacy of the newly declared state. He had been writing in Somali well before the introduction of an official script. At the age of ten he was sent to stay with an uncle in Yemen to study there. He learned to read and write fluent Arabic and at high school he also learned a certain amount of English. Through English he learned the Latin alphabet and when he began to compose poetry, he wrote down the words phonetically using Latin characters. Some of his contemporaries made similar experiments, but since there was no standardized orthography, it was as if each were writing in his own private language. Hadrawi returned to Somalia in 1967. He wrote and performed poetic plays and as his fame grew he was invited to teach at the National Teachers' Education College, near Mogadishu, one of the new universities that had sprung up with independence. In 1972, in collaboration with three other young poets, he wrote a play called *Knowledge and Understanding*, which called openly for a written Somali script. It opened just months before the launch of the government's literacy campaign.

On the evening of October 20, 1972, the third anniversary of the coup that brought Barre and his socialist Supreme

Revolutionary Council to power, most of the population of Mogadishu was lining the streets along the parade route. Suddenly, a helicopter swooped down and began to drop thousands of brightly coloured leaflets on the crowd as if in a heavenly dispensation. People picked up the pamphlets and puzzled over them. They were not in a language that anyone in the crowd recognized: they were not in Arabic, or Italian or English. 'They began to fight with their tongues to read the new writing,' the government English-language newspaper later reported. At first they were baffled, the paper reported, then they realized: 'This was Somali!'

Since only a tiny percentage of the crowd could read, the written message was reinforced on Radio Mogadishu by songs proclaiming the new script. In the homely metaphors of nomadic verse:

> In the history of the world, our Language was taking no part;
> But the sunrise appeared uncovering our Language from darkness;
> The fence was cleared, so the livestock could graze.
> Give me your pen, the words I write for you.
> It is not a Foreign Language; the tongue does not slip,
> Like milk, it can be swallowed smoothly.

There are more than 1,000 indigenous African languages, but only a few—Swahili and Amharic, for example—have written forms. European colonization meant that European languages, principally Portuguese, French and English, became established as the unifying common languages in territories which had many different tongues (Zaire alone has 320 of them). But European colonization came late to the nomadic population and semi-arid land of Somalia—in the late nineteenth century, when the Italians occupied the south and the British took over the north. It was bitterly and often successfully contested, and the colonists (especially the British) rarely strayed far from the coast. As a result, literacy began much later than in other African colonies, and by the time of the Somalis' independence in 1960, less than ten per cent of the population could read—one of the lowest literacy rates in Africa. And rather than unifying the country, the colonial languages had divided it. For some time after independence official documents had to be produced in both English and Italian and as few people spoke any foreign languages and hardly any spoke both well, the result was a bureaucratic disaster. The solution was obvious.

Somalia was one of the few African countries where nearly everyone spoke the same language; to speak Somali was to be Somali, a linguistic nationalism which had helped the push for an independent, unified Somali state. A written form would open the world of government and power to all citizens. But what form should the script take? This became a paralysing political issue. Arabic script, which some Somalis learn at religious schools as children, does not have vowel symbols, and so is not suited to the Somali language which has twenty-two different vowel sounds, more vowels than consonants. The Latin alphabet appeared a more practical solution: its five vowels could be used in different combinations to approximate the intonations of Somali speech. Educated Somalis who had studied English or Italian already knew Latin letters and the government could continue using its store of European typewriters. But the Latin alphabet faced stiff political opposition. The Muslim sheiks coined a clever slogan, 'Laatiin, *Laa Diin*,' playing on the similarity between 'Latin' and the Somali word for 'godless'. Somali nationalists viewed the Latin script as a residue of the country's colonial domination. When the government tried putting up a few street signs in Somali with the Latin alphabet, a riot broke out. Some nationalists insisted that to be truly independent Somali must have its own indigenous alphabet and several Somali intellectuals created their own sets of symbols which they proposed as alternative scripts. Soon there were twenty-three competing candidates, each of them backed by different Somali clans. Faced with this babel, the early independent governments chose the path of least resistance: doing nothing.

The paralysis was emblematic of the inefficiency, corruption and inter-clan squabbling that paved the way for Siad Barre, who after a bloodless coup promised order, progress, socialism and an end to the clan system. He was met with wild joy in the streets. 'I welcomed the revolution like everybody else,' Hadrawi said. 'We were nationalists.'

His enthusiasm for the new politics soon turned sour. Emulating Mao and Castro, Barre sent all high school and university students into the countryside for a year to teach the nomads in the bush how to read and write about the feats of the revolution. He kept strict control of all publishing and it was even difficult to own a typewriter. The official newspaper, the *October Star*, printed a picture of Barre on its front page every day and was written in the hagiographic style of the average socialist dictatorship. With so little to read, most Somalis had no motive for literacy. Hadrawi said of Barre: 'He should have translated world knowledge into Somali. Instead he only used the script for political propaganda.' Barre also tried to control the flow of poetry. 'He used it for his own influence with power and money,' Hadrawi said. 'He tried to control all the poets and everything else in the area of literature. All the Somali media, Radio Mogadishu, Radio Hargeisa, were harnessed to broadcast propaganda for the regime.'

It was at this point that the cheap cassette players arrived. 'That's when the underground literature started,' Hadrawi said.

The tape recorder amplified an ancient Somali tradition: the poetic duel. Somali poetry is based on the alliteration of a particular letter or sound in a poem rather than a rhyme. In a poetic chain, or 'duel', one poet will write a poem on a given theme, using a particular alliterative scheme, and other poets will then answer addressing the same theme and using the same alliteration. The chain has a competitive element, with the poets vying with one another to come up with unusual words or clever neologisms, but its metaphors allow difficult political and social problems to be aired without provoking conflict. 'Allegory cools down speech,' according to an old Somali proverb. It was also the perfect way to avoid government censorship. The standard tropes of Somali poetry—'a bitter drought' or 'a cleansing storm'—could carry a subversive meaning or simply be about everyday life. 'Somalis like to sit around in the afternoon and listen as they chew khat,' Hadrawi said. 'So everybody would listen to the tapes and then compare interpretations the next morning.'

One of the reasons for his popularity is that Hadrawi was one of the few poets who refused to use his poetry to praise the Barre regime. Several of his poems, set to music by one of Somali's leading singers, became popular favourites. One of them, 'Saxarla' (pronounced Saharla), sparked off a poetic duel known as the 'sin-ley' poems, meaning 'S-chain' in Somali. Although it was ostensibly a love song, its main character, Saxarla, a blind woman, was thought to represent Somalia, groping around in the dark, and its tone of impatient longing suggested covert political parallels. The desire to rescue Saxarla was interpreted by some as a desire to free Somalia from dictatorship and by others as a call to liberate the Somali-speaking territories in Kenya, Ethiopia and Djibouti.

Soon poems on cassette began pouring in from different parts of Somalia and from Somalis in other countries. All kinds of symbolic devices were employed: five little sheep, or five lamps, to represent the five regions of Somalia; a spear served for a cryptic discussion of the government's military might. They allowed people to discuss topics that were impossible to talk about openly.

Siad Barre is said to have amassed a formidable collection of these tapes. In 1973 he summoned Hadrawi to the presidential palace and offered him any job he wanted on condition he stopped writing poems against the regime. Hadrawi retaliated with his most overtly political poem to date. His poetic play *The She-Camel* described the slaughter for a feast that is enjoyed by a few while the multitude watches from a distance; a clear reference to the corruption and cronyism of the Barre government and a portent of its end.

> With the news of a slaughtered she-camel
> Everybody hurried to the scene.
> The fun will be to see the others
> Who saw the smoke from the high peaks
> And will come rushing down the slopes and the ridges.

The play was performed before the censorship board, the vice-president and two government ministers. They demanded numerous changes, but Hadrawi refused to make them. The play was never performed in public and Hadrawi was put under house arrest in isolation about 350 miles from Mogadishu. Meanwhile *The She-Camel* was set to music and distributed widely on tape.

During his detention between 1973 and 1978, Hadrawi refrained from writing political poetry, both to avoid further trouble, he said, and to maintain his sanity. But on his release he found a political situation he could not ignore. In 1977 Siad Barre had declared war on Ethiopia in order to annex the Ogaden region, where many ethnic Somalis lived. In 1978 the Ethiopians counter-attacked, driving hundreds of thousands of Somalis across the border into Somalia and creating the beginning of a twenty-year refugee crisis.

Barre had no desire to resolve this crisis. The presence of refugees in Somalia was a cash cow for his regime, and the refugee numbers were deliberately inflated to increase foreign aid. Since Ethiopia was supported by the Soviet Union, Barre became the West's man and got arms and financial help from the US and Europe. Almost overnight, the father of Somali socialism had turned into the leading anti-Communist in Africa. Domestically, however, his policies amounted to little more than an increasingly brutal grab for power and money.

Not long after Hadrawi's return from detention he was woken at 5 a.m. by Barre's agents and taken to the palace. Barre, a chronic insomniac who chain-smoked throughout the night, was in the habit of summoning people from their sleep in this way. 'He told me to bring various men of literature with me and he tried to convert us to his ideas,' Hadrawi said. They listened politely but were unmoved. In one poem from this period, Hadrawi answered Siad Barre's request for support with a direct slap in the face.

> How can I say something good about you?
> Where shall I start?
> You are not brave enough.
> You are not kind enough.
> You are not wise enough...
> You are made of a bad clay.

And then, in December 1979, Hadrawi and fellow poet, Mohamed Hashi Dhamac (known as 'Gaariye'), decided to launch a poetic duel that would directly confront the regime. The duel was composed of poems beginning with the letter 'd' and has become known as the 'de-ley' (or 'D-chain') poems. The 'sin-ley' poems were ambiguous in their meaning, but now the poets directly addressed

Alexander Stille

the new reality of Somalia, and the people who had grown rich from stolen foreign aid. In this poem, 'Debatiel', Hadrawi wrote:

> Where does all this money come from?
> It doesn't come from people's work.
> Who has paid for
> All these colourfully decorated houses?
> Where do these Japanese cars come from
> When most people have nothing?
> They do not come from the sky.
> These people are flaunting their wealth instead of hiding their shame.
> Don't they know that they will have to stand for their crimes?
> That there will be a day of reckoning?

About sixty other poets joined in the chain, contributing a total of more than a hundred poems. The regime tried to ban the poets, but people continued taping as they had before. 'We were expecting to be imprisoned every night,' Hadrawi said. 'If Barre had had the support of the people, he could have smashed us in a minute as he did in 1973. Instead, it shook the foundation of the state.'

The view that the 'de-ley' chain was a crucial turning point in Somali life is also shared by many non-poets. 'The poetry was more important to us than guns and cannons,' said Abdulrahman Yousseff, a fighter with the Somali National Movement (SNM), one of the first armed groups to oppose the regime. 'These songs opened up discussion for people. They were becoming educated and informed. They would sit around listening to the songs and talk. People generally didn't listen to these songs alone. They listened with other people and they had to screen the people whom they were listening with and so these were the basis of political groupings. So Siad Barre was not wrong to be afraid of the poets.'

The SNM was formed in January 1981, about a year after the beginning of the de-ley chain, and operated from a base in Ethiopia. The majority of its members were from Northern Somalia, where opposition to the Barre regime was particularly strong. Hadrawi and Gaariye remained in Mogadishu until May 1, 1982, when, taking advantage of the May Day holiday, they slipped out of the city, were driven north to Hargeisa and across the border into Ethiopia. On the day they left, there was an announcement on SNM's independent radio that the poets had joined the opposition. 'I said: "Hargeisa, awaken!"' Hadrawi recalled. 'And the armed poetry started.'

Their support lent prestige and respectability to the armed resistance and the SNM frequently broadcast their poetry from a radio station in Addis Ababa, the capital of Ethiopia. When Barre made peace with Ethiopia in 1988 in order to convince Ethiopia to expel the Somali resistance groups, the SNM used a mobile radio transmitter which they transported strapped to the back of a camel.

After Barre's fall in 1991 the country was divided into clan-based areas, each controlled by a clan warlord. There is a widely held view among African scholars that the lack of a solid tradition of written law has forced many African countries to fall back into their ethnic and clan affiliations, and that this, in turn, has contributed to the massacres in places such as Rwanda, Liberia and Uganda as well as in Somalia itself. (Radio broadcasts are not always benign; they played a key role in the genocidal killings of Rwanda.) Somalia has since disintegrated into a lawless, stateless nation, its public infrastructure destroyed by civil war. In Somaliland, however, the situation is more reassuring.

With almost no international aid, this northern part of Somalia has rebuilt itself with remarkable speed. Hargeisa, which was a semi-deserted pile of rubble with only a few thousand residents in 1991, is now a lively city. Somali refugees are returning from the West or remitting money which their relatives can invest in new businesses. Schools are reopening. There is a functioning bus service. Couriers deliver mail. A maternity hospital is under construction.

The oral and written cultures in Somaliland are mixing in curious and innovative ways. The northern Somalis have formed a 'parliament of clans' as a means of securing peace. They have also downloaded the text of a Nigerian law from the Internet in order to work out a new constitution that would prevent any one clan from dominating their country. Somaliland offers its citizens a choice of justice: they can abide by traditional clan justice (where the clan of the victim works out a settlement with the clan of the perpetrator) or by the written laws of the government court system.

As I was preparing to leave Burao, a local video shop owner arrived at Hadrawi's house to sell me one of the first edited copies of the Hadrawi wedding tape. 'It will be seen in Toronto, Minneapolis, Norway—wherever there are Somalis!' Hadrawi said with a wry kind of pride. Paradoxically, his wedding video is part of his current poetic strategy of fighting the pressures of Westernization and urging a return to tradition. He is aware of the contradictions of using Western technology to combat Western culture, but he feels he must fight fire with fire. He is worried that the same technology that helped to make him famous, and which he continues to use, will pull Somalis further and further into the global consumer economy that is transforming Somali society.

In recent years, this has become the dominant theme of his poetry. The world in which he grew up, a pastoral nomadic life that developed over centuries in isolation, is disappearing. Hadrawi said: 'Poetry was a repository of all our knowledge. It was our dictionary, our encyclopedia, it told you everything you needed to live. In the past, there was actually a competition over how much knowledge a person could carry in him. People knew the names of all the plants and trees and what their properties were. Man felt at home in his environment. A great deal of knowledge that has been slowly accumulated for hundreds and hundreds of years is now coming to an end. My work will remain in books, but the future generations will not understand it because they will speak the language of technology.' □

GRANTA

AN AMATEUR SPY IN ARABIA

Norman Lewis

PHOTOGRAPHS BY
NORMAN LEWIS

Norman Lewis, 1930s

In the 1930s I wanted to travel and I wanted to write. In 1935, I published my first book—about a journey to Spain. It was not, however, my writing ability that brought me to the attention of a Rex Stevens of the Colonial Office in London. He was attracted by my interests in photography and foreign languages, particularly Arabic. One day this Mr Stevens called on me to enquire whether I might be interested in a journey to the Yemen, which until then had been hardly visited by Western travellers, and of which little was known.

Having succeeded in awakening my interest, Stevens passed me on to the Foreign Office, where an official outlined the drawbacks to the kind of expedition Stevens had in mind. Such unsolicited incursions were regarded by the country's suspicious and xenophobic rulers as espionage, to be punished by chopping off the offender's head. 'So far only two Englishmen have travelled in the country. There are no roads as we understand them. There's no electricity and you will be unable to eat the food. I would strongly recommend a further discussion with Stevens before you commit yourself.'

When I saw Stevens again, he shrugged his shoulders. 'These men are professional pessimists,' he said. 'Do you still feel you might want to go ahead?' I told him I did. 'In that case you must meet Ladislas Farago,' he said. 'He'll be coming along.'

'Didn't he write that book about Abyssinia?'

'He certainly did, and if you haven't read it I've got a copy here.'

Stevens fumbled in his briefcase and brought out a copy of *Abyssinia on the Eve*, which at that moment was in all the bookshops. 'It's the most extraordinary book of its kind I've ever read. Absolutely riveting. Farago's a remarkable man. Anyway, why don't you join us?' Stevens said. 'You'd find it of immense interest, I assure you, and full of amazing adventures.'

'I can imagine,' I said.

In the end it was decided that I should meet Farago if that could be done, and later that day I took a phone call from Stevens to say that this had been arranged for the following Friday.

This gave me a couple of days to read the book, and I settled down to an account of the extraordinary year Farago had spent in Abyssinia.

Farago was a Hungarian-born journalist who worked for the

Associated Press. He had a reputation as a great miser and bluffer. A couple of years earlier he had been sent to Abyssinia on the eve of the Italian invasion, which began in October 1935 and was completed by May 1936. He discovered a country that had never freed itself from the Middle Ages—nor had it wished to do so—ruled by Haile Selassie, its emperor, and a tiny aristocracy which enjoyed total power. Here they had even dispensed with prisons. If a man killed another, the nearest armed guard would execute him on the spot, and there were buffalo-hide whips and branding irons ready in the street to be used on minor criminals. Proven liars were scourged, and debtors chained to their creditors. Slave markets existed in the remoter towns, and Farago described naked slaves of both sexes being exhibited for sale.

On the Friday, as arranged, the meeting with Ladislas Farago took place in Stevens's office. My first impression of Farago was favourable. Reading his book I had been carried along by a robust sense of humour, and now I was impressed by his modesty—highly commendable in a successful author. It was evident that he had experienced considerable relief at being able to put Abyssinia behind him. In his view nothing in European history had existed to compare with the tragic condition of the poor in that country.

So had he finally turned his back on the place? Stevens asked. Farago raised his eyes to the ceiling. 'I have no plans to go back,' he said.

Stevens turned to the Yemen project, which had clearly been under discussion before my arrival. 'So, Ladislas, I can take it you're quite happy with what's suggested?' he asked.

Farago laughed. 'I have to do something for a living. Who do we see about all the details?'

'No one but me, I'm afraid,' Stevens said. 'We're dealing with a closed country. There's no one we can talk to except a number of Bedouins who trade across the border. We know nothing of what goes on at the top, which is what interests us. We're starting from scratch.'

'When do you expect we'll be making a move?' I asked.

'As soon as we can. Sir Bernard Reilly, our man over there, is giving us a letter for the king and I've managed to fix up passages for a dhow from Aden. The first thing we do when we get there is

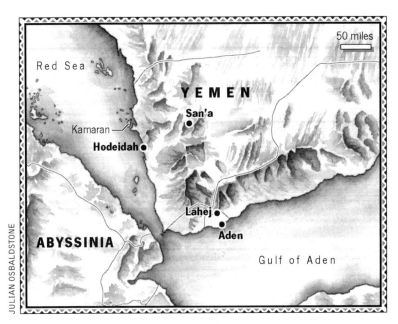

see the skipper—he'll ask us to sign a paper saying that we believe in God. Be another week or so before they collect all the passengers and we can set sail,' Stevens replied.

'Things move slowly,' I said.

'They do, but you soon get used to it,' Stevens told us. 'The only port in the Yemen is Hodeidah. It takes five to fifteen days to get there, according to the weather. What happens next, heaven only knows.'

'And once again, what is the objective of the expedition?' I asked. It was a question which produced one of Stevens's secret smiles.

'The answer,' he said, 'is that we will gain valuable information. You will busy yourself with your camera, and Ladislas, I'm sure, will write another excellent book. Just think of the photographic possibilities. It's still illegal to take photographs in the Yemen. Did you know that?' he asked.

'No, I did not.'

'Something to do with the Prophet's ban on graven images. Which being the case, you'll want to get shots of practically everything you see.'

95

'Naturally.'

Little remained to be settled after that. Stevens spoke to his travel agent, and a week later we boarded the SS *Llansteffan Castle*. We reached Aden in nine days. The year was 1937.

Aden was then one of the great destinations of the world. Sitting in the middle of the trade route to India, it was of immense strategic importance and had been ruled by the British since the 1830s. A constant, almost uncontrollable influx of travellers poured through it, as if through a cosmic filter, from all parts of the Eastern and Western worlds. Newcomers passed through a climate of bewilderment, frustration, hope, relief and despair before finding salvation in the neutrality of a hotel.

Though we had arrived late in the day, the heat was still intolerable. Fortunately the Marina Hotel to which we had been delivered possessed a roof terrace on which beds were lined up ready for the night. From this point there was a distant view of what we were assured was the last of the 'Towers of Silence', with vultures flapping over it round a corpse abandoned for disposal. The mutterings and squawks of nocturnal animals destroyed any hopes of sleep and I got up and moved down to the bar which was still open. Here I was instantly approached by a courteous young man who handed me a visiting card engraved with his name, Joseph, and his profession: Senior Officers' Pimp. We talked for a while of his occupation and he assured me that Aden City and the smaller towns of the Protectorate possessed in all 8,000 prostitutes, and that those under his protection were not only of exceptional beauty and charm but with the education necessary to be included at reasonable prices in any family party. There were a few who could perform tricks at such gatherings, even causing the guests' enemies to disappear and be seen no more, although they naturally demanded a higher fee.

Stevens was soon busy making our arrangements. After a visit to Sir Bernard Reilly, the Governor, he was handed a letter to the Imam Yahya—at the time on the verge of official recognition as the Yemeni king. Sir Bernard hoped that our visit might do something to improve the somewhat flaccid relationship between Britain and the Yemen in recent years. Obtaining our permit, however, proved

MUST REMEMBER TO SUBSCRIBE TO GRANTA.

RIDICULOUS TO KEEP BORROWING IT FROM FRIENDS/BUYING COPIES IN
BOOKSHOPS, WHEN I GET THE EQUIVALENT OF A FREE ISSUE WHEN I
SUBSCRIBE, AND HAVE IT DELIVERED TO ME AT HOME.

OH AND LOOK. I DON'T EVEN HAVE TO SCRABBLE AROUND FOR A STAMP.
AND APPARENTLY THEIR SUBSCRIPTIONS DEPARTMENT IS FAMOUSLY
EFFICIENT AND PLEASANT TO DEAL WITH (AND THERE'S NO 'VOICE-MAIL'
SYSTEM TO CONTEND WITH).

NB: GIFT SUBSCRIPTIONS. CLD BE USEFUL.

GRANTA

SEE OVERLEAF...

FREE ISSUE OFFER

Every issue of Granta features outstanding new fiction, memoir, reportage and photography. Every issue is a handsome, illustrated paperback. Every issue is special. That's why Granta is published only four times a year: to keep it that way. Subscribe, and you'll get Granta at a big discount, delivered to your home. (A subscription makes a great gift, too: thoughtful and lasting.)

- A one year (four-issue) subscription is £26.95. You save £9 (25%) on the bookshop price (£8.99 an issue). That's equivalent to getting a whole Granta, **FREE**.

- A two year (eight-issue) subscription is £50. You save £22 (30%).

- A three year (twelve-issue) subscription is £70. You save £38 (35%).

E S S E N T I A L R E A D I N G

OBSERVER

GRANTA

I'd like to subscribe for myself, for: ◯ 1 year (4 issues) at just £26.95 (25% off)
◯ 2 years (8 issues) at just £50 (30% off)
◯ 3 years (12 issues) at just £70 (35% off)
Please start my subscription with ◯ this issue ◯ the next issue

I'd like to give a subscription, for: ◯ 1 year (4 issues) at just £26.95 (25% off)
◯ 2 years (8 issues) at just £50 (30% off)
◯ 3 years (12 issues) at just £70 (35% off)
Please start the subscription with ◯ this issue ◯ the next issue

My details (please supply even if ordering a gift): Mr/Ms/Mrs/Miss _____

Address _____

_____ Country _____ Postcode _____

Gift recipient's details (if applicable): Mr/Ms/Mrs/Miss _____

Address _____

_____ Country _____ Postcode _____

01JBG750

Total amount* £_____ paid by ◯ £ cheque, enclosed (to 'Granta') ◯ Visa/Mastercard/AmEx:

card no: / __ / __ / __ / __ / __ / __ / __ / __ / __ / __ / __ / __ /

expires: / __ / __ / __ / signature: _____

* Postage. The prices stated include UK postage. For the rest of Europe, please add £8 (per year). For the rest of the world, please add £15 (per year).

◯ We occasionally permit compatible organizations to mail our subscribers. Please tick here if you'd prefer not to receive their literature through the post. (Gift recipients are automatically opted out.)

▣ **Post** ('Freepost' in the UK) to: Granta, Freepost, 2/3 Hanover Yard, Noel Road, London N1 8BR
Phone/fax: tel 44 (0)20 7704 0470, fax 44 (0)20 7704 0474 **Email:** subs@granta.com

difficult. Money could provide a variety of entertainment in Aden but when it came to taking a dhow to the Yemen even financial solidity came second to religious faith.

We were soon assured that, by the greatest of good fortune, a dhow had just arrived in port that would serve our purposes. It would shortly be taking cargo for destinations on the Red Sea, including Hodeidah. Unfortunately it had run into a storm on its way from Al Mukalla, necessitating repairs involving an uncertain number of weeks. We were taken to inspect it and welcomed on board. It bore the name *El Haq* (Truth), and had been somewhat nonchalantly berthed in an angle of the waterway. It smelled of bad breath. A man in a yellow jacket of the kind in compulsory use where outbreaks of the plague were suspected was splashing the deck with disinfectant from a can, while another had withdrawn to a corner for evening prayer. The inflated corpse of a dog drifted past on a sluggish current. The dhow was smaller than expected and would have been much improved by fresh paint. It was impossible to ignore the massive, roughly carpentered chair in its surrounding cage, known in Arabic as 'the place of ease', which would be hoisted high in the air over the waves as soon as the ship was under way.

By the end of the sixth week of our stay, we had become very familiar with the situation in Aden. Investigating the city, we had, worryingly, identified many Italian soldiers in mufti, though Ladislas assured me that they had been drawn there by the presence of a singular attraction. This was, in fact, the best-kept brothel in the Mediterranean, with a complex of charming and spotless chalets said to have been designed by a lapsed Roman Catholic priest, based on a vision of Paradise that had drawn him to the place. It was heavy with the perfume of the jasmine plants that trailed over all the houses, and ruled over by a dazzling young lady of fourteen named 'Halva' (Sweetness), who made no charge for her services for suitors who presented themselves with an acceptable poem. But we had also soon become aware of the presence of many secret agents, and there was no longer any doubt in my mind, and certainly none in Farago's, as to the immediate purpose of our presence there.

This had been instantly confirmed when, on the spur of the

moment, I had visited Stevens in the lodgings he had taken to escape the noise of the hotel. He had put aside a map he had been studying but it was clearly one of southern Yemen, showing an area encircled in red ink. A whisky bottle close at hand may have accounted for his immediate frankness. He shook his head. 'Really it's all a matter of who gets there first—the Italians or us,' he said. 'Everybody realizes that something has to happen. Any leads on the situation? I suppose it's early days.'

'I wasn't sure how urgent this was,' I said. 'I talked to a man who could be useful yesterday. Belongs to an organization called the Whisperers, based in Lahej. He could find us a professional guide and bodyguards if necessary.'

'Good,' Stevens said. 'No chance of a trap, I hope?'

'I doubt it,' I said. 'It's something the Arabs don't seem to go in for.'

'What's special about Lahej?' Stevens asked.

'It's practically on the border, and half the population are Yemeni refugees. They'd be on our side.'

'And you feel like going there then?'

'Why not? Better than hanging about in Aden.'

'Well, don't get yourself killed,' Stevens said.

I was pleasantly surprised that it should be possible to take a taxi to Lahej, although I noted that the driver wore a gun, tucked into an armpit holster. We covered a few miles through Aden's slatternly outskirts before reaching an open road flanked by the muted outlines of the shipbuilding yards of prehistory. Lahej came rapidly into sight, surrounded by shining oases. The initial brilliance of its surroundings proved on closer approach to be something of a deception, for the town itself was subject to dust storms, its buildings being pallid with a greyish powder that stuck to its walls. Worst of all, the palms grouped by the hundreds in its open spaces released cascades of dust at fairly regular intervals when shaken by gusts of wind. A touch of fanaticism in its religious observances kept the citizens of Lahej more frequently at prayer than elsewhere in southern Arabia. They fasted, made donations to the poor, nurtured the sick, dressed without ostentation, played nothing but religious music, and had outlawed the gramophone. With all that they contrived surely to be the most friendly and companionable people it was possible to imagine. I had hardly released myself from the taxi when a passer-by pushed himself to the front of the small crowd that had gathered, and proceeded to offer me, using a simplified form of his language employed in conversation with foreigners or children, the hospitality of his home. I had already been warned of the almost embarrassing kindness of these people so I was able to excuse myself with a reasonable amount of grace. I then hastened to take refuge in one of the town's inns, in which Bedouin and their camels were lodged without distinction, before someone else, seeing me at a loose end, could implore me to become a guest in his house.

I was to spend two days in Lahej, enchanted by the rigidity of its customs. It was immediately clear that this was the great playground of the desert, and that these people of Bedouin origin remained Bedouin at heart and were the prisoners of pleasure. A man at the inn had told me, 'Parties go on all the time. We're addicts of them. If a man sells a few sheep he's likely to join with a friend and they hire a tent. It holds 200 people and they put it up in two days. Often it's for a wedding and everyone is invited. I could take you to a party now, and they'd rush to grab your hand and say *"Ahlan wa sahlan"* (Your very good health).'

The next day was a Friday, when the Sultan accompanied by his numerous family and the nobility of this minuscule realm walked in procession to pray in the mosque. I witnessed an inspiriting scene in which the Lahej army, composed of about one hundred British-trained soliders, marched both to the rhythm of native drummers and to the music of the only saxophone permitted by the religious authorities to be imported into the state.

In the evening I was invited to a party attended solely by men, at which the chewing of khat—the leaves of a mildly narcotic plant—was general, although this produced only a mild hilarity. A number of the guests had visited the barber earlier in the evening to have themselves cupped and a few arrived still wearing cows' horns covering gashes on various parts of their bodies. No disquiet was evident when, despite the illegality of photography, I used my spy camera to take pictures of this weird effect and other scenes likely to be of interest to Stevens. But my use of the camera—never seen and hardly even heard of—aroused interest and speculation in Lahej. 'I'm making pictures for the people back home,' was my reason given, whether or not understood.

Lahej was within 300 miles of one of the greatest of earth's total deserts, but it had a temperate climate and substantial rainfall. A guest at the party told me that this was due to the mountain range to the north, the beginnings of which were almost within walking distance. He offered to take me in his camel cart into these mountains, and we set off together the next morning. The distance was covered at a remarkable pace and within two hours we found ourselves in a flowering landscape.

We were now in the forbidden land of the Yemen, passing through countryside watered by mountain streams and covered with a profusion of green vegetation. It was too early in the year to enjoy the summer maximum of this scene, but on all sides the aloes and tamarisks, date palms and banana trees protruded from among flowering aromatic shrubs. My friend, Said Hamud, was a man of education who stressed the fact that the climate of his land, although a part of Asia, was more like that of a country lying far away to the north by the waters of the Atlantic. In winter, he said, there were stiff frosts within fifty miles of Lahej, although no snowfalls. A little later, in season, I was told, these mountain flanks would be clothed with jasmine, clematis and wild briar, and also—incredibly enough with bluebells and forget-me-nots. The more accessible valleys had already been cultivated with coffee beans, and fruits of all kinds. My friend pointed out the monkeys in the trees, and as a lover of birds I was delighted to identify the hoopoe and the golden oriole. A pre-Islamic Arab writer had said of this country that, 'Its inhabitants are all hale and strong; sickness is rarely seen, there are no poisonous plants or animals, nor blind persons, nor fools, and the women are ever young. The climate is like Paradise, and one wears the same garment all winter.'

What we had seen that morning explained the eagerness of certain colonial powers to grab whatever they could of this country and it was fear of the colonialists, we were later to learn, that had induced the Yemeni priest-king Yahya to step up his military and spiritual offensives. Ladislas claimed to have discovered that the Imam had purchased 15,000 defective rifles from the Polish government, and in the same week had trebled the amount of compulsory public prayers. The kingdom's postal services, he believed, had become a tool of international spies. Thus Sir Bernard Reilly's letter on our behalf was carried to the Yemen by one of Yahya's personally appointed postmen, qualified not only to deliver the mail but to preach in the mosque. Such were the methods by which the king hoped to hold nemesis at bay.

When I got back to Aden I sensed a change in the atmosphere of the place but some time passed before I decided that this was due to another influx of Italian soldiers. They were all officers, splendidly uniformed and courteous—if slightly aloof in their manner— still perhaps a little dazzled by their recent victory in Abyssinia. They congregated in the lounges of the better hotels, bowing and smiling slightly when introduced to foreigners, but above all demonstrating a slight superiority, where their British counterparts were concerned, by never appearing to have had too much to drink. It was in the bar on the roof terrace of the Marina Hotel that I spotted Farago, who had been mysteriously absent for most of our stay. He was with an Italian, grinning broadly and gesticulating as he sometimes did. A second Italian officer joined the pair and the soldiers exchanged fascist salutes. At this point I moved behind a potted fern to give some thought to the possible implication of this scene.

That afternoon I located Farago in another part of the hotel and he told me that he had been to Djibouti—clearly at Stevens's behest. 'But why on earth Djibouti?' I asked, 'isn't it French?' He grinned. 'These places change hands all the time,' he said.

It seemed better to change the subject. 'A lot of Italians about the place,' I suggested.

'I noticed that,' Farago laughed. 'They're quick off the mark. No Italian stays longer than he has to in Abyssinia. This must be like coming home to them. Just say *"Buon giorno"* and *"come va?"* You'll find they're all right.'

'Any news of the permit?' I asked.

'None whatever. I can assure you that Sir Bernard Reilly has given it up as hopeless and so have I. All we have to do now is take the dhow to Hodeidah with a pocket full of fivers and talk to the immigration people there.' He laughed again—a sound in this case finishing in a whine like a dog's.

'When do we leave?'

'Impossible to say. The dhow people probably don't know themselves. Also they keep as quiet as possible until the last moment, to trick the devil who preys on ships. All we can do is be ready with the luggage and sit down to wait until the omens are right. That's something that can take two or three days.'

'This sort of thing goes on all the time, I imagine?'

'All the time. Same as in Abyssinia. They had prayer groups there. You went down to the port and joined a group praying for a change in the wind, or whatever it was that was holding things up. A mullah led the prayers and collected his fees.'

'And they do that here?'

'Probably. We'll soon see.'

Later the news came through that the dhow would be leaving that night, and after some hurried packing we arrived at the harbour in the early evening. Here, having delivered our gear to a crew member, we climbed aboard by a rope ladder and picked our way over piled-up boxes and bales in search of a place to put down our belongings. Most of the passengers had already settled in and scooped out nests for themselves among what could be shifted of the cargo. A few, perhaps braving the sea for the first time, and nervous in these surroundings, had apprehensively wrapped clothes around their mouths. I was told that this was in reaction to a local belief that at such moments of tension the spirit may suddenly endeavour to make its escape from the body. We had been given deck passages, and this came as a relief, for when we had first looked the dhow over we had noted a stagnant odour rising through the gangway from the depths of the ship.

The dhow's captain—the nakhoda—told us that he hoped to set sail in the early hours of the next day. But an hour after we had embarked a canoe came alongside, bringing a messenger from the city with an invitation for the dhow's crew and passengers to attend a wedding of a Hadrami family which had settled in Aden. This was

instantly accepted and the nakhoda announced that work for that day was finished.

We were delighted to find ourselves included in the invitation. For one reason, we hoped that the marriage celebrations would afford us an excellent opportunity to get to know our future sailing companions. Of equal importance was our suspicion that, whatever the promises, we might still have several days on our hands before the dhow sailed. We were soon to discover that, as feared, sailing would be postponed due to exceptionally strong headwinds. These winds, our new friends told us, were provided by Allah whenever there was a prospect of a good party. It would have been ill-mannered not to agree, and thus we made our way to the main entertainment, held in a large tent that had been put up on a waste space at the back of the town.

Inside, cushion-covered benches, forms and, above all, packing cases had been arranged in rows. This was the main gathering place for the 200 guests. Shortly before sunset the nakhoda and the crew of the dhow appeared. They lined up facing each other and, to the rhythm of pipes and drums, performed a sword dance. They pranced and gesticulated, advancing threateningly and retreating a number of times. Then, as the music and chanting reached a climax, they rushed to meet each other, leaping high in the air. The dances of the Hadrami, like most Arab performances, are violent and warlike. Swords must be clashed as often as possible and if the party is going well—as in this case—someone will shoot out the lights.

When the dance was over, night had fallen, and we joined the guests, led by torch bearers, to the house where the bride's family lived, for the signing of the legal documents. An overflow sat down at tables that had been set out in the street, where they were served by members of the bride's family with coffee and sweets. Some, perhaps bored—even a little drunk—went to sleep, and these were approached by a soft-footed servant, who sprayed them with perfume. After about an hour had elapsed, the witnesses came out of the house. A basket filled with jasmine blossoms was passed round and when each guest had taken a handful, embraced each other and praised God, the party broke up for the night.

The wedding party was held next day in the great tent. Inevitably in southern Arabia, it was, like our party in Lahej, devoted to the chewing of khat—a drug guaranteed not to provoke argument or improper conduct of any kind. The guests stripped the leaves from their bundles of khat, pulled out their narghiles, refreshed themselves with mouthfuls of water and listened to the musicians. The host's two younger brothers were with him, as bridegrooms are never left unattended during the ceremonies, theoretically to protect them from evil spirits, but actually to avoid overindulgence.

The all powerful barber-surgeon was master of ceremonies, and as each newcomer entered the tent the barber played a few notes on a pipe and announced his name. Guests went up to the dais, placed a gift of money in the bowl set before the bridegroom and gave a small coin to the barber in recognition of his services in arranging the wedding. The low social standing of the barber was curious in view of the essential services that he performed. His most important function was that of surgeon, and however fearsome the wounds he was called in to treat, his services were preferred in this Islamic community to those of physicians with medical degrees—suspected as sorcerers and quacks. The barber in southern Arabia, like the sweeper and the troubadour, was often recruited from the depressed Subis, thought to be descendants of the enslaved remnants of the Persian and Abyssinian invaders of the Yemen. But because the bonds of caste were loosely drawn, it sometimes happened that a barber, escaping his destiny, would rise even to become the governor of a province.

Morally and philosophically I did not think we had much to offer of advantage to the East. But, generally speaking, the ills of the body were not well understood or capably treated. Bloodletting was the remedy for most ailments. The traveller returning home after a long journey made for the barber's parlour and had himself slashed wherever he had felt pain while away. He sat down in a chair, stripped to his loincloth, and the barber cut into the areas that had given trouble. Then heated cows' horns were cupped over the razor cuts and left there as long as necessary.

Even khat may produce special effects when taken in abundance. Some of the guests began to sing quietly to the accompaniment of the *rebaba* and the violin of the musicians. Others fell into melancholy silence. Outside the tent the Hadrami seamen who had been chewing for hours on end laughed and clapped their hands and danced a kind of farandole in the torchlight. An unveiled Subi woman exorcized evil spirits with a prolonged and quavering howl. She was answered by the faint yapping of the pariah dogs that came down from the mountain slopes to devour the Parsee dead and to wander among the tombstones of the ancient Jewish cemetery. A few Yemeni Bedouin looked on with uneasy fascination. It was remembered in the Yemen that the Prophet, when he heard the music of pipes, had put his fingers in his ears, although recently Yahya had written a poem in music's praise, mentioning that its use promoted calm and the dutiful acceptance of the orders of those placed in authority.

Finally the feasting and the many delays were at an end. Two days later we rowed out to the dhow and climbed the rope ladder again. Half an hour later, at six in the evening, we put to sea.

The nakhoda raised his arms and gave an order. Several of the crew scrambled down to the bows and heaved up the anchor. Others grasped the rope and began to hoist the sail. This task, like the others on the dhow, was done to a rhythmic chant. A leader set the time by cries of 'He bab', and, with each heave, the haulers roared all together, 'Allah karim'. Some of the passengers went to help the crew with the sail. Before it was halfway up the mast, a chance breath of wind caught it and the dhow began to move slowly forward. Immediately, the helpers let go of the rope and clambered hastily to the sides to say goodbye to their friends. The air resounded with parting cries of 'God keep you', and 'Go in peace'.

It was a hot and airless evening. The burnished breast of the harbour curved gently with a sinuous movement from the depths and, in places, a vagrant breeze frosted its surface with changing designs. Momentarily the great triangular sail filled with wind and strained billowing at the mast. Then just as suddenly it drained out and hung down loosely. We moved so slowly that looking at distant objects we seemed to be stationary. Only a gentle straining of timbers assured us that we were under way, and in the water thin streams of iridescence spread out and curled into rings over the gently heaving wake as the ship's sides disturbed the oiliness of the surface. Even the gull perched on the mast remained standing trance-like on one leg, and, as night drew close, stirred only to put its head under its wing.

While we were still a distance from the mouth of the harbour the sun began to roll down the sky, gilding the ship with yellow light. Some of the Yemeni who had previously wound cloths round their mouths now covered themselves completely. They believed that the rays of the setting sun were harmful and, for this reason, in the Yemeni capital, San'a, the houses had no ordinary glass windows facing west, but in their stead, round or oval apertures with panes of thin alabaster. These they called '*qamar*' (moon) on account of the moonlight effect they gave.

The sun reached the horizon. Silhouetted against the brilliant sky were the tall raked masts of the dhows that still lay between us and the open sea. The faint stir of urban noises reached us across the still water, rising above the soft splash of oars and the lapping of the water against our ship. At the sonorous '*azaan*' of the muezzin the nakhoda turned from the wheel and, facing east, raised a quavering voice in the call to salvation. Now the evening air came up over the bows, cleansing the ship of the staleness of sacking and dried fish and bilge. We clumsily moved the packing cases about to clear a little area of private space, and laid down our blankets. Most of the passengers who had come aboard with us lay huddled up asleep, but the Hadrami from the eastern end of the coast collected in the bows and began to sing the quavering songs of their country.

We soon became friends with our neighbours on the deck, and this quickly spread to the majority of the passengers and then to members of the crew. Possibly only the Western world tends to regard questioning of strangers as impolite. On the dhow curiosity was even a demonstration of good manners. A young man in temporary possession of a few spare yards on the other side of the deck leaped to his feet at my approach, and smilingly said, 'Ask me something about myself.' I asked him whether he was married and what he did for a living, and scribbled his replies in my notebook. At this he was clearly gratified.

These Yemeni folk were strikingly handsome, with the refined features of a people locked away in their deserts for thousands of years. I was to notice that they seemed sometimes to respond to questions that were not asked, as if with our increasing familiarity they were mysteriously able to read my mind.

It was the practice on dhows like ours to carry a 'fortunate lady'. That night I was to catch my first glimpse of her. When the families were asleep the nakhoda summoned her for a tour of the deck, and as she stole past trailing an aroma of jasmine blossom I was astonished by how much beauty the faint gleam of her torch revealed in her face.

This young Somali girl was rarely mentioned in conversation. In Europe she would have been called a prostitute; here she was respectfully referred to as '*Sa Mabruka*' (the fortunate one). A few days later I asked through a crew member if she would permit me to photograph her, to which she agreed. She proved to be as charming and beautiful as the sailor had suggested. But as she could not appear on deck I had to take the picture in the dim light of her windowless cabin; the result was poor.

The moon came up; the breeze died away, and we lay motionless on a sea that glistened with phosphorescence, white as a frost-flecked desert. The sail stretched above us like a dark wing cancelling out the stars. Sometimes it gave a single flap and the mast creaked faintly. A stifling exhalation rose from the bowels of the ship and filled it to the brim, and the chanting of the Hadrami died away as if oppressed. Against the silence that followed could be heard the strong hum of mosquitoes, which the dhow harboured by the thousand. We soon found that protecting our exposed flesh from their torment meant unmaking our improvised beds and covering ourselves completely with our blankets.

The morning brought no freshness. Aching and sticky with heat we climbed to the side and looked around us. We were adrift in an expanse of steaming silk. Just over the stern, unexpectedly, the rocks of Aden were still imminent and huge after the night of travel. The harbour from which we had sailed the day before was only two or three miles away, but the short distance that separated us from the city's ash heaps had wrought a change. The rocks had lost their sharp outlines and had become pale and spectral, as if on the point of floating away.

As the sun rose higher, a canvas awning was unrolled and stretched over part of the ship to afford shade to the passengers. This was a doubtful blessing, because the awning held in the intolerable odour of staleness and decay which the sun seemed to scorch away

wherever it was allowed to penetrate. We felt greatly tempted to cool ourselves by swimming in the sea around the ship, but on attempting to climb over the side, we were held back by the Arabs, who showed their alarm and pointed meaningfully at the water. We saw no signs of sharks, but the general nervousness impressed us and we abandoned our project.

For half the day we stayed motionless. Then a faint breeze began to blow from the shore, and to make the most of it the nakhoda had the sail changed for a larger one, and at last we moved again.

The Arabs began to prepare the main meal of the day. The cook was of slave origin and almost pure African in type. He was heavier, more thickset and more muscular than the average Arab, and his voice was deeper and more melodious. His face was pockmarked and twisted into an almost permanent grin. He prided himself on his professional artistry, and spent a great deal of time pounding and blending the ingredients for each meal. He filled in the intervals between his work by dancing and, as far as was possible, he used to dance even while the cooking went on. Up in the bows he kept an open fire on which he baked unleavened bread. The fire used to menace our lives by throwing out sparks which the breeze took and spread among the cargo. We were thankful that this was not especially flammable. Until recently, kerosene and petrol had often been carried by our dhow. This practice had been discontinued when four petrol-loaded dhows in succession set sail from Aden for Madagascar and never reached their destination.

A feeling of unity and fellowship quickly sprang up. Chance had brought together on this ship some thirty men of different tribes and social classes, coming from places in Arabia as far apart as Athens is from London. Their bond was the common compulsion that had sent them out from their own people to travel to a far country. They were all intensely religious, and it was clear that practically all their actions were carried out in accordance with the precepts of the Koran. We found ourselves part of a community in which the issues of life were suddenly simplified and the essential virtues became of importance once again.

The moral atmosphere was perhaps similar to that of a medieval pilgrimage. Divisions between passengers and crew ceased to exist. On the rare occasions when there was work to be done everyone joined in, and at meal times all hands were dipped into the common dish. Arabs press food on those who eat with them. Ashore, sometimes, when we ate at table our host would become impatient of our mincing manners and, snatching our plates away, would heap them with mutton and rice, strewing the food all over the table in his prodigality. The same spirit was present here, but we found *qishr*—a drink made from coffee husks—and unleavened bread like lead on the stomach.

Supreme command of all those gathered together on this ship was vested in the person of the nakhoda, who was tall, lean and grave. His beard was dyed red, but his eyebrows and eyelashes were long and white. His hands were so thin and long that they looked like the hands of a skeleton. His eyes were clouded and tired looking, but he frequently screwed them up and shaded them with his arm, pointing out some elusive, half-obliterated landmark on the distant shore. Five times a day the nakhoda gave the call to prayer in his old, croaking voice. The first time he called *'Allahu akbar'* the words came falteringly and could hardly be heard up in the bows, but he cleared his throat and started again and by the time he reached the *'Haya ala'l falah'* his voice was strong. Besides the call to prayer, the nakhoda led the chanting at night, and sometimes when we were all resting he would tell a tale of the wit of some merry thief of old or the wisdom of a great king.

The nakhoda lived aft on a little platform from which the dhow was steered. This was as sacred to him and his officers as is the bridge to the captain of a ship. Out of respect it was usual to offer him the first piece of unleavened bread and to give him the first cup when the *qishr* was poured out. He always accepted it gravely, saying 'May God increase your blessing', or 'God be pleased with you'. When there was work to be done, such as hoisting or changing sail, the nakhoda hauled on the rope with the rest, but he always maintained the dignity that became a man of his position. When something went wrong and damage was done, as was to happen later in the voyage, he did not raise his voice or wave his arms; instead he displayed the self-possession and restraint expected of an Arab gentleman.

Our steersman was from Kuwait in the Persian Gulf. He was a

young man who had once been a trainer of falcons and he still looked like one. He had also been a fisherman and he claimed to know the names of all birds and fishes. He used to point to the seabirds flying overhead, naming those that were good to eat. These, he said, he could attract by a certain call before flying his falcon against them. He told us of strange animals that his falcons had killed, including a bird that was larger than a man. He boasted that he possessed abnormal strength of vision—he used to point over the sea to towns and villages that remained invisible to us. To his credit it must be said that when we were on the lookout for a landmark or an island he was always the first to see it; often a man had to be sent up the mast to confirm the sighting.

Our sailors for the most part came from Bahrain, where they had originally been pearl fishers. They were not paid wages but received their food and a very small percentage on the sale of the cargo. One of them was keen to try his luck with the Italians in Abyssinia, and another had saved a little money and hoped to become a trader in Jeddah, where he had relatives. The experience they had gained as fishermen came in useful, for they trailed lines behind the dhow at certain times of the day, particularly towards the evening, to catch barracuda and rock cod.

As for our fellow passengers, these were people drawn from a variety of walks of life. As well as a restaurant owner with his family, we carried a man who sold masks and magical cures, a pearl merchant, and a circus performer who was to demonstrate how to ride a unicycle. Not everyone, however, travelled with such peaceable motives. On the deck just behind us sat a tribesman of the Beni Zaranik who was on his way to fight for what was left of free Abyssinia. These people lived in the coastal region of the Yemen, south of Hodeidah. Until a few years before they had been indomitable sea pirates and slavers, who had fought off invaders so successfully that they had always managed to retain their independence. Thus they were to prove one of the greatest impediments to Imam Yahya's campaign to rule the whole of the Yemen. Yahya's method of keeping these tribesmen in order was to take the sons of chiefs hostage, and of these he eventually had several thousands. But even with his hostages the system failed to work. Finally, in December 1939, Ahmed Seif-el-Islam, the Imam's son, marched against them, and after a short but bloody war the Zaranik was exterminated.

Our Zaranik friend was not the only would-be soldier travelling with us. We also carried a Yemeni Bedouin without a penny to his name, but full of hope for the future. This Bedouin had been a shepherd, but his ambition was to become a military man in some country where soldiers wore imposing uniforms and did not have to buy their own rifles. After emigrating from the Yemen, he had worked for a short time as a coolie in Aden. There he had lived in one of the caves in the rocks to keep his expenses down. He had bought himself a shirt and an old black coat with his savings, with the idea of impressing future employees. He still darkened his eyelids, however, with antimony powder and bound his calves and his hair with sprigs of sweet basil.

The more than leisurely progress of the dhow came as a surprise. Occasionally a breeze tightened the sails, but by the end of the first full day at sea we were to learn that we had covered only ten miles, and by the next morning we were in a flat calm. It was a situation accepted almost with jubilation both by the male passengers and by several members of the crew. Many of the passengers had brought fishing tackle along, in readiness for forced inactivity, and now they baited their hooks and lowered them into the sea. Within minutes the first catch had been landed. The shores of the Red Sea were devoid of human population. Thus the Red Sea abounded in fish.

To the fishing enthusiasts who travelled with us only a few kinds were acceptable. Barracudas, which flourished in these waters, were caught at intervals of a few minutes without showing fight. But rock cod and big rays, the other favoured catches, put up a great struggle. These and a few lesser kinds free of suspicion were handed over to the cook, the rest being immediately thrown back. Occasionally a shark took the bait, usually snatching the line from a surprised fisherman's hand.

At this moment I was made aware of a new facet of Ladislas's personality. Someone had offered him a line to join in the fishing, but this he refused with a shake of his head. I was surprised. Why not join in with the others? His reply was to stagger me. This was a man who had spent his life as a witness and reporter of so many terrible scenes. 'I find fishing cruel,' he said, and I knew that he meant just that.

After supper that evening we settled under a hurricane lamp for a discussion of the events of the day. Some reference to meals consumed in barbarous circumstances prompted me to mention an episode in *Abyssinia on the Eve*. There Ladislas had described a banquet, said to have been the biggest in national history, given by Haile Selassie on the eve of the outbreak of the war with Italy. Among those who took part were 2,000 accredited beggars and the main tent in which Ladislas found himself held 4,000 guests. As a matter of etiquette the Emperor himself and the dignitaries of the nation squatted on the ground with the rest of the invitees.

'And they actually threw food about the place?' Stevens asked.

'In a ritual way, yes. At the end of the tent newly slaughtered oxen were hung up and the servants cut off slices of the warm flesh and threw them to the guests.'

'To the Emperor as well?'

'Of course. A great shout went up when he caught a slice of meat and tore a strip off with his teeth. They drank a kind of alcohol called *tetsh*, and spat it out of the corners of their mouths so that it would mix with the blood.'

Next day the sea was as flat as ever, with all lines in the water and a massacre in progress of so many beautiful fish. Several passengers including myself were on deck at first light, prey to a compulsion only to be satisfied by coming to terms with the dhow's 'place of ease'. This proved an atrocious experience when it could finally no longer be avoided. It was hard to believe that a contraption of this kind should be so difficult to gain access to. For technical reasons it swung loose on its ropes, thus partially freed from the wallowings of the ship; but for this reason only a calm sea permitted easy access and reduced feelings of extreme insecurity. Whatever the weather it was difficult for a European, buttoned up in his garments, to make use of the contrivance without loss of dignity, and in a period of storms which could last up to a week the problems involved became acute. We were to discover that in rough weather the victim would be lowered by the wallowing dhow at one moment into the cavernous belly of a wave, and thereafter hoisted high into the air over the cargo.

For three days we sailed slowly through calm water. On the fourth day the nakhoda told us we were about to turn into a storm of exceptional violence. We looked down at the pellucid green sea and watched tiny wavelets slapping at the dhow's sides. It seemed hard to believe that a storm was coming, but the nakhoda, his usual calm if pessimistic self, warned us of what was about to happen. All baggage would have to be stowed away below deck and the nakhoda recommended that we take cover there, too, as soon as he gave us the signal. Male passengers, he warned us, might be forced to shelter in an area below, normally reserved for females, and would be called upon to swear a religious oath not to molest them in any way. Second thoughts caused him to shake his head doubtfully. In our case, since we were not people of the Book—within reach of the salvation of Islam—such oaths would carry no weight. Were we, he wondered, prepared to change our faith for the period of the emergency? I said that it was a possibility to be considered.

We returned to the temporary sanctuary of our deck space, where the bad news was under discussion. One of our friends who had been in situations of this kind before assured us that anything was possible on the Red Sea. A few months ago a two-masted decked vessel bound for Jeddah had hit the south-west monsoon somewhere in this area and simply disappeared from sight.

Watching the western horizon we saw a powdery vapour spread over the sky and slowly lift itself from the water. It brought with it a humming that could only be the roar of a distant storm. Five crew members were on deck busying themselves with the sails, but they were too late, for the first blast of the wind to reach us ripped the mainsail to shreds. At the last moment, the nakhoda swung the dhow around to face the tempest head on; confronting it, the boat bowed very slightly, as if to a worthy adversary, before a mountainous wave smashed over its bows. A torrent of water rushed around us, over us and through our collection of struggling men, and the Koran held over us by the nakhoda was torn from his hands.

The storm waned, the sea calmed, and the nakhoda and his
second in command went off with their lamps to inspect the damage,
for by this time the loss of the mainsail had reduced our speed to
barely two knots. The news that followed was bad. Not only was
the mainsail shredded, the steering gear was damaged and we had
sprung a leak. Our remedy was to make for the desert island of
Kamaran, where whatever repairs were required could be made.
Kamaran was actually further off than our destination, Hodeidah,
but the wind favoured it, or so the nakhoda said.

The prospect filled passengers and crew alike with dismay.
Kamaran was seen as a place of supernatural terrors, of mysterious
sickness and mania. Sailors shipwrecked there, even if physically
undamaged, were said never to be the same again—they were prone
to foolish behaviour and notably lost interest in their wives. Assuring
his crew that there was no alternative, the nakhoda closed his ears
to their pleas.

We were in a paradise of nature that went unobserved. Long-
winged terns encircled the boat, performing a kind of serial ballet
before diving with infinite precision and grace to snatch fish from
the waves.

But the mood of the passengers, crammed together in appalling
heat on a seemingly endless voyage, had changed. Little local feuds
broke out among erstwhile good friends—often as they chased the
small patches of shade that constantly shifted across the deck. There
was an attempted suicide by a young man who, we learned, suffered
from bouts of chronic depression. The 'fortunate lady's custom of
appearing on deck at night to serenade favoured males came to an
end when she was doused by infuriated wives with urine.

Two days later, as the sails snatched at the last flicker of breeze
and fell limp, and as the belief spread that another night would be spent
at sea, Ladislas groaned with despair. He loathed dhow journeys, he
said, complaining of their terrible dependence upon the weather and
their inevitable delays, the fetid breath of the bilges and the infernal
creaking of timbers that robbed the night of sleep, the dire poverty of
most of the passengers, and the religiosity of the nakhodas, who
virtually enforced the attendance of travellers at prayers. Rex Stevens,
who carried with him a small collection of classical books in readiness

for such moments, passed Ladislas a volume of Smollett's *Travels*, but Ladislas put it aside. In a way boredom was his undoing—it was to cause him to drop his guard and take me into his confidence in matters which had previously been excluded from our talks.

That afternoon, I was to hear for the first time that Ladislas had had far closer contacts with the Italians in Abyssinia than I had ever imagined. He admitted that he had spent five months in Rome as correspondent of the London *Sunday Chronicle*. He had even been received by the Duce, for whom he had been provided in advance with a made to measure address of eighteen adulatory words. Remarkably, too, Ladislas had confided to Stevens after our first meeting that he would be particularly happy to work with me as I looked like an Italian, and reminded him physically of the fascist General Balbo with whom he had been on exceptionally close terms.

These revelations were followed by an assurance that he knew every Italian worth knowing in Aden, and that although Aden had been promoted to the status of a Crown Colony, Italian settlers—most of them in British employ—surpassed in numbers, wealth and prestige those of the resident English. The shadow of Mussolini, Ladislas emphasized, had fallen across this great settlement of uprooted foreigners by the sea. The Aden press, he told me, was manipulated by the Italians so as to present the Abyssinia war as a one-off situation, with Ethiopia remaining the single constituent of the Duce's Roman Empire. But nothing was more relentless, said Ladislas, than the Duce's determination to go ahead with territorial acquisition. The Arab state of the Yemen was small and weak, and nothing, said Ladislas, could be clearer than the fact that the Yemen, too, would ultimately be snapped up by one or other of the European powers. Our Arab friends on deck took this news with their characteristic fatalism. Whoever their rulers, they assured us, their situation was unlikely to change.

With the dhow in the doldrums it was an excellent time to fish, and while the children were left to quarrel happily among themselves our friends caught fish of all sizes, shapes and colours, forcing us into acceptance of the choicest prizes. Stevens withdrew with a book into a square yard of shade in search of the comforting unrealities of Suetonius. But Ladislas was not to be diverted from the magnificence of the new Roman Empire. Finding a passenger recently returned from

Abyssinia, Ladislas questioned him on the quality of life under the Italians as compared with their Ethiopian slave masters, and the Arab told him there was absolutely no difference. In the afternoon's heat even the ship's timbers sweated gently, and here and there tiny scorpion-like creatures pushed their heads for a split second out of crannies in the blackened wood. Somewhere nearby a colony of cicadas clicked and hissed, and Ladislas wrapped a wet towel round his head.

Another mystery soon became clear. In the seven weeks Ladislas had been booked in at the Marina Hotel he had rarely been available to callers, and he was now quite happy to offer an explanation for these absences. 'I was away in Perim and Al Mukalla,' he said. 'Also Hadramawt. Ever been there? The name means "the Presence of Death". Understandably, too.'

'What made you go to all these places?' I asked.

'We were wasting our time in Aden. We were supposed to be going to the Yemen, but nothing happened. I knew people who could help us. I know the Sultan of Perim, and also the Sultan of Lahej.'

'We knew Sir Bernard Reilly. He did all he possibly could.'

'He didn't have the connections—people who count for something. The king of the Yemen has four wives and twenty-nine children. One of his nephews worked as a porter in our hotel. You would have done better to talk to him.'

'Well, there it is. We're committed to this now. We can only hope for the best.'

Years were to pass before the real explanation behind Ladislas Farago's mysterious journeys in southern Arabia appeared. His book of our travels, *The Riddle of Arabia*, was published in 1939 but, despite his fame as an author, it received little publicity and disappeared from the booksellers' windows within days of publication. The explanation generally offered was that it was in the course of reprinting, but the leading bookshop that had taken my order for a copy was never able to supply it. My attempts to find the book in the London Library proved fruitless. Finally in 1999 a friend unearthed a copy for me and the puzzle of Farago's unexplained absences from Aden was solved.

In his book Farago describes how within days of our arrival in Aden he was lucky enough to meet a Monsieur Klar, a dealer in furs just back from Paris where he had attended an auction of hides and skins by the Hudson Bay Company. 'He gave me a letter in which it stated that I was a fur merchant and his representative. Without Monsieur Klar's letter I would never have reached the forbidden shores of the Yemen.' As the agent of an established trader all doors were open and a permit for the Yemen was immediately arranged. Travelling on the Portuguese steamer *Ayamonte*, he visited Hodeidah where he was comfortably housed and well looked after in the forbidden city. After completing whatever business it was that had taken him to the Yemen, a secret which he was never to reveal, he returned to Aden and checked in again at the Marina, this time in preparation for boarding the Arab dhow which was to take us all (in his case for the second time) to Hodeidah. This was the way, as he was to insist so often in our discussions, that operations of this kind were arranged.

Yard by yard the dhow edged forward through the night. Seven weak lamps lit the deck after nightfall, providing a gentle and soothing environment by comparison to that of the brash illumination of the day. The passengers, nevertheless, had wrapped scarves round their heads to protect them against the threat to their health of weak moonlight. Most had fallen asleep, and so they remained until the softest of winds picked up once again and Kamaran surfaced from the sea in the first flush of dawn.

Kamaran's romantic name, meaning 'two moons', was ascribed to the belief that under certain conditions the moon's reflection was visible in the water on both sides of the island at the same time. The first accounts of the island spoke of a race that had learned to harness cormorants in such a way as to carry human passengers in short aerial journeys over otherwise impassable territory. Subterranean galleries, said our guidebook, in which the population had taken refuge from piratical attacks still remained to be explored. Kamaran had been part of the kingdom of the Yemen until a few years before our arrival, when quite suddenly, and without explanation or published excuse, it had been taken under the control of a British administrator.

A freak of the dawn light revealed not desert sand as expected, but sparkling crystals by the thousand, heaped all along the edge of

the tide. These, as we drifted in, separated into innumerable slivers of mother-of-pearl and shells tossed away by pearl fishermen, still asleep by their canoes in postures that mimicked death by exhaustion.

The nakhoda nodded and the anchor was dropped into the incomparably clear water. The families bustled into the boats to be taken ashore while their menfolk waded through the bright mud and glittering nacreous rubbish to the beach. Smoke curled up as the first of the stoves was lit, the children chattered excitedly, the nakhoda prayed, and within minutes one of the pearl fishers raised himself with obvious reluctance and came scrambling into view. There was a primitive elegance about the scene. The supreme effort and the simplicity of the pearl fishermen's hard lives had left them with flat stomachs, protuberant ribcages and eyes brightened by peering into the depths. It was a breach of custom in all these isolated societies to ask questions, but we were to spend many days in Kamaran while our timbers were strengthened and our sails repaired, and answers were provided readily enough without questions being put. Nothing grew on the island and in these pearl-fishing waters there were no fish except the occasional shark. 'If we eat nothing but oysters we cannot have children,' we were told by one of the wives. A husband had to take himself off to the mainland and live there for a month like a mainlander until his virility returned.

We sat down by a stove and struck up a conversation with one of the divers. 'We use a petrol can with a glass plate in its bottom,' he said. 'The shells are so large that only one at a time can be held in the hand and brought to the surface. Here we are all what they call shallow divers and we shall live to reach fifty years. Some of our friends are deep-sea divers. Their pearls are better than ours, but those divers will not last so long. At forty they're finished. It is all a matter of luck. A hundred shells were brought up yesterday, but of those only two produced pearls of reasonable size, and both were yellow and misshapen.'

Our surroundings were of the most austere beauty. The sea was dazzlingly green and vivid, and when—as we were later to discover—the dhows set sail for the fishing banks soon after daybreak, their keels could be seen so clearly through the water that they sometimes seemed to be floating out upon the air.

The British occupation of the island was still considered 'questionable', even by the press of the Crown Colony of Aden. Many maps still included it in the kingdom of the Yemen, and some even referred to it as Turkish. At its nearest point this long sliver of land—hardly more than a vast sandbank—was only some five miles from the coast, but its usurpation had aroused little concern or excitement in the Yemen. It had never been peopled except by a few transient pearl fishers. Its land was without water and produced nothing; and there were few hotter and drier areas in the world. Despite this, the British annexation had been carried out in a final flush of empire-building—a house was put up for an official 'administrator' who had in reality nothing to administrate, plus barracks for the handful of soldiers sent to support him in his duties.

Kamaran's administrator at the time was Captain David Thompson, and as soon as we had recovered from our journey we set out to present ourselves at his headquarters, a mile or so away. The captain and his young wife were possibly the two loneliest people I had ever seen. Up until a few years before Thompson had been a military attaché at the British Embassy in Tehran, which he described with enthusiasm as one of the few cities of the Middle East where the good life was still to be found. The solution, Thompson told us, to the problem of their present isolation was to create occupation at all costs, and he lost no opportunity for keeping himself busy. With this objective in mind he had persuaded Aden to provide them with a Model T Ford and in this, despite the lack of roads and the presence of many areas of sinking sand, he was to keep a benevolent eye on the island's people. These, he said, were no longer just a handful of pearl divers, but now included some settlers from the mainland who had arrived a year ago. He had persuaded them to stay and taught them how best to fish away from the pearl-diving area.

Our visit to the Thompsons was a resounding success. Writing of this occasion in *The Riddle of Arabia*, Farago admitted that the days on the dhow had been some of the worst of his life, hardly less awful than the few days he had spent due to a police mistake in prison in Addis Ababa. (On his release he had received an apology from the Emperor himself.) By comparison with the long days and nights of the dhow, the island, though 'a sea-lipped desert', 'came close to paradise' and the Thompsons' bungalow was upgraded to 'a mansion where I enjoyed refrigerated drink and all the comforts of an English country house'.

Farago had something in common with Thompson, for although they had not previously met he had been sent to Tehran by the *Sunday Chronicle* to cover a difficult political situation while Thompson was there. Rex Stevens, too, was on home ground with his background in colonial government. Later, when Mrs Thompson joined us, Rex Stevens and her husband wandered off for a few words in confidence on colonial matters into a garden in which a single rosebush had struggled to survive under the protection of a small tent. This plant was regarded almost with reverence by the locals, who had seen no more by way of vegetation than a few blades of grass in all their lives. The Thompsons' serving girl even addressed it politely by the name of 'Ayesha'.

The nakhoda sent news up to the house that the repairs to the dhow would take some days, even weeks, to carry out. Thompson himself confirmed that he could not allow the dhow to leave until it was fully seaworthy once more. Nevertheless, the future was not wholly depressing, for a radio message came in that a steamer bound for Hodeidah was due to call in ten days' time. There was nothing to do but relax and occupy oneself in the meanwhile with whatever activity Kamaran might offer. For me it was to provide an opportunity to study the hard existence of the island's pearl divers, who were at the bottom of the human pyramid of one of the world's luxury trades.

Thompson, whom I would have described as far from a social reformer, told me that, 'There is something about the pearl business, like the wealth mined from the earth—say gold or oil—that seems to exclude mercy. These men are the sweated labourers of the sea.' The youngest of the divers were ten years of age and only a handful reached fifty—as my friend on the beach had told me—by which time their active life was at an end and they depended upon the charity of the community to survive. They were battened upon by a sequence of exploiters. A third of their catch became the property of the dhow owners who took them into deep waters. The price of what was left was negotiated between the agent the divers were compelled to employ and the pearl merchant—described by Thompson as a man of education and charm. Eventually the pearls would be packed up and sent off to be sold in Bombay, at a price estimated by the administrator at some fifteen times that received by the men who risked their lives and ruined their health gathering them from the sea.

Thompson had done his best, he said, to rectify the worst of the abuses of the pearl-fishing trade. He had been promised a resident doctor to remedy a situation in which men, elsewhere accepted at their age as in the prime of life, were seen in the island as worn out. Above all, ferocious punishments had been abolished. Formerly a diver discovered in attempting to dispose of a pearl secretly for his own profit had been given a can of water and set adrift in a canoe without oars. 'We're far more civilized now,' Thompson said. Nevertheless his own description of the pearl fisher's standard of living was that it was 'no higher than that of the labouring poor in the most downtrodden countries of Europe'.

Later on the conversation turned to the eccentric lives of those working Europeans—usually Englishmen—bold enough to take on rarely offered employment in Hodeidah, or in San'a. A Britisher, the head of a foreign commercial undertaking in Hodeidah, had found himself in difficulties for importing a gramophone. This he was eventually allowed to play but only in a room close to the shore where, with all windows closed, the music would be deadened by the sound of the waves. He was soon under investigation for teaching his servant to play tennis, which the Yemeni proposed to ban on the grounds of its being a dance and therefore atheistic.

In the Yemen, most human activities apart from those linked with actual survival were banned as being 'against the will of God'. Apart from beheadings prescribed for all major crimes, thefts of petty objects or even food were punished by the amputation of a hand, and a whole range of minor punishments were inflicted for trivial offences seen as possibly against the wishes of the Almighty. It was illegal to sing, and even more to whistle, but retribution could also result from giving a horse a human name, walking backwards, climbing to the top of certain mountains and—seen in this case as a reprehensible superstition—pointing at the full moon. In Hodeidah and San'a watches could be worn, but only if they were left unwound as ornaments. Harsh penalties were imposed for smoking. The Britisher in Hodeidah who was forced to close all his windows for playing his gramophone distributed cigarettes among a group of labourers who worked for him. The penalty for smoking them in public turned out to be three months in chains.

Ten days later, as expected, a small cargo steamer, the SS *Minho*, called in to pick us up, its only other passenger being a gunrunner who boasted of the fact that he had just sold the Yemeni a cargo of defective weapons.

It seemed that Sir Bernard Reilly's appeals on our behalf were at last to bear fruit, for when our ship dropped anchor a quarter of a mile from the Yemeni shore a reception party of notables came chugging out in a motor boat to meet us. The newcomers, including Hodeidah's remarkably bejewelled harbour master, climbed aboard, and Rex Stevens and I were told that our party's permit to enter the country had been granted, and that a house had been placed at our disposal for our stay in Hodeidah. With that the visitors climbed back into their boat and returned to the port. We settled to await their return to be escorted to the promised house, and a longish period of suspense ensued. After an unexpectedly long delay it occurred to Stevens and myself that some problem might have arisen over the fact that Ladislas, who had been running a high temperature that morning, had not been present for our meeting with the Yemeni officials. 'His Majesty's permit granting your entry into our country,' the harbour master had said, 'was for three persons. Where is the third?' It was explained to them that Ladislas was suffering from an attack of fever, which we took to be malaria. Stevens asked if there was a doctor in the port, and they shook their heads. There was none.

Two hours passed slowly with no sign of the return of our friends and doubt began to settle in our minds. Could something have gone wrong? Could Ladislas's absence from the interview have in some way aroused suspicions? There was no way of knowing. It now occurred to me that Farago's sudden temperature had come as a surprise. He had passed some hours on the Minho before its departure from Kamaran, and during this time he had appeared normal in every way. But now he was complaining of a severe attack of malaria. He held out a thermometer which registered, he said, a temperature of 103 degrees. His face was twisted with anguish. It was impossible for him to talk to the Arabs, he insisted, because he was just about to be sick. A lurking doubt appeared in my mind as to whether Farago genuinely intended to go with us into the Yemen or whether, for some reason that remained wholly obscure, he did not. At this point I didn't, of course, know of the incredible subterfuge by which he had already crossed the frontier on his own as a fur-trading agent of Monsieur Klar. At the time I thought it possible, as Captain Thompson had insisted, that as a newspaperman Ladislas would be automatically refused entry to the country, and that his non-appearance was a ruse to enable him to sneak by the officials.

That afternoon the harbour master and his accompanying officials were back and our intuitions were confirmed. These men had discarded their masks of shallow amiability, and now proclaimed by their expressions that they saw through us. The harbour master told us that His Highness, the king, had assumed we were there to sell them arms for the defence of their country. If we could offer the latest models of rifles and machine guns for sale, His Majesty wished to be shown samples of them, but if our intention had been only to travel in his country and study its defences, our entry would be refused.

The turbaned dignitaries of the town solemnly arose from the chairs we had put out for them, and pressing our hands one by one they silently withdrew. They were returning, the harbour master said, to obtain further instructions from His Majesty. Then he went. We knew from that time that only unofficial visits could be made to the Yemen.

Rex Stevens went back to tell the Portuguese ship's master that we would be ready, tides permitting, to put out at any time, and I was left alone on deck to take in a final view of the memorable front of Hodeidah—gateway to the Yemen.

This, like all the prospects of southern Arabia, was different in many subtle ways from the models that had inspired it. In the great tidal wave of escapism that had followed the end of the First World War, rich Arabs from north Africa and the Yemen coast had sought temporary refuge from the asceticism of their lives by visits to such European playgrounds as the Côte d'Azur. Overcome with admiration they had strolled down such avenues of social display as the Promenade des Anglais at Nice, determined on their return to repeat these northern splendours in the sweltering tropics from which they so rarely emerged. The result was charming in a wan sort of way, but it reflected the inbred asceticism of Islam rather than the high spirits of European holidaymakers. The people of this coast had been trained from birth to draw their pleasures from fasting and prayer, and Hodeidah was the result of a temporary compromise between two faiths. Decoration and architectural exuberance were restricted in these buildings to the top storeys 'because they were nearest to heaven'. At street level they were plain and mute. There were doors but no windows.

I had been cautiously taking my last photographs of the scene when I noticed that a thin, ant-like stream of distant humans had come into view on the previously vacant and inanimate seafront. Putting my camera out of sight, but continuing to watch, I saw that these people soon branched off on to a narrow track that led eventually into the port. A few minutes passed and a black vehicle like a delivery van came up from the rear, pushing past the pedestrians that blocked its way. It turned off into a cleared space among a collection of hutments close to the water's edge where it came to a halt. As the bystanders closed in, two uniformed men climbed down from the front seats, went back to open the rear doors and reached into the van. Moments later they reappeared with a man who was clearly a prisoner, since his arms were fastened behind his back.

The Portuguese captain was now at my side. Neither of us spoke while the guards hauled the prisoner into the centre of the cleared space, now kept empty by the arrival of two more guards. The two new arrivals took charge of the prisoner and forced him to his knees. 'This man has been brought here to die,' the captain said. 'Soon the executioner will come and cut off his head. If the people ask for him to die they will shout "na'm". If they are not wishing this they will make faces, and groan.'

'Why are they killing him? Is he a murderer?' I asked.

'No, he is not murdering. They are bringing him here because there are foreigners on the ships offshore and they wish them to see.

127

Norman Lewis

This is the penalty for spying. The executioner will dance before he cuts this man's head off.'

'But why on earth should he dance?'

'It is custom. The executioner is dancing to give the people good heart. Before he strikes with the sword he will call out "*Ya akhuya*" which is meaning "Oh my brother" because he is sad for this man's death. Perhaps then he will sing. You must understand me these are not cruel people. All people in Hodeidah are kind. Only God is cruel.'

The crowd closed in and we caught a final glimpse of the executioner as he leaped and cavorted in his dance. Nothing more was seen of his scimitar but streaking reflections snatched from the sun. 'Listen to the crowd,' the captain said. 'Now they will call for the end.' But the only sound to reach us was a faint *ah*, whether of pleasure or despair—like a murmur to be heard distantly on some sporting occasion.

The captain shook his head. We turned and walked back over the deck and I moistened my dry lips. 'So now we will go to Jeddah,' he said, and the change in his voice suited his recall to duty. 'What is it like?' I asked.

'Well, it is still Arabia,' the captain said. 'At least we may say it is better than this.'

'That is certainly to be hoped.'

The captain said, 'In Hodeidah at this time there are three foreigners and all the Arab people are poor. Jeddah has many foreign people who are coming for a better climate, also because they may smoke, drink and maybe even fornicate with women in hotels. The Lord is everywhere in Hodeidah to punish men who do these things. In Jeddah, Almighty God is remaining in the mosque when the cruising ship is in port. That is important for Jeddah. That is why Jeddah is one rich city while Hodeidah is very poor.'

He turned away, then remembered our patient. 'So Mr Farago will be travelling to Jeddah with us?'

'Yes,' I said. 'When he next takes his temperature I'm sure it will be normal. He will travel with us as arranged.'

GRANTA

THE SEPARATE
WORLD OF
SEAPORTS

Photographs by Alex Majoli
Text by James Hamilton-Paterson

Santos, Brazil

Salvador de Bahia, Brazil

Genoa, Italy

Sergei, Murmansk, Russia

Diana, Santos, Brazil

Murmansk, Russia

Murmansk, Russia

Murmansk, Russia

Mação, Portugal

Paolinho, Santiago Beach, Luanda, Angola

Bombay, India

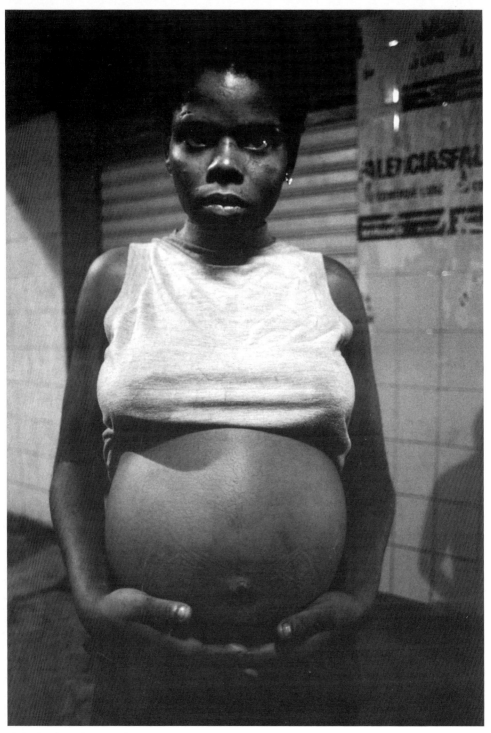

Salvador de Bahia, Brazil

'Enza', Genoa, Italy

Murmansk, Russia

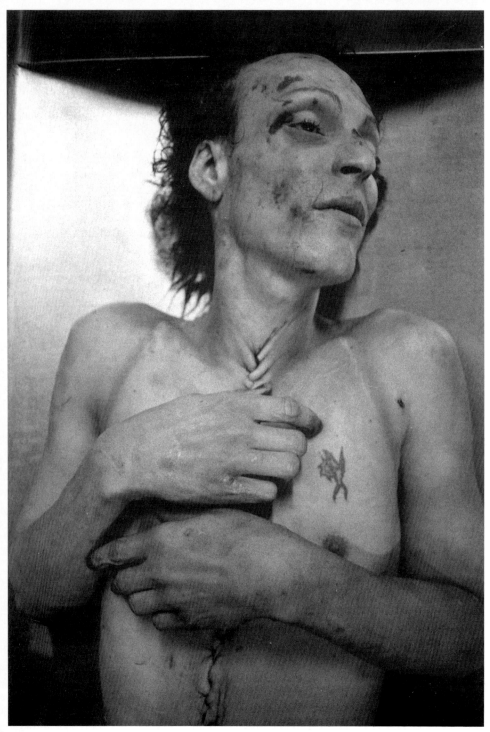

Marzia, Santos, Brazil

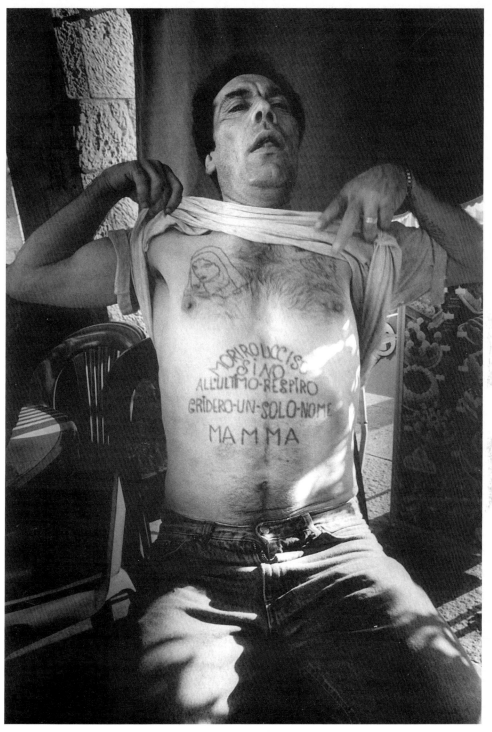

'When I die, the word I shall utter will be "Mamma"'. Genoa, Italy

'Nada', Salvador de Bahia, Brazil

Staglieno cemetery, Genoa, Italy

Luanda, Angola

Santos, Brazil

I am aged eight or nine, on a family outing by Thames water bus in London. We go upstream as far as Teddington, back down to Westminster Pier and on to the Pool. I think it is 1950. Certainly the South Bank by Hungerford Bridge is a mass of cranes and girders as the Festival of Britain site takes shape in the shadow of the Shot Tower, itself an intriguing structure when it is explained that in 'the old days' they used to make lead shot by dripping the molten metal from the top of the tower so that by the time it reached the bottom it had hardened into ball shot for the army's rifles. Less interestingly, the Royal Festival Hall and the Dome of Discovery are well on the way to completion, but the embryonic Skylon is indistinguishable among the general confusion of scaffolding and RSJs—if indeed it has even been started.

The skipper of our water bus is a relentless fund of information about the buildings on either bank as we pass. I don't give a fig for any of them, really; it is the Thames itself that grips me. This is the first time I have ever been on the river and I'm besotted by its khaki smell which so precisely matches the water's colour. The smell is compounded of freshwater mud as well as of sour tidal flats mixed with oil and bilges. It is both melancholy and bracing. While the boatman uses his tin megaphone to tell us about the Mother of Parliaments and a lot of historical grandees, I am out of reach in the bows with my hair streaming in this fatal tainted breeze, watching the tugs with their strings of lighters and deep-laden coal barges heading upstream to Battersea and Fulham power stations. These pass close by on either side of us with flurries of smoke and steam and bulges of displaced water that set us wallowing. 'We call this rolling butter,' says our skipper in a phrase so archly sea-doggy I have remembered it to this day. His passengers smile gamely and brace themselves.

My impression of the Thames that morning is of industry. The river was busy with craft all whizzing in different directions: tugs, water buses, Port of London Authority and Trinity House cutters, River Police launches, cargo vessels. The wind smelled of seagulls and coal gas. Dead rats lapped in rainbows of spilled oil bumped against the slimy timbers of the wharves as we passed. Everything was a curious mix of the static and the bustling. There were derelict bomb sites where nothing moved but weeds; but there were also the nodding cranes and the bascules of Tower Bridge opening and closing every few minutes. The very air seemed dark and sulphurous, pierced here and there by white tufts of steam. Smoke lolled greasily from funnels and chimneys. Am I grafting on to a half-remembered scene the settings of stories I liked at the time describing a London that even then was out of date? Does Sherlock Holmes's hectic boat chase down the Thames at the end of *The Sign of Four* mingle with Percy F. Westerman's tramp steamers of a later era to cast a pulse-quickening but fallacious cloud of soot and yellow fog and derring-do over a perfectly ordinary post-war London morning? Maybe slightly, but no more. Any photograph of the time shows how busy the Thames was then, especially the Pool of London. What a photograph doesn't know, any more than I did, was how diminished the activity already was compared with what it had been between the wars. Nor had I any idea of how the same view was to change in only a decade or so when the docks began closing for good and London's river was demoted from being one of the world's great mercantile arteries to a mere water resource. And what might I have said had I been told that those infamous places whose names rang with squalor and violence—Wapping, Shadwell, Limehouse, the Isle of Dogs—would for a future generation shed all their slumland associations of Lascar seamen and opium dens and become sought after addresses for the new rich? No doubt I shouldn't have minded; eight-year-olds are not nostalgic. To them, everything is new and pretty much value free. And everything is taken personally.

This is certainly how I took the docks when our water bus reached the Pool. I can't now remember which we visited: whether we nosed into the West India dock or Millwall dock or slipped on past Blackwall to the Royal Victoria in Silvertown. No doubt our skipper was as informative about them and the Empire they served as he was about everything else, but I doubt if I was listening. I was entranced instead by big ships seen close up for the first time, by the moan of winches and the whistling of stevedores. What I remember as much as the docks themselves was my father's reaction to them. So far that day he had played the adult, preserving a dreary parental pretence of being interested in the historical sites we passed; he came alive only when we entered the docks. He knew a lot about ships and the sea. He had been born in China in 1915 and in due course sent 'home' to school in south London. As with most child exiles of his period, the ships that carried him at horribly long intervals to and from his family acquired the most pungent associations, some of the world's most famous ports (Suez, Bombay, Rangoon, Singapore, Shanghai) taking on individual significance much as the Stations of the Cross might have for a devout pilgrim. As a teenager he had wanted to become a naval architect. Now, in whichever dock we had entered, he perked up. 'Ooh look,' he grabbed my arm and pointed. '*The Bengal Star*. I last saw her in Karachi, oh, it must have been in '31 or '2.'

I have before me as I write my father's 1930 edition of *Ships & Shipping*, with its lists of vessels belonging to the world's principal fleets. It is marked everywhere by his schoolboy's annotations: stars against ships he had seen (an early version of I-Spy) with laconic comments like 'Caught fire and burnt out in Amsterdam, 11/32.' To judge from its sun-bleached cover and generally battered appearance it must have travelled everywhere with him. Its pages would have been opened to tropic noons as he leaned over the rail of a P&O liner in Calcutta or Port Said, noting down the other ships in harbour. 'And good Lord,' he said on our absurd water bus, dwarfed by the towering bulk of the cargo vessels in dock, 'there's the old *Ariadne*. Obviously she survived the war, too. I remember her ramming the wharf in the Whampoa.'

That day there was something in my father's manner, rather than in any piece of information he imparted, that fixed in me forever the sea's poignancy as well as its more conventional romance. I became fascinated by details of the ships as evidence of their having knocked insouciantly about the world. The fouling and encrustations on their hulls that had come into view as they were unloaded, the noticeable dent in one ship's bows (when had that happened? Where?), the scent of hardwood and pepper drifting down from open hatches. I looked up into incurious faces of several colours hanging over rails far overhead and wanted to be them. (That ship's where they live!) The stench of bunker oil, the trapped patches of sick-coloured scum and flotsam—spoiled fruit, torn sacking and the odd bobbling turd—I loved it all. As we filed carefully over the short gangway back on to unsteady dry land in the shadow of Big Ben, I must have looked back at the Thames as having been more than just the setting for a day's outing because for years afterwards whenever I sat dreaming at a school desk I was always embarking on long voyages from the London docks. This was not an error: I knew perfectly well that the big liners went from further downstream at Tilbury. But I was a merchant seaman: a boy adventurer not a cosseted passenger. I treasured my trite perception that you could set keel to water in London and reach any seaport in the world without once leaving water. The sea simultaneously linked all destinations, which in a mysterious way made them contiguous.

This banal but magical discovery has never quite left me. By comparison the equally true (and even more banal) notion that everywhere on earth is linked via the air we breathe made almost no impact. Before the Seventies and the beginning of mass air travel, airports had even to me represented footholds of endless possibility on strange continents, but they never held the romantic appeal of seaports. They were too flimsy in some way: too arbitrary, too obviously plonked down in handy fields (often still called airfields) that gradually became more covered in concrete and terminals and all the identically anonymous furniture of modern passenger throughput. One can land at an airport without having arrived anywhere.

Seaports were never like that, and most still aren't. The last thing they are is anonymous, as Alex Majoli's haunted photographs show. The faces glimpsed in them may be framed by similar kinds of dereliction whether in Murmansk or Brazil, but they remain individuals. That peculiar symbiosis of town and waterfront often seems to densify the national character even as it lends people a faint air of being in transit. Tie up at Piraeus or Surabaya and you are truly pitched into Greece and Java; while in Belém the freshwater of the Amazon embraces your hull, bringing you the heart of a continent with its floating logs and flakes of gold. Most ports have been established for centuries and some—like certain Mediterranean ones—for millennia. They are there for sound geographical (rather than purely convenient) reasons: because they are sheltered, because the water is deep, because a river connects them to inland towns and cities. Which is why ports are so often in places of considerable natural beauty, backed by hills, guarded by cliffs or enclosed by islands. Still, it is true that many of the world's larger commercial ports have acquired container terminals that are almost as anonymous as any airport, just as container ships themselves are scarcely proper ships at all, being little more than seagoing juggernauts with drivers rather than skippers.

Yet no matter how mechanized and vast the port (for in order to accommodate today's ships wharves may be a mile long), and no matter how empty because intensive human labour is no longer needed, a wharf still represents land's end, the last of terra firma. Here at one's toecaps flexes the mystic boundary where the ocean begins, the old anarchic element the same as ever was, a law unto itself. A few miles out effective policing stops and the ships fan out, bending their various courses around the globe, passing on their way other ships being sucked inward towards this port as though by a local vortex. Their wakes efface themselves in the trade winds.

There is no question that the great increase in air travel and air freight is having an effect on all things maritime, especially on ports themselves. Today's cargo vessels require fewer crew just as modern cargoes such as bulk petroleum and cars need separate terminals and storage pounds that are usually some way from the city port. Whole economies die back and old ports die with them. The port of Glasgow is a shadow of what it was, and so is Chatham. The same can be said of Lowestoft or Hull. Similar changes are repeated around the world. Ports that rely almost exclusively on a single industry by being home to a fishing fleet or a naval base or else the point of export for a region's steel are the least able to remain viable. With luck they may eventually cater to a different clientele such as cruise ships or weekend sailors. A sure sign of this bogus rehabilitation is a marina. A marina is to an old port what a prosthesis is to an amputee. The historic all-purpose busy port relied largely on variety, on tramp steamers like Masefield's coasting from place to place carrying a mixed cargo, picking up some timber here and dropping off fifty tons of copra there. That was also how to offset the loss of revenue once the great fleets of passenger liners dried up and no longer needed their numinous staging posts. The sort of local, decentralized economy that needs coastal cargo vessels still exists, but not in northern Europe. It flourishes in places like South-East Asia, where ports can be as wildly rank and seamy as they ever were.

On the whole I am thankful I never sought my living on the high seas, and especially not in the British merchant navy which over a few decades has shrunk from dominating the world to impersonating a ghost. I am glad to have taken my chance once, back in the Sixties, when I hitched a lift on a Hapag-Lloyd cargo ship, the *Hilde Mittmann* out of Hamburg, and worked my passage up the Amazon to Manaos by scrubbing down the engine room bulkheads. I fear this sort of casual travel would be almost impossible these days, what with unionized crewing and the security regulations of marine insurance companies. That, too, tarnishes some of the sea's romantic gleam. I am snobbishly out of tune with the idea of cruise ships, floating pleasure palaces of hideous and unnautical design, which may nonetheless help restore the fortunes of the world's more photogenic ports. They roll down to Rio, all right, though not much up to Calcutta or Vladivostok. Anyway, cruising is not the same as travel, which no matter how dreamily undertaken is nevertheless full of intent. The whole point of cruising seems to be that of distraction: of diverting attention at all times away from anything as humdrum as a journey and on to bars, restaurants, casinos, saunas, gyms, discos and the other beguilements of city life, until there is no obvious reason for being afloat.

To have grown up dreaming of oceanic horizons inevitably dates me. To have narrowly inherited (even if only by a few years) the culture of an island people, a nation of seafarers with a vast overseas empire, is an ironic mischance. None of us aboard our water bus in the Pool of London that day could have known quite how dead and overtaken by history the reality already was, any more than we could have guessed that a New Elizabethan era was about to dawn that had not the slightest affective connection with the world of Drake and Raleigh.

These days I still gravitate towards the nearest port, drawn as if by a pheromone carried on the wind. I like to stand at dusk on an outermost jetty or mole and gaze out to where the first navigation lights are lit on the ships riding at anchor in the roads. There may well be a stubby lighthouse at my back, a stroller or two, the odd dog sniffing around the bait boxes of the usual anglers in battered straw hats. The lights of the port are coming on, bouncing off the dimpled water, ladled back and forth between glittering cups. I think of all those boys and young men who over tens of centuries must have stood dreaming on wharves and strands while gazing seaward, imagined futures stretching gloriously beyond a horizon tingling with danger and promise. One would say they had surely gone, at least from Europe's shores, overtaken by air travel, work permits and decimated merchant fleets, except that people everywhere still compulsively stare out to sea, just as they do into an open fire.

One of the reasons I like to return to the village beside the South China Sea that I have known for over twenty years is because it enables me still to fight my way on and off decrepit inter-island vessels in ports that Conrad would recognize. Another is that it holds echoes of an old order. This is no colonialist nostalgia but a purely maritime one. At dusk it is possible to glimpse silent youths sitting on the beach staring pensively towards the last gaudy rags of a tropical sunset. I do not have to invent a wistful look in their eyes. From daily conversation it is obvious they are rehearsing the fabulous possibilities that surely await them as soon as they are old enough and qualified enough to set sail from their impoverished archipelago and go adventuring at large on the oceans of the world. As Filipinos they will be joining the greatest single diaspora of merchant seamen, so their dreams are by no means pure fantasy. Foreign ports... Despite the forty years between us, I know how they feel.   □

James Hamilton-Paterson

WWW.GRANTA.COM

On the Granta website this month: Ian Jack's Notebook, Neil
Belton's Notebook, interviews, essays, extracts, archive, events, fo-
rums, and special offers—including one on our new anthology,
'Granta: the First Twenty-One Years'. ('A wonderfully readable anthology with a splendid succession of pieces.' Spectator)

GRANTA

GRANTA

LITTLE SISTER
Anne Enright

Anne Enright

The year I'm talking about, the year my sister left (or whatever you choose to call it), I was twenty-one and she was seventeen. We had been keeping our proper distance, that is to say, for seventeen years. Four years apart—which is sometimes a long way apart, and sometimes closer than you think. Some years we liked each other and some years we didn't. But near or far, she was my sister. And I suppose I am trying to say what that meant.

Serena always thought she would overtake me some day, hence the under age drinking and the statutory sex. But even though she was getting into pubs and into trouble before I was in high heels, I knew deep down and weary that I was the older one—I always would be the older one, and the only way she would get to be older than me, is if I got dead.

And of course, I liked it too. It was fun having someone smaller than you. She always said I bossed her around, but I know we had fun. Because with Serena you were always asking yourself what went wrong, or even Where did I go wrong? But, believe me, I am just about done with all that—with shuffling through her life in my mind.

There was the time when she was six and I was ten. I used to take her to the bus at lunch time, because she still only had a half day at school. So I spent my break waiting at the bus stop with my little sister instead of playing German Jumps in the playground, which is not me complaining, it is me saying that she was cared for endlessly, by all of us. But there are just some things you cannot do for a child. There are some things you cannot help.

This particular day, we were walking out of the school lane and on to the main road when a girl sailed through the air and landed on the roof of a braking car. Serena said, 'Look!' and I pulled her along. It was far too serious. And as if she knew it was far too serious she came along with me without a fuss. A girl landed on the roof of a braking car. She turned in the air, as though she was doing a cartwheel. But it was a very slow cartwheel. There was a bicycle, if you thought hard about it, skidding away from the car, the pedal scraping the tarmac and spraying sparks. But you had to think hard to remember the bike. What you really remembered was this girl's white socks and the pleated fan of her gymslip following her through the air.

The next day there were rumours of an accident, and my mind

tells me now that the girl died, but they didn't want to tell us in case we got upset. I don't know the truth of it. At the time there was just the two of us on an empty road, and a girl turning her slow cartwheel, and my hand finding Serena's little hand and pulling her silently by.

That was one incident. There was another incident when she was maybe eight and I was twelve when a man in plaid trousers said, 'Hello girls' and took his thing out of his fly. Maybe I should say he let his thing escape out of his fly, because it sort of jumped out and curled up, in a way that I now might recognize. At the time it looked like giblets, the same colour of old blood, dark and cooked, like that piece of the turkey our parents liked and called 'the Pope's nose'. So we ran home all excited and told my mother about the man in plaid trousers and the Pope's nose, and she laughed, which I think was the right thing to do. By the lights of the time. And we had three ordinary brothers, who went through their phases of this or that. Nothing abnormal—though the year Jim wouldn't wash was a bit of a trial. Look at me, I'm scraping the barrel here. We had a great childhood. And I'm fine, that's the bottom line of it. I'm fine and Serena is no longer alive.

But the year I am talking about, it was 1981 and I was finished at uni and starting a job. I had money and was buying clothes and I was completely delighted with myself. I even thought about leaving home, but my mother was lonely with us all growing up. She said she felt the creak of the world turning and she talked about getting old. She cried more; a general sort of weep, now and then—not about *her* life, but just about the way life goes.

I came home one day and Serena was in the doghouse, which was nothing new, because my mother smelled cigarettes off her, and also Something Else. I couldn't think what this something else might be—there was no whiff of drink—perhaps it was sperm, I wouldn't be surprised. It was three weeks before her final school exams and Serena was trashing our bedroom while my mother stood in the kitchen, wearing her coat, strangely enough, and chopping carrots. I went in and sat with Mam for a while, and when the silence upstairs finally settled, I went to check the damage. Clothes everywhere. One curtain ripped down. My alarm clock smashed. A bottle of perfume snapped at the neck—there was a pool of Chanel No. 5 soaking into the chest of drawers. I had a boyfriend at the time. The room stank. I didn't blow my top. I said, 'Clean yourself up, you stupid moron, Da's nearly home.'

None of us liked our father, except Serena, who was always a little flirt, even at the age of three. I don't think even my mother liked him—of course she said she 'loved' him, but that was only because you're supposed to when you marry someone and sleep with them. He had a fused knee from some childhood accident and always sat with his leg sticking out in front of him. He wasn't a bad man. But he sat looking at us shouting and laughing and fighting, like we were all an awful bore.

Or maybe I liked him then, but I don't like him since—because after Serena he got a job managing a pub and he started sleeping over the shop. So that's another one, now, who never comes home.

For three weeks the bedroom was thick with the smell of Chanel, we did not speak, and Serena did not eat. She fainted during her maths exam and had to be carried out, with a big crowd of people fanning her on the corridor floor. All of June she spent in the bathroom squeezing her spots, or she sat downstairs and did nothing and wouldn't say what she wanted to do next. And then, on July 14, she went out and did not come home.

We waited for ninety-one days. On Saturday, September 13, there was the sound of a key in the door and a child walked in—a sort of death-child. She was six and a half stone. Behind her was a guy carrying a suitcase. He said his name was Brian. He looked like he didn't know what to do.

We gave him a cup of tea, while Serena sat in a corner of the kitchen, glaring. As far as we could gather, she just turned up on his doorstep, and stayed. He was a nice guy. I don't know what he was doing with a girl just out of school, but then again, Serena always looked old for her age.

It is hard to remember what it was like in those days, but anorexia was just starting then, it was just getting trendy. We looked at her and thought she had cancer, we couldn't believe this was some sort of diet. Then trying to make her eat, the cooing and cajoling, the desperate silences, as Serena looked at her plate and picked up one green bean. They say anorexics are bright girls who try too hard and get tipped over the brink—but Serena sauntered up to the brink. She looked over her shoulder at the rest of us, as we stood and called to her, and then she turned and jumped. It is not too much to say that she enjoyed her death. I don't think it is too much to say that.

But I'm stuck with Brian in the kitchen, and Serena's eye sockets are huge, her eyes burning in the middle of them. Of course there were tears—my mother's tears, my tears. My father hit the door jamb, and then leaned his forehead against his clenched fist. Serena's own tears, when they came, looked hot, like she had very little liquid left. My mother put her to bed, so tenderly, like she was still a child, and we called the doctor while she slept. She woke to find his fingers on her pulse and she looked like she was going to start yelling again, but it was too late for all that. He went out to the phone in the hall and booked her into hospital on the spot.

Ninety-one days. And believe me, we lived them one by one. We lived those days one at a time. We went through each hour of them, and we didn't skip a single minute.

I met Brian from time to time in the hospital and we exchanged a few grim jokes about the ward. A row of little sticks in the beds, knitting, jigging, anything to burn the calories off. I opened the bathroom door one day and saw one of them checking herself in the mirror. She was standing on a toilet seat with the cubicle door open and her nightdress pulled up to her face. You could see all her bones. There was a mile of space between her legs, and her pubis stuck out, a bulging hammock of flesh, terribly split. She pulled the nightdress down when she heard the door open, so by the time I looked from her reflection to the cubicle, she was decent again. It was just a flash, like flicking the remote to find a sitcom and getting a shot of famine in the middle, or of porn.

Serena lay in a bed near the end of the row, a still shape in the fidgeting ward. She read books, and turned the pages slowly. I brought her wine gums and fruit pastilles, because when she was little she used to steal them from my stash. Serena was the kind of girl whose pocket money was gone by Tuesday, and spent the rest of the week in a whine. Now, it was a shower of things she might want, Jaffa Cakes, an ice-cream birthday cake, highlights in her hair, all of them utterly stupid and small. We were indulging a five-year-old child and nothing was enough and everything was too late.

Then there was the therapy. We all had to go, walking out the front door in our good coats like we were off to mass. We sat around on plastic chairs, my father with his leg stuck silently out, my mother in a welter of worry, scarcely listening, or jumping at some silly thing and hanging on to it for dear life. Serena sat there, looking bored. I couldn't help it, I lost my temper. I actually shouted at her. I said she should be ashamed of herself, the things she was putting Mam through. 'Look at her,' I said. 'Look!' I said I hoped she was pleased with herself now. She just sat through it all, and then she leaned forward to say, very deliberate, 'If I got knocked down by a bus, you'd say I was just looking for attention.' Which made me think about that car crash when she was small. Perhaps I should have mentioned it, but I didn't. Brian, as official boyfriend, sat in the middle of this family row with his legs set wide and his big hands dangling into the gap. At the end of the session he guided her out of the room with his palm on the small of her back, like he was her protector and not part of this at all.

It takes years for anorexics to die, that's the other thing. During the first course of therapy they decided it would be better if she moved out of home. Was there another family, they said, where she could stay for a while? As if. As if my parents had a bunch of cheerful friends with spare rooms, who wanted to clean up after Serena and hand over their bathroom while she locked herself in there for three hours at a time. We got her a bedsit in Rathmines, and I paid. It was either that or my mother going out to work part-time.

So Serena was living my life now. She had my flat and my freedom and my money. It sounds like an odd thing to say, but I didn't begrudge it at the time. I just wanted it to be over. I mean, I just wanted my mother to smile.

Five months later she was six stone and one ounce, and back in the ward after collapsing in the street. I expected to see Brian, but she had got rid of him, she said. I went to pick up some things from the flat for her, and found that it was full of empty packets of paracetamol and used tissues that she didn't even bother to throw away. They were stuck together in little lumps. I don't know what was in them—cleanser? Maybe she spat into them, maybe her own spit was a nuisance to her. I had to buy a pair of rubber gloves to tackle them, and I never told anyone, not the therapist, not the doctor, not my mother. But I recognized something in her face now, like we had a secret we were forced to share.

I went through her life in my head. Every Tuesday night before the goddamn therapy, I sifted the moments: a cat that died, my grandmother's death, Santa Claus. I went through the caravan holidays and the time she cried halfway up Carantoohill and sat down and had to be carried to the top. I went through her first period and the time I bawled her out for stealing my mohair jumper. The time she used up a can of fly spray in an afternoon slaughter and the way she played horsey on my father's bocketty leg. It was all just bits. I really wanted it to add up to something, but it didn't.

They beefed her up a bit and let her go. A couple of months later we got a card from Amsterdam. I don't know where she got the money. The flat was all paid up till Christmas and I might have taken it myself, but one look at my mother was enough. I could not do a thing to hurt her more.

Then one day I saw a woman in the street who looked like my gran. I thought it was my gran for a minute, just before she died, out of the hospice somehow ten years later and walking towards St Stephen's Green. Actually, I thought she was dead and I was terrified—literally petrified—of what she had come back to say to me. Our eyes met, and hers were wicked with some joke or other. It was Serena, of course. And her teeth by now were yellow as butter.

I stopped her and tried to talk, but she came over all adult and suggested we go for coffee. She said Brian had followed her to Amsterdam. She looked over her shoulder. I think she was hallucinating by now. But there was something so fake about all this grown-up stuff, I was glad when we said, 'Goodbye, so.' When I looked after her in the street, there she was, my little sister, the toy walk of her, the way she held her neck—Serena running away from some stupid game at the age of seven, too proud to cry.

The phone call from the hospital came six weeks later. There was something wrong with her liver. After that it was kidneys. And after that she died. Her yellow teeth were falling out by the end, and for some reason she grew a bit of a moustache. All her beauty was gone—because, even though she was my sister, I have to say that Serena was truly, radiantly beautiful, in her day.

So, she died. There is no getting away from something like that. You can't recover. I didn't even try. The first year was a mess and after that our lives were just punctured, not even sad—just less, just never the same again.

But it is those ninety-one days I think about—when it was all ahead of us, and no one knew. The summer I was twenty-one and Serena was seventeen, I woke up in the morning and I had the room to myself. She was mysteriously gone from the bed across the room, she was absolutely gone from the downstairs sofa, and the bathroom was free for hours at a time. Gone. Not there. Vamoosed. My mother, especially, was infatuated by her absence. It is not enough to say she fought Serena's death, even then—she was absolutely intimate with it. To my mother, my sister's death was an enemy's embrace. They were locked together in her own sitting room, in the kitchen, in the hall. They met and talked, and bargained and wept. She might have been saying, 'Take me. Take me, instead.' But I think—you get that close to it, you bring it into your sitting room, everybody's going to lose.

So, it was no surprise to us when, after ninety-one days, Serena walked back into the house looking like she did. The only surprise was Brian, this mooching, ordinary, slightly bitter man, who watched her so helplessly, and answered our questions one by one.

I met him some time after the funeral in a nightclub and we ended up crying at a little round table in the corner, and shouting over the music. We both were a bit drunk, so I can't remember who made the first move. It was a tearful, astonishing kiss. All the sadness welled into my face and into my lips. We went out for a while, as though we hoped something good could come of it all—a little love. But it was a faded sort of romance, a sort of second thought. Two ordinary people, making do. Don't get me wrong, I didn't mind that he loved Serena, because of course I loved her too. And her ghost did not bother us: try as we might, it did not even appear. But I tell you, I have a child now and who does she look like? Serena. The same hungry, petulant look, and beautiful, too. So that is my penance I suppose, that is the thing I have to live with now.

I am trying to stop this story, but it just won't end. Because years later I saw a report in the newspaper about a man who murdered his wife. The police said he was worried she would find out about his financial problems, and so he torched the house when she was asleep. He made extraordinary preparations for the crime. He called out the Gas Board to complain about a non-existent leak and he started redecorating so there would be plenty of paint and white spirit in the hall. He even wrote a series of threatening letters to himself, on a typewriter that he later dumped in the canal. I read the article carefully, not just for the horror of it, but because his name was Brian Dempsey. The name of the broody, handsome man that I had slept with, and who had slept with my sister. Which sounds a bit frank, but that was the way it was.

Brian. I could not get those letters out of my head. He started writing them two whole months before he set the fire. I thought about those eight weeks he had spent with her, complaining about the dinner or his lack of clean shirts, annoyed with her because she did not, would not, realize that she was going to die. I even wanted to visit him in prison before the trial, just to look at him, just to say 'Brian'. When the case finally came to court, there was a picture in the paper, and I thought he looked old, and terribly fat. I looked and looked at the eyes, until they turned into newspaper dots. Then, when I read the report, I realized it was another Brian Dempsey altogether, a man originally from Athlone.

That was last month, but even now, I find myself holding my breath in empty rooms. Yesterday, I set a bottle of Chanel No. 5 on the dressing table and took the lid off for a while. I keep thinking, not about Brian, but about those ninety-one days, my mother half crazed, my father feigning boredom, and me, with my own bedroom for the first time since I was four years old. I remember the way we lived from one phone call to the next, the skipped meals, and each of us, some days, forgetting to dress. I think of Serena's absence, how astonishing it was, and all of us sitting looking at each other, until the door opened and she walked in, half dead, with an ordinary, living man in tow. And I think that we made her up somehow, that we imagined her. And him too, maybe. And I think that if I made her up now, if she walked into the room, I'd kill her all over again. □

THE INVENTION OF THE RESTAURANT

Paris and Modern Gastronomic Culture

REBECCA L. SPANG

"This prize-winning academic historical study is a lively, engrossing, authoritative account of how the restaurant as we know it developed...Rebecca Spang is consistently perceptive about the semiotics of her theme, and as generous in her helpings of historical detail as any glutton could wish."
—THE TIMES [UK]

"Spang has written an ambitious, thought-changing book. Until now, most restaurant history was pop history, filled with canned 'Eureka!' moments and arch legend-making...Spang's book is an example of the new 'niche' history, and, like the best of such books, it is rich in weird data, unsung heroes, and bizarre true stories about the making of familiar things."
—Adam Gopnik, NEW YORKER

Harvard Historical Studies • 27 halftones
New in paperback

HARVARD UNIVERSITY PRESS
US: 800 448 2242 • UK: 020 7306 0603 • www.hup.harvard.edu

GRANTA

IN BETWEEN TALKING ABOUT THE ELEPHANT

Jackie Kay

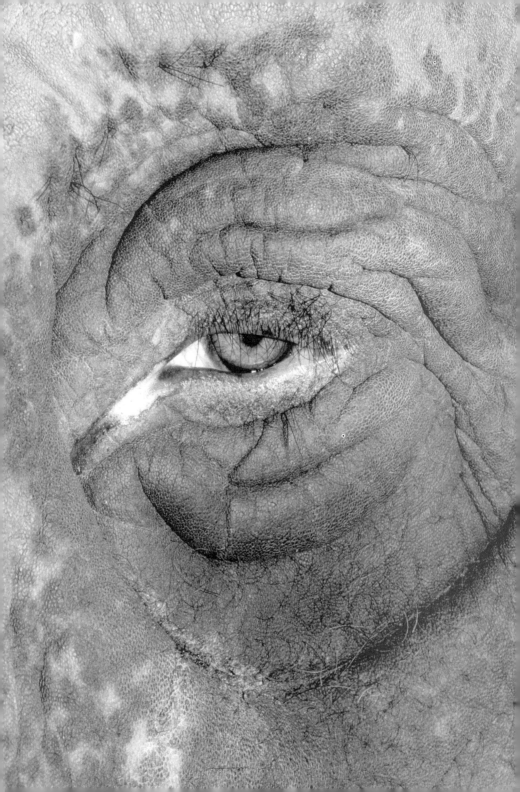

I discover some rough skin on her elbow. I run my tongue along it. I kiss her again then I fetch an apple. A polished red apple. I watch her eat it, even the core. It is thrilling. She holds the apple close to her face and munches slowly and stares at me while she bites into it. The juice from the apple, frothy, slips down the side of her chin. We get out of bed.

We sit down in the middle of the floor in our living room. We are on the twenty-fourth floor. We've got quite a view of our city. Up here, we feel apart, high and holy. I go out as little as possible. I look into her eyes, ready, full of a terrible trembling excitement. I can't wait. It is really all I want to do. It is all she wants to do. My mouth is dry with anticipation. My heart beats faster. I wonder how we lived before, what we did, how we passed our time. It all seems incredible to me that we could have thought life had meaning, significance, depth. How naive we both were. How shallow. It is not too late. Every day counts.

'The elephant herd,' she says, and I feel a surge of happiness, a pleasure so intense I can feel it in my bones. 'Can you picture them, their brown skin, their long trunks, their vulnerable tusks, their columnar legs, their big feet, with such carefully defined toes, walking in Ceylon before Ceylon was Sri Lanka? Can you just see their big bulging foreheads? Their massive, gifted ears? Imagine the profound feeling they have, elephant to elephant, a clan, a tribe, a family. Oh, they know they are similar and different. They know each other's bones!' she shouts out. I feel faint, giddy. I grip the wooden leg of the sofa. 'They're trundling along, together, united in their elephantness, their trunks swaying, their huge hides swinging. And suddenly one of them falls down and dies. The weight, the crash, makes the earth groan. Maybe it's the matriarch. The other elephants try and get her up: one pushes her with his trunk; another tries putting food in her mouth; another tries to mount her. Some of the elephants stroke and stroke her with their trunks. A calf kneels and tries to suckle. Then the elephant herd circles the dead elephant, round and round. It's a circle of hope, of disbelief. If they just walk round and round this dead elephant, they think they will bring her back to life. Or this elephant is not dead, they think; they refuse to believe it. This elephant wouldn't do that to us, they think, one heavy, thunderous step after another. Or perhaps they don't think at all; they carry out actions that are just like our thoughts.

'Still, the dead elephant does not move. The others are tired, the top lids of their small eyes heavy and sad and lined. She will not move. What do they do then for her, for our elephant?' She's started to cry. I have tears flooding my face. I wipe them away to the side of my hair with the palm of my hand. She is sniffing into a tissue. I feel protective, aching. We have to get back into bed.

I kiss the tears from her face. If a human being cries from emotion, there is protein in the tears. I lick them. The tears on her cheeks are salty and plump. She moans and sobs and she sounds just like an animal. She moves her head from side to side; her hair is thin, light, feathery.

'When the circus elephant was whipped for not learning her trick,' I tell her after, 'she lay on her side and wept and real tears fell down her elephant's face. The trainer couldn't believe it, the racking sounds of her sobs. He never punished her again. I think some men feel more shame than others when they mistreat an animal. Isn't it odd how animals can reveal the real man?' I feel pleased with myself.

The light in her eyes has gone out and the dull look has come back. I think she prefers to do the talking. She doesn't like it when I do the talking. I try to make my voice sound soothing, calm, like a balmy hot summer evening in a very foreign place. I try to picture us on some veranda with the sound of foreign birds singing in the heat and trees shuffling gently in the breeze. I imagine us, under the mosquito net, tilting cold drinks down our throats. But my voice can't lift her and take her away.

The phone rings. It will be her mother. 'Don't get it,' I say. 'We're up to our ears here.' Her mother's voice comes on the machine. It grates even though her mother has quite an easy voice. It never used to grate. It has only been an irritant since the elephant. 'Hello, it's me. I'm just ringing to see how you are,' she says. Her voice is too cheerful.

The sky is huge outside. A lot is happening in it. Before the elephant we just watched the sky, watched the sun go down in flames and fury and the moon appear cool and serene, we watched the clouds conceal, reveal, conceal the moon. But then the elephant came. And now the sky is just a big sky outside the window. What more is there to say about the sky. When an elephant arrives, you must talk about the elephant. It is impossible to ignore. You must talk about the elephant until you are blue in the face. Because the elephant is massive; because the elephant's brain is larger than yours; because elephants know all about sorrow.

I pull myself away from her to pour a glass of water. The tap runs for a long time and I listen to the sound of the water running. I put the glass to her lips. Go on, I say. Go on. And she does. Oh, she does. Her throat is dry at first, so I push the glass of water into her hand and watch while she takes a few careful sips. It's been a long time since we've cooked a proper meal. We've lost interest in food. We eat apples, potatoes and carrots. Mostly we eat them raw, grated. Raw is good, raw is best. I can't wait for the next instalment. I am glued. If it wasn't for the elephant, I don't know what we would do with our time. 'If it wasn't for the elephant, where would we be?' I sing, but she raises her hand to stop me. Concentrate, she must concentrate. Her face is intent, intense.

'The elephant tribe circles the dead one several times until it comes to an uncertain stop. Then the tribe faces outwards, their trunks hopelessly hanging down to the ground. They tread slowly, slowly, slowly,' (her breathing is uncertain here, difficult) 'circling the dead one. Still they face outwards because they can't face what they see or because that is just their elephant way of doing things. They must know for certain now that all the circles in the world will not bring the dead one back. So they tear off branches from nearby trees, they rip grass clumps from the vegetation and they bring all that back and drop it on the dead one to bury her, to cover her, to show some respect.'

I know what she means. Nothing is lost on me. I listen with huge flapping ears. I could hear her voice if she was miles away and not up in this small living room on the twenty-fourth floor in the city. I hear the voice underneath the voice she speaks with. I hear what it says. If I go out to the shops quickly to get a few essentials, I hear it on my skin. I stand at the till willing the woman to count my change quicker. The money looks strange to me. So do the cars. I rush along the street in the rain with her voice trembling on my skin. She hates me to go out. The lift doors openly slowly no matter how many times I press the button. I hurry out of the lift, my key already in my hand.

When I get in, she is awake with the elephant look on her face. I know she has been dying for me to get back. 'Did you know,' she says slowly, 'that when two related groups of elephants meet up again after a long time, there is quite a to-do? Yes!' she says, struggling to sit up, 'They run towards each other screaming and trumpeting. They twine their trunks together like twins. They click their tusks as if they are saying "Cheers". They spin around each other, rubbing their elephant skin against each other, up and down, up and down. Oh, can you see it? Can you just imagine the elephant pleasure of it? All that screaming and rumbling and trumpeting.' I am already at her side, my arms around her. I rest her head on my chest. She is quite out of breath.

We are tired again. We get tired so easily talking about the elephant. Only an elephant can bear an elephant load. We must take it bit by bit. Don't rush. Easy does it. We need to get back into bed. There is nothing else that matters to us.

The sheets are all crumpled so I take them off the bed and I put on fresh white sheets and I lay her down on the bed. Then I go into the bathroom and run the bath and pour some washing powder in it. I throw in the sheets and I take off my shoes and my socks and my jeans. I trample up and down, up and down on the sheets, getting the sweat out, getting the tears out. It is a timeless thing cleaning our sheets like this. We have a washing machine but we don't want to use any of our modern things since the elephant. The sound bothers her. It is a fast whine, a dizzy spin, then the terrible, thunderous rumbling. But I imagine the sound of my feet, walking up and down the bath, slopping and splashing in the soapy water, is soporific. She is falling asleep whilst I clean our sheets.

When I am sure they are clean, I fill the bath again with cold water and I trudge up and down rinsing out the soap with my bare feet. The water is so cold it makes my feet sting and buzz with a terrible awareness of themselves. I pull the plug and let the water run away and I pick up the sheets and wring them, twisting and turning and mangling them with my bare fists till I squeeze out as much water as I possibly can. Squeeze and squeeze and squeeze and squeeze. I carry them through in a basin and hang them on the clothes horse. 'Imagine I am a mahout,' I say, coming into our small, crowded bedroom, with its jungle of clothes hanging everywhere. But she has already dozed off by now.

So I get into bed beside her and I kiss her shoulder softly. With my eyes closed, I gently trace her jawbone with my finger. I run my finger round her clavicle, down her breastbone, past her ribs. Every bone is so distinct: hip bone, femur, patella, fibula, tibia, ankle bones. I stop there and work my way up, on the other side this time, going up her back. I know her spine intimately. I open my eyes to find her looking at me. She likes her bones being traced. Suddenly she sits up and her eyes are bright and elephanty again. We struggle out of bed and I take her arm along the short corridor into the living room where we sit down on the carpet. Whenever we are talking about the elephant, she likes to sit on the carpet.

'This proves it!' she screams. 'There were two African elephant lovers and one died. The other one could not move from the spot where his partner had died. He just stayed and stayed. His herd had to move on without him on through the open grassland, the dry savannah, but he refused to move. It was once thought that elephants went to special places to die, that they had elephant graveyards. In that exact spot in the forest, he stayed. He'd bring things to the spot where she died every day, gifts—branches, leaves, long grasses, a special piece of bark. Years passed and his elephant partner disintegrated bit by bit till all that was left was her bones. He picked up her tusk, his favourite bone of hers, running his trunk over the bone and smelling it, turning it over and then he went off with it. Elephants have always had a strong interest in bones. He walked and walked for several days and several nights until he found his herd. He was carrying her tusk in his mouth. They all gathered round and stroked the tusk with their trunks. They knew who it was, don't you see! A baby calf once found her mother's jawbone and lay stroking it for hours because she recognized her mother's face. You would recognize mine, wouldn't you, darling,' she says, sighing pleasantly. 'If you just found my jawbone, you would know it was me, wouldn't you, sweetheart.' Of course I would, I tell her. I put a cushion under her head for her to doze a little. Perhaps she might dream a dream about the Indian elephant, the *Elephas maximus*.

Our house is so quiet. There is the sound of my lover breathing, that's all. I go into the kitchen to make some broth, some potato broth. Everything has to be very simple. No oil. I chop the shallots small and put them in our soup pot adding a small amount of water. No garlic—much too strong. No salt, no pepper, no caraway seeds. I can't risk any flavour at all. I peel the potatoes. Skins are too difficult now. I bring it to boil then simmer. Last week I made a stew. But we are beyond stews now. Simmer, soup, bed, elephant. My life is right down to the bare essentials now. I clean up after myself. The elephant has changed me into a very tidy person. These days mess makes me weep. I have to have clean bare surfaces. She has to have clean sheets. I long to rip all our clothes off our hangers, to strip our wardrobe till we have very little left. If I could stare into our dark wardrobe and see empty space, I would feel uplifted.

So I pull back the crisp, clean sheets and tuck her in. She is exhausted and her limbs are thinner than the day before and the day before that. 'The Indian elephant is sometimes said to weep,' I whisper in her ear, before she drifts off to sleep. 'Darwin said that.'

A little later, she manages some of my broth. Perhaps four whole teaspoons full. She seems to gain some strength from my broth, some sustenance. It is astonishing when she comes back round like this, her eyes alert and her voice strong. 'You know Ganesh,' she says. 'You know the Hindus have an elephant God.' She drifts off again and doesn't say any more for two days.

I feed her the juice of an orange one day. When she sleeps, I polish my shoes till they shine deep and dark. If I have to go out, I hurry down and grab what we need from the corner shop, then I rush back up. It seems bizarre to me that people are still going about their business. The minute I come into our flat I can smell her smell. My nose is so strong now. I wipe it with my arm. There is nothing for me to do. Our kitchen is bare and clean. I fill the kettle and make two cups of tea. I put sugar in both cups even though neither of us has sugar. I know the night ahead will be long and dark and will seem as if it could go on forever. At some point, the point I will be waiting for, the night will turn round and be heading at last for morning. Like a ship coming in to the shore.

We slip in and out of sleep and in and out of each other's dreams, tossing and turning and sometimes she cries out. In the middle of the night she sits bolt upright and wants to make it down to the carpet again. I carry her into our living room, beside myself with tiredness, not knowing if I am up to the elephant in the middle of the night. I bring a sheet and cover her.

She needs water, but she can't manage it on her own. I get a straw from the kitchen and she attempts to suck it up, but even that is too much for her. I fill a flannel with cold water and squeeze it into her mouth. Her tongue comes right out and licks the drops. I put my fingers in a glass of water and then put them in her mouth. I rub her tongue with my wet fingers. I know her tongue too. I know all of her. 'There was an elephant, who got separated from her herd and couldn't find a waterhole,' I begin, but she grabs me and whispers urgently, hoarsely, 'Tell me about the ears!'

'You know what they say about elephant ears?—they can hear low sounds from miles away, they pick up the sonic booms? A deep rumbling, a vibrating sound. The elephant can hear the sound through its own trembling skin.' She nods, her eyes closed, but I can tell she is listening. Her cheeks are open and wide, almost new. I lightly touch her face. Her eyelids flicker for a second, she takes me in and then closes her eyes again. I take her hand in mine and she holds it for a moment. Then she starts to pluck at the sheet with her hands, pluck, pluck, pluck. 'It comes after the trumpet signal has been given. A herd of elephants lived in a free park in Zimbabwe many miles away from another herd of elephants who were about to be culled. On the day of the culling the free elephants, miles and miles away, rushed to the very back of their park. They wept and the sound of those elephants weeping was electrifying.'

I imagine them. They fill my whole head. She falls off to sleep again and I pick her up and carry her to our bed. She is light now, skin and bone and there is nothing I can do. There is nothing I can do. Only the elephant can help, only the kind, compassionate, understanding elephant can help us now. I love to see the excitement in her eyes, the tenderness, the elephant empathy. It is quite exhilarating. We could never have said the things we say to each other, were it not for the enormous elephant.

Perhaps she sleeps for an hour, at the most two. But suddenly she wakes up, screaming. She is having the nightmare. I rush and get her medication and give it to her with some water. I'm here, I tell her. Don't worry. Try and sleep. But she is too restless. I carry her into the living room again and try to make her comfortable.

'Did you know about the baby African elephants that witnessed their families being slaughtered by poachers, witnessed the tusks being cut off their bodies? These baby African elephants woke themselves up in the night for months afterwards, screaming. Elephants scream, don't they? The scream comes out of their long trunk and goes right up into the air.' I am keeping my promise to her. Don't stop talking about the elephant till it happens, she said when we heard. She smiles at me, the weakest of smiles. Her eyes take me in and then she loses it. I want her to stay awake. 'Did you know elephants can draw pictures?' I ask, certain that this will make her open her eyes. 'They draw pictures on the ground with sticks.' But she has drifted off; she won't come back.

I go to the kitchen to make her some hot potato broth. It is the middle of the night and I am here making soup. I open the curtains in our kitchen and look down. I can see the lights from cars move slowly along the roads, the lights from other buildings sparkle and spray. They look alive, the lights, dancing and twirling, pretty. The road is a long black scarf and the lights are jewels. I used to love being driven in a car at night, watching the bright lights outside. It used to make me feel safe. I stare down for ages. I see a tiny man in the dark along the street. I can even see that he is smoking from here. A tiny light is in his hand. Everything is really very small.

I know that if I can just get her to take a few spoonfuls of soup, she will be the better for it. I try and sit her up and spoon-feed her my broth but her mouth won't accept it. Her eyes won't open. Her body is heavy. She can't be hungry. I put a pillow under her head and sing to her. I stroke her long bones, her damp hair. It is sparse now, her hair, thin on the ground. She is not her usual colour. She is grey. I walk round and round her facing out towards our window. I walk around our small flat, going from room to room. From our bedroom to the bathroom, from the bathroom to the living room, from the living room to the kitchen. I find a shell and a stone in the bathroom. I carry them into the living room. I find an old photograph of her mother. I lay it beside her. I search for her favourite scarf, ripping things out of her drawers till I find it. I hold it to myself first. It is full of her smell. The sun is frail and rising in the sky. The light outside is pale and weak. I look down again out of our window. Down there, the whole world looks different in the day. There are many bright cars on the motorway. I can't see speed from up here. They seem to float. I look across at all the buildings, the shops and the offices and the houses and the homes. I look down at the trees. It all looks pretend. When birds fly past the window, I can't believe they are real.

I sprinkle her with spring water. I go back to our room and carry all of our pillows through and lay them around her. I try kissing her, touching her. But she doesn't respond. Her body is warm but she will not move. I rest my head on her chest and hold her cheek. For a split second I am sure I can feel her breath on my face. Then I realize it is my own breath coming back to me. I trudge round and round her again. I keep on going, around and around, treading the light from the hard hours. I face away from her. The light outside darkens. It seems to darken inch by inch by inch. I know what to do. We have talked about this. I bring sheets from our bed and cover her and then I lie down beside her and I hold her. I won't leave her. I will stay with her. I won't leave her. Outside the big bulk of darkness presses against our window. There's a sliver of moon in the sky like a tusk.

□

UNDERSTANDING THE WORLD

Global Sex
Dennis Altman

"Altman thoroughly analyzes the way globalization has influenced sex in various cultures around the world. He discusses the worldwide ramifications of various aspects of sex—AIDS, beauty pageants, prostitution, abortion, sterilization programs, genital mutilation, and others—always showing the complexities of the problems.... Most of all, Altman shows that sex and sexuality are not just personal and private matters but have much more to do with global politics and economics."
—*Library Journal*

Cloth £15.50

Rock of Ages, Sands of Time
Paintings by **Barbara Page**
Text by **Warren Allmon**
With a Foreword by
Rosamond Wolff Purcell

Each of the 544 contiguous painted panels by Barbara Page that make up *Rock of Ages, Sands of Time* depicts a million years of the history of life on earth in glorious full color and three-dimensional texture. This book contains crisp color reproductions of each painting, together with an accessible essay by paleontologist Warren Allmon giving the scientific context behind the art.

Cloth £28.50

The Energy of Nature
E. C. Pielou

In *The Energy of Nature*, E. C. Pielou draws on a wide range of scientific disciplines as well as on her own lifelong experience as a naturalist to explore energy's crucial role in nature—how and where it originates, what it does, and what becomes of it.

Cloth £16.00

The University of Chicago Press
1427 East 60th Street, Chicago, IL 60637
www.press.uchicago.edu

GRANTA

EVERYTHING IS DIFFERENT IN YOUR HOUSE

Adam Mars-Jones

JOHN VINK/MAGNUM PHOTOS

Everything Is Different in Your House

At the end of the year, an ambulance brought Suseela home from hospital to die. It wasn't any sort of errand of mercy. She was being dumped, no bones about it. They were cleaning house. The patient was done for—but the hospital would pull through.

Ramana was cutting my toenails at the time. That gives a false impression of what we are to each other, a houseboy impression, but it's the fact. Ramana is my 'little brother'—my *tambi*—and I'm his 'big brother', his *annan*, but the quotation marks around those endearments mean nothing in the day-to-day. Big brother, little brother, looking after each other, that's the set-up. Ramana was Suseela's grandson, and he was nineteen when she was doing her dying. He could just as easily have been playing his GameBoy, though batteries aren't cheap and they come out of his wages, or he could have been having a cigarette out of my line of sight. He smokes. I know he smokes. He knows I know he smokes. But a little brother doesn't let his big brother see him smoke. The rules aren't so much about who does what as about who sees what. The one time I manoeuvred myself so he could catch sight of me watching him indulge, he laughed but he wasn't happy. I repented of putting him under pressure, by misguidedly playing around with the ground rules. I have a right not to mind him smoking, no right to impose my permission on him. Cultures always clash, they clash even when they kiss, but here I must remind myself that it's so.

And when the ambulance arrived he was cutting my toenails. I've taught Ramana what chiropodists have taught me, that it's important not to follow the tempting curve of the toe, but to cut straight across, even to leave the edges longer than the middle. That way you lessen the odds of ingrowing toenails. There are toenails that need all the help they can get.

I've imposed Western ways in the matter of toenail-clipping, though I'm sure there's an Indian tradition with thousands of years behind it. There's a tradition for everything, and a thousand years seems to be the minimum age for them. There's certainly an Indian tradition of hair-cutting, which I've witnessed with wonder. Of course it's not unisex. Nothing whatever is unisex here. No one sees everything. Everything is a secret from someone.

I just go for a tidy-up—there's a deaf barber I favour out of disabled solidarity—but there are grades and degrees of tidy-up. Rural barbers will happily trim the hairs round a client's anus. It's just that the client has to adopt the position that makes it possible, kneeling with his bum in the air. He must take his weight on his knees and his head, and use his hands to pull the bum cheeks helpfully apart. And there you have it: a short back and sides, the Tamil Nadu way.

The time you spend having your hair cut is always profitable thinking time, even if like me you don't actually transfer laboriously to the rickety stool that qualifies as a barber's chair. I stay put, but the thoughts flow just the same.

It's one of my idle fantasies to imagine translating *Nineteen Eighty-Four* into Tamil. I don't see how you could do it. In one vital respect, Orwell's Newspeak wouldn't work in Tamil, but the problem isn't too much distance but too little. There's a deceptive overlap. As far as 'Big Brother' goes, Tamil is Newspeak already. That's the problem. Call him *annan* and everyone will side with him. They might easily decide that Winston Smith is a bad *tambi* because he doesn't love his *annan*, and the whole searing indictment would fall flat. It's something that I laugh at inwardly, in this society where I can share everything but a few jokes. Here's another: in unworldly, backward Tamil Nadu, where fathers keep their sons in total dependent ignorance of economics, it's nevertheless true that time is money. That is, the word for 'time' is pronounced 'mani'.

Tamil is a language both quaint and amorous (rather than erotic), but quite startlingly earthy about the functions of the body. The proverb that means 'You can't be too careful choosing your friends' actually says 'If you wipe your arse with too small a stone, your fingers will stink all day.'

Stones are the traditional cleaning medium, in the absence of water—as they were for the ancient Greeks (three stones in succession, no recycling). Aristophanes could always get a cheap laugh, I seem to remember, out of a soiled-stone joke. That's the sort of thing I need to wait until I'm back in Britain to look up.

With certain subjects, though, Tamil resorts to a roundabout approach that is like Newspeak in a different way. You can say 'bad' without resorting to 'double-plus ungood', but you can't say 'ninety-three' just like that, you have to say 'getting on for a hundred plus three'. I suppose it's not so different from French breaking 'ninety' down into 'four twenties ten', so let's not be snooty. Still, it's odd that the language fumbles numbers, though the most naturally gifted mathematical mind in history, Ramanuja, was born just down the road and presumably spoke it. Even when he was imported at great expense to be a genius in Cambridge, it was a goddess from his birth village who dictated theorems to him in his dreams.

If you can't say 'ninety-three' in Tamil, it's not too much of a shock that you can't say 'homosexual', either. You can say 'number nine', but that's different. For some reason that means a transvestite. Here I'm just a man 'who doesn't like ladies'. As for whether there's even a roundabout concept of orientation here, it's hard to tell. The insults are all heterosexually based, if that's evidence. The commonest is 'sisterfucker', which can be a rather risky term of endearment, between very good male friends, where there's no possibility of taking offence. Men can't take their hands off each other and no one says a word.

Policemen walk hand in hand in the streets of Tiruvannamalai, and if you ask why they should do so, people are mystified and just say, 'Because they are lovely friends. Why would they not?' The root taboo is against something else, unmarried expressions between male and female, *lingam* and *yoni* seeking each other out without blessing. Ribald jokes are fine, but actual contact is different.

If I did 'like ladies', there would be no question of me being allowed to build a bungalow here. Even if I was married, there would be something of a question mark against me. I might be on the prowl for a *stepney*—a mistress. In the ashram canteen in Tiruvannamalai I sometimes warn Western couples that out of town they will be given a warm welcome, but they can't expect to stay the night. It won't be allowed. Their unmarried union is a ritual pollution. Even their holding hands is a provocation, an obscene gesture. Kissing is an arrestable offence, though foreigners get away with it.

Not that my immunity to ladies was accepted without question. Ramana is my little brother and companion, and his uncles and boy cousins with their relentless massage skills are intimates in one way or another, but it was always Suseela's husband Sadasivam who was the key to my happiness here. Who gave permission for the building of the bungalow. Who gave me a real home in this world. It all started in 1985, with a hyperactive boy pestering me adorably outside a temple—who turned out to be Sadasivam's youngest son. But it was the father who gave my happiness an anchor.

Still, he had to be sure of me first. So years ago he sent his daughter Mani Megalai to give me a massage. In his Solomon shrewdness he wanted to find out if I responded to female touch despite everything I had said. She went about the massage with downcast eyes that missed nothing, and I passed the test. She gave witness that I was very friendly, but that truly I did not like ladies, wherever they were so bold as to place their hands.

It was Sadasivam, shrewd as Solomon, patriarch farmer of eleven acres, presiding over fields of rice and tuberoses, who first suggested that this odd boy Ramana would be a good person to look after me, that he deserved a chance. He was certainly an odd boy then, withdrawn and dreamy, as well as being so skinny I wasn't sure he'd be up to it physically. He'd given me massages, but I didn't think he was strong enough for anything more than that. It's the first question that flashes across my kind when I meet someone—could they carry me safely up a flight of stairs? And Ramana looked like a borderline case for John-toting duties, quite apart from his blankness. He'd been brought up in another village, with his father apparently treating him almost as an idiot. I imagine that was the order of events, first the father's rejection and then the withdrawal that seemed to justify it. So at eighteen he was pretty, with long eyelashes and a nice smile, but he just flopped around holding hands, holding hands with family and friends. He wasn't a useful sort of person, too weak for field work. The sun gave him headaches. Everyone remembered that he was born with a misshapen head, a head like a cone.

It turned out we all underestimated Ramana, his grandfather included, but the old man had been shrewd enough to want him given a chance. I say 'old man', but of course Sadasivam is younger than my own father. Ramana's lively spirits came out remarkably soon from behind the cloud of what was almost autism. He blossomed, he became social. I suppose this could only happen in a culture which doesn't despise the caring arts. Where devotion has a good name.

One thing about Ramana that hugely appealed, but which I resisted as a sort of temptation, was his own good name. What devotee doesn't want to be able to call on the guru, wholly naturally, all along the day? Holy naming, a reflex prayer quietly in progress the whole time. My guru is Ramana Maharshi, my guru and the reason I came here in the first place. Guru is a word that was worn right down in the 1960s and 70s, I know, but it has never lost its shine for me. The guru isn't a god, he's a conduit to divinity. He's my modem, my service provider. Ramana Maharshi is where I plug in.

The guru can speak through anyone's lips at any time. The guru is a dispersed function as well as a condensed presence, so perhaps it was the guru speaking through Ramana's grandfather's mouth, giving an odd boy a new start. Perhaps runaways look after their own. Ramana ran away and came to his grandfather's village when family life became too much for him, and so in his more serene style did my guru.

In fact Ramana took to his new role from the beginning. He could do moderate lifting, and he was particularly good at finding things. He could go into a room at night and come out with what I wanted—even a toothpick—without turning on the light. But then he was brought up in a house without electricity. 'Dark' for him was a relative term, nothing he flinched from.

After a month or two Ramana's father came to visit and I was nervous. But it turned out I wasn't the only one. Ramana's dad thought I was going to scold him for maltreating a boy who was so tender and industrious, so he couldn't wait to tell me that Ramana wasn't his any more. 'I give this boy to you,' was what he said. 'Now he is your son.' Scolding is a tremendously powerful instrument in India, a feared force, but it hadn't occurred to me until then that I was in a position to do any.

Perhaps it was the guru speaking through the lips of the librarian in Bourne End in 1968, when I sent Mum there to find me a book. I was convalescing from my hip replacements at the time. McKee pins. Before then it was either stand up or lie down—take your pick, just don't expect to bend. They were early operations of their kind, but I have no complaints. They're still in there, though their maximum useful life is supposed to be fifteen years. It helps that

I don't weigh a lot, and I don't use my legs all that much, so the mileage is low. In fact: one careful owner.

I'd always been interested in yoga, in the idea that there was something you did with your body that had a spiritual aspect. If the word 'holistic' existed I didn't know it at eighteen, but that was certainly the drift of my interest. The only thing was that my body couldn't do any of the basic movements. Meditation I'd always done—it's something that develops automatically if you spend years in bed before school age, with instructions not to move. But that's different. What I was really looking for, when I sent Mum out with a vague request for a book about yoga that didn't require flexibility, was what she came back with: a guru with arthritis. To be exact, Arthur Osborne's book *Ramana Maharshi and the Path of Self-Knowledge.*

I suppose I'm a seeker, and there are any number of types of seeker, and types of guru correspondingly. The odd thing is, I wanted a guru who would turn my life upside down, largely because my life consisted of being looked after by my mother, and being reassured the whole time that I'd never be able to manage without her. The man in the book emphasized a principle that a seeker of my type least expected and least wanted to hear: do nothing to change your life. Your outer life.

Ramana Maharshi didn't set out to be a guru. A Brahmin who as a child showed no particular spiritual promise except a talent for deep sleep, he travelled to Tiruvannamalai at the age of sixteen. The distance from his birthplace was short in miles but symbolically huge. He had the tuft of hair at the back of his head removed, and completed the renunciation of caste by throwing away the sacred thread. This all happened in 1896. He stayed here until his body died in 1950.

It was a holy place already. The mountain Arunachala had been sacred time out of mind. You pay your respects by walking round it clockwise and barefoot, a journey of eight miles. The prescribed style is not downcast but grave and proud: you must walk 'like a pregnant queen in her ninth month'. So when Ramana Maharshi added his sanctity to the area it was a sort of merger of spiritualities, the mountain and the man.

He didn't eat, so he was assumed to be fasting. He didn't speak, so he was thought to have taken a vow of silence. In fact there was no element of mortification involved, just the indifference of bliss. When ordinary people meditate, it's like lowering a bucket of water into a well. The two waters become one, but the bucket and the rope are still there, ready to winch you back to unenlightened being. Ramana Maharshi's meditation wasn't like that. The rope was cut, the bucket was dissolved in the well. He would eat, but only if food was put into his mouth. He became covered with mosquitoes and infested by ants, but made no attempt to peel them off his skin. He simply meditated, and a shrine grew up around him. As his fame spread, there were attempts to restrict access to him, to control admission. He retreated from the manipulation of holiness, and meditated in greater seclusion; even there he became a focus of devotion.

Even when he accepted the role of guru, his teaching was undogmatic, almost subversively serene. He said that the unenlightened soul was like a man on a train clutching his suitcase in his hands. It's safe to put down your baggage. He didn't say, throw it out of the window, like most religious teachers, let alone throw yourself out, as a few do. Just put your baggage down. That's all. You don't need to carry your bags, the train is carrying them anyway, if you only knew. Everything is coming with you already. Everything is on its way.

In Tamil Nadu the ambulance is a Janus truck. It points towards treatment and towards death. Ambulances don't have sirens—the only thing that makes them ambulances is the word painted on the side. There's a difference in the way they sound the horn, depending on which way they're going. They sound the horn when they take you to hospital—for all the good it does, when there are signs saying SOUND HORN on the back of every lorry and the air is saturated with the blasts. When they bring you home again, when nothing more can be done for you, they don't bother with the horn. They bring you home because the taboo of death mustn't be allowed to contaminate a hospital. Of course death is also taboo in Ukay (as we call it here) but it operates the other way round. Same horror, different priority. It's people's homes that no one wants stained with last moments.

Adam Mars-Jones

It was actually Christmas Day when the ambulance delivered its
burden of taboo, but in this part of the world that isn't a huge event.
Christianity is a minority religion, Christmas a marginal festival. One
year it was even postponed, when a politician died. The revised date
was December 27—my own birthday, as it happens. As a child it
always seemed as if my birthday happened in the shadow of His.
There was pique, I suppose. But here was Christ sidling over, after
four decades, to share my celebrations. It unsettled my prejudices
when a fixed and overweening feast came over all movable. Since then
I've been mellower towards that callow godhead. I still think he's
callow. Christianity is such a young religion. It's teething.

Everyone in the village knew how ill Suseela was, but we weren't
expecting her back. I just looked up and saw the ambulance, the van
with the word on its side. The ladies laying a path between the houses
cried out, 'She's dead,' and started to scream. There was only the
driver in the ambulance, apart from Suseela's daughter Porkodi, so
her sons ran over and lifted her out. Once the driver had a hundred
rupees, he was gone. He'd done his work, now that the hospital—
or the Rangammal Health Centre—was out of danger. He'd
completed his errand of reverse mercy. That's why I say that the
patient was done for but the hospital would pull through.

For years before the ambulance dumped her, I'd known what
the matter was with Suseela, medically. She'd had a hysterectomy a
few years before, and it had affected her badly, but it was her heart
that was the real trouble. I even knew the technical term for the way
her heart misbehaved: mitral stenosis. It's a painful condition in which
the valve lets blood back into the heart. It's a stabbing leak. I also
knew I couldn't help. There's an intervention that corrects it, but
that's in the West. There's medication to control it, but that's in the
West. In Tamil Nadu Suseela sits for a few years in the corner of the
kitchen watching the cooking happen without her, and dies on
Christmas Day.

It wouldn't be hard for any Westerner in Tamil Nadu to get a
reputation as medically knowledgeable. In fact it would be hard for
a Westerner to get any other sort of reputation. We grew up with
aspirin, Savlon, *Emergency Ward 10*, and they didn't. It's that
simple. Say 'Feed a cold, starve a fever', and you'll make a huge

impression here, though traditional medicine in any culture is full of similar wisdom and nonsense. If I have extra knowledge, it's because I was on the receiving end of a lot of medical attention from an early age, and I learned to ask questions and, later, to follow up references. If I had to choose between the Bhagavad Gita and my MIMS, the Monthly Index of Medical Specialties, I hope I'd choose the Gita. But it could go either way.

I don't always hold back from intervening when it's a simple emergency. When diarrhoea strikes, people don't know about sachets of replacement salts and sugars to reverse dehydration, but you can give them green coconut milk, which works in much the same way. It's rich in potassium. I read a report prepared by the World Health Organization on the effectiveness of green coconut milk, directly from the fruit into the vein. Of course diarrhoea is one of the main killers worldwide.

Diagnosing appendicitis is more ambitious, but it's no great feat—there are only so many explanations for pain in that area of the body. So when a local girl had that pain, I told her to go to the hospital, and when she returned with a diagnosis of tummy ache, I sent her straight back with a note saying please look again. Then when it turned out to be what I'd said, the surgeon was so embarrassed-grateful that he sent it to me. The appendix. In a bottle, delivered by a messenger. A grey flange of flesh in pickle. That was how I got my honorific, the one I try to live up to, the one I try to live down. Not just 'Doctor' but 'John, Doctor of Doctors'. The one who knows what doctors don't and corrects their mistakes. Though it's really only the most rudimentary knowledge.

Then once as I was being wheeled along, we came across a cobra by the side of the road. It was only a baby, its markings faint, but it struck its instinctive posture of aggression. It spread its hood, which in so modestly sized a specimen looked only endearing. It was like a child frowning and shaking a fist. Its hiss was almost too faint to be heard. I reached out my cane, and the baby cobra struck out at the ferrule. Then it retreated, seeming to flow backwards away from us, its little hood still spread.

The whole event I found thrilling. In a life where the adventures have mainly been subjective here was something out of books I once loved, Rider Haggard, Jules Verne. Ramana and two of his uncles were murmuring prayers of relief, but I felt I couldn't let that tiny drop of toxic nectar on the end of my cane go to waste, without any kind of homage or investigation.

It was awkward work turning the cane round so that the handle was down and the tip was up. Ramana and his uncles were shouting, 'No, very dangerous, not to touch,' but they didn't quite dare to stop me. And I couldn't resist it. I put my tongue out and touched it to where the poison was, a little patch of dampness. Cobra venom is supposed to be milky, but by torch light I couldn't make it out. Still, I couldn't pass up the opportunity of experiencing something so rare, and I admit I liked the idea of adding it to my repertoire of connoisseurship back in Ukay. I'd frown while I sampled my half of Greene King IPA, in the Rising Sun back in Isleham, where I don't need to specify the stemmed glass that my hands can manage, and I'd claim to detect notes of immature cobra venom, poised to strike at the palate from among the malt and hops.

I thought my tongue could detect a faint bitterness, but I couldn't swear to it. I'm not in the habit of licking my cane. Maybe it always tastes like that. Ramana and the uncles were beside themselves, saying they must take me to a doctor or a hospital, but I was able to reassure them little by little. Nothing will happen to me, I told them, I'll come to no harm.

Of course cobra venom is a circulatory poison, it can't do you any damage unless it reaches the bloodstream. My digestion was under no threat. I told Ramana that if I was ill in an hour he could take me to hospital, and he calmed down a bit. Snakes play a big part in Indian religion—some divinities are represented with the cobra's hood protectively spread behind them, as a sort of reptile halo. So perhaps their worry had a ritual element to it, an overtone of taboo.

Next morning Ramana woke me, which isn't something he would normally do. He was very gentle about it, he just laid a hand on me. But he couldn't wait any longer to be reassured that I was really only asleep, not in a cobra coma.

In Western terms I'm penniless, but in India pennilessness goes a long way. I have a few more or less ethical stocks and shares, but my attendance allowance from Ukay is my only income. Technically I'm breaking the rules by going away for six months at a time, you're not supposed to do that, but if I was in an institution I would be costing the state a lot more, which can't be right. I'm not happy with the deception, but there it is. Didn't Christ tell his followers they must be as wise as serpents, not just as harmless as doves? Ramana Maharshi used guile when he left home to travel to Tiruvannamalai, saying he was going to a special class on electricity. You could even say he stole, since he took three rupees with him that were supposed to go towards his brother's college fees.

What money I can spare I spend on the most efficient mechanism for changing things, the education of girl children. Parents here will still always put their boys first, but the best hope for the world is the education of girls.

Education of girls is the great planetary bargain, the single most effective use of funds. I run tuition schemes, but tuition means nothing without vegetables, so I run vegetable schemes also. My vegetable schemes differ from the charitable ones round here because I favour giving vegetables to the whole family, when a crop fails or the monsoon doesn't come, rather than the named child. I don't see how the daughter can float when her family sinks.

It sounds an absurd thing to say, but there are remarkably few women in India. Outside the cities, they're hugely outnumbered by ladies. Being a lady isn't a matter of money or caste, or there wouldn't be any round here, among the farmer castes. Being a lady is a matter of how you're brought up, and round here girls are brought up with the very strong idea that Boys Are Nasty. The only boy in the world who isn't nasty is the one you will marry.

In Tamil Nadu even a career woman, by which I only mean a lady who has a job, perhaps as a health visitor, will not expect any extra status to come from that. She will still wait for her husband to finish eating before she even starts, and then she eats his leftovers. If there are to be spectacles in the family then he will be the first to have them, even if his vision is perfect and hers is poor. Theirs isn't a two-car family, not by a long chalk. It isn't a car family at all. They aren't even a two-pairs-of-glasses family. They're a one-pair family, and the man of the house wears them happily round his neck, while his wife squints in poor light at her paperwork.

But if Tamil Nadu isn't a society where girl children are more welcome than boys, then it's hardly an exception. In fact there's only one daughter-treasuring culture in history that I know of. In (was it?) ninth-century Japan noblewomen kept control over their assets when they married. In fact their husbands were no more, really, than senior lovers, not allowed to stay the night after intimacy any more than their juniors were, but expected to compose a poem before dawn like all the others celebrating the encounter. To be evaluated by the lady on the basis of inspiration, technique and penmanship.

Ramana and his uncle Arumugam will say, if asked, that they would like to have a daughter first, then boys, but it may be that they're humouring me, and if they're not then their attitude is a minority one. The state is pretty low-tech, with electricity unreliable and far from universal—the most influential Western innovation is actually the non-stick frying pan, which has pushed the local diet from soups and stews towards pancakes and fritters. But when ultrasound scanning finally arrives in these parts, there's not much doubt there will be a prenatal cull of daughters in most of the castes.

In the meantime there isn't infanticide, not as such. It's just that sometimes people will put rice straw in a girl baby's feed, to shorten the odds of a providential choking. And yet when a boy baby does come along, it's common to dress him as a girl for years. That's one of the things I haven't worked out about the culture—what that means.

Still, our ignorance is mutual, Tamil culture and I. I asked one of Ramana's relations how much he thought I earned, and he said, 'Sixty thousand pounds each week,' which would put me up there with the Queen of England, but it's an understandable mistake. From their point of view my economics must have a royal ease and power. My money comes from the other side of the world, and it isn't actually the fruit of my labours. I'm like a personified bank.

I did what I could to help Suseela, but medicine wasn't really a part of it, unless all small acts of love count as medicine. I have to ration what I've been prescribed anyway. I have to restrict it to close family. So if a girl in the village has fallen off a wall and wrenched her ankle, and all her mother can think to do is massage it until she writhes in agony, then I'll contribute one of my precious aspirins—but only if I don't have a sugar pill handy. The placebo effect is the cornerstone of medicine.

Aspirins wouldn't do anything for Suseela, though. The only thing I could do for her was give her a couple of Coproxamols once in a great while. They're strong stuff. They'd make her light-headed but the next day she'd thank me and say, 'That was nice.' She was grateful for a little blurring, a few hours without edges.

I used to send Ramana round with the wheelchair now and then to pick Suseela up. I'd get comfortable in a chair, and then dispatch the wheelchair next door as if it was some rudimentary taxi. When she arrived I would feed her English tea-time treats, international dainties. She didn't like the food at home, she said, but it may just have been that someone else, her daughter-in-law, was cooking it. Her daughter-in-law was also her niece—kinship structures round here are rather intricate. There are some nuances within first-cousinship, for instance, that the anthropologists may not have caught up with yet.

I gave her cardamom trifle (the spicy flavour is in the custard powder). Veggie burgers, also from a packet, but with home-made onion sauce. Dumplings from scratch. Exciting food, to someone raised on millet broths and watery stews, once she had the courage to try it. I'm an instinctive abstainer from meat, living among poverty vegetarians, who wouldn't touch beef or pork but would have no objection to chicken or fish if it appeared on their plates, nor to goat meat, which does turn up on the menu once or twice a year. Lots of Indians won't try new things, but Suseela would, having nothing to lose. She was always appreciative. She'd say, 'Everything is different in your house.' My house, to which her husband had made only two contributions. The permission and the plot.

When I first came to India I was afraid that everyone would ask me the same question: What did you do? Not a biographical question but a karmic one. What did you do in a previous life, to be punished in this one? The question has come once or twice, but that is not on the whole how I am regarded—as a casualty of past misdeeds. Partly it's being a European exotic, but over time I've realized that the wheelchair plays its part. This is a caste where vehicles of any kind are treasured, and children aren't spoiled by prams and buggies. If a family is lucky enough to have a motorcycle, then it appears in every photograph, and not just in the background as a trophy but as a prominent family member in its own right.

It's actually the Western approach which is more likely to offend me. In India curiosity can sometimes be shameless, but it is never perfunctory. In Britain people are quite capable of asking, 'So what's Still's Disease, exactly?' because they've been brought up to think it's polite to 'show an interest'. These days I just give them the address of a non-existent website.

I have a curiosity of my own, about this culture that has taken me in, this tactile culture, this language by turns earthy, playful, amorous and quaint. If curiosity is something that dies down as the soul becomes enlightened, then I still have many lives to pass through before I am ready to give it up.

And what does Tamil culture make of me? Children will follow the wheelchair in crowds, laughing and touching it. The closest thing to buggies locally are the little carts in which images of the gods are trundled on special occasions, and that dignifies the wheelchair by association. I'm a human effigy riding my tiny juggernaut. Once a boy who must have been about ten called out, 'Ramana, what's that dolly you're pushing in the cart?' When he found that the dolly had working blue eyes, a fair complexion and spoke Tamil he wasn't repulsed or embarrassed, it gave him glee. He laughed and asked if he was allowed to push me for a bit. Disability would be very different without the wheels.

Still, the gods in their trolleys don't have to dismount every now and then, as I do, for a discreet leak at the side of the road. Even then I'm likely to be followed by a small crowd of boys and men, eager to see if the cock I produce from my trousers, with Ramana's help, is a pink one—or a brown one after all.

It all swells the karmic murmur, the way my strangeness is domesticated in my Indian home. I can't claim that my roots are here, but if my life has fruits and flowers they are here, the fruits and flowers. People turn to me in tender mischief and say, 'Jarn,'—it's closer to Jarn than John—'we think you were a doctor in a previous life, because you like to make people better. We think you were a cook in a previous life, because you like to feed people and make them happy. And we know you were a prostitute in a previous life, because you love to lie down with all the boys.'

Here I am understood without being known, without needing to be known. Everyone sees something—nothing stays a secret from everyone. Suseela's illness made her unable to keep control of the cooking and household management that is all and everything for women here. For her, illness was more than anything the experience of an unwanted privacy. She would watch others preparing meals with a sort of dry grief. But at least I could feed her puddings—apple-and-raisin duff with custard was a favourite.

I could give her a transfusion from my own status, which is high and not even, any more, precarious. At first I was embarrassed that any leftovers from Suseela's little feasts, when I offered them to anyone else, were treated as *prasad*—as holy. Then I came to accept the naturalness of their response, here where there is a sort of constant updraught of spirituality. Nothing stays profane for long. Friendship becomes devotion, and puddings can acquire an aura. In any case, *prasad* doesn't entail the sort of fierce sacramental symbolism that goes with the communion wafer. It's not food in a state of grace, exactly, but there's grace involved. Grace in the form of food, perhaps.

If it had been treated simply as food, the amount left over for the family would have seemed pitifully small. But they would eat it with exaggerated delight, and always said it made them sleepy. They would even ask, without disapproval, if sleeping pills were the secret ingredient.

Perhaps that's just a placebo effect. I respect placebos. The placebo is as real as the illness, which is as real as the flesh, which isn't very. In any case English traditional cooking does use gluten in quantities that aren't customary in India. They would sleep like snakes replete, gluten taking their digestions by surprise. If my duff helped Suseela to sleep I'm glad of it.

Perhaps Ramana's first impulse, when Suseela was unloaded from the ambulance, was to leave me and run from the bungalow to her house, but I'm not sure. That's not something a little brother does, any more than a little brother will smoke in front of an older one.

He was desperate to go to Suseela, but he waited for me to give the word. Otherwise he would finish trimming my nails, as a dutiful *tambi* should. And of course I told him we'd better both go. Normally I ask Ramana not to hurry with the wheelchair, but not this time. We probably did need to hurry, and if I was going to have a bumpy ride that was just too bad.

One thing I miss about the West is a certain basic mechanical awareness. I don't mean that everyone in the West can lay a drystone wall, fix a car or even put up a set of shelves. Obviously they can't. But a Westerner pushing a wheelchair knows that when you come to a change of level you don't just carry on regardless. You have to finesse the wheels up or down or the person you're pushing gets jarred. But on this occasion it would have been unfeeling to put any brake on our progress.

In this supremely tactile culture people seem to lose the grace of their instincts when they're not actually in physical contact. It's still a lot easier to teach people in India not to crash the wheelchair at a change of level, than to teach most Westerners how to touch without self-consciousness. I've seen lots of European visitors who blossom for a few hours or days in this hothouse of touch, but then want nothing more than to be left alone. It's a release and a treat for them to drop their defences, but they soon need to re-establish their boundaries. Unrequited love is the West's big thing, and here all love is requited.

Tamil culture and I are a perfect match: I will never have enough of being touched. There will never be a moment of satiety and recoil. As long as I live, I'll never say, 'No massage for me today, thanks all the same.' I've made my choice. I'm never going to tell Ramana's uncles, 'I'll give "healthful semen-release" a miss today, if it's all the same to you.'

As the wheelchair bumped and careered towards Suseela and her death, along the half-laid path, I was trying to focus my attention on what was going to happen. Every bump along the way seemed to crash my on-board cranial computer, accustomed as it was to being cushioned on its travels.

There was already a crowd outside the house. In fact we could hear them before we set off, the noises of ritual distress. In this part of the world, 'my family' and 'my village' are different ways of saying the same thing, and there was no question of anyone being kept away. Privacy is in any case an elusive commodity in Tamil Nadu—

an undesirable state, come to that, at least among the farmer castes. People sleep together piled up like puppies, and it wouldn't occur to anyone to pull a door shut when, say, taking a shit, since they do it out of doors and without shame. The first time I saw human waste just lying there on the ground I must admit I was amazed. The mustard seeds in the mess were intact, they hadn't been broken down.

The path between the bungalow and where Suseela lived was still being laid, and Ramana had to negotiate it with care. Where Suseela lived was a converted cow shed. 'Converted' puts it too high. More accurate to say that a cow shed had been cleaned and repopulated. The main sleeping area was a covered veranda, and that was where she was. She lay there twitching and open-eyed, but not responding to what was going on around her.

Grieving of the sort that was going on in Suseela's house is one of the occasions in Tamil culture when no limits are set to the expressiveness of women. It is the men who hang back, and the women act out in its fullest traditional form the horror of leaving life. The men make sporadic noises, but the women beat their breasts and wail. Every individual takes a breath now and then, but the effect is of a continuous shriek with an undertow of savage thumping. The noise was already terrifying when we were outside, and much worse when Ramana persuaded the people in the doorway that they should let us through.

I'd said to Ramana, '*Tambi*, can you take me to your grandfather?' I knew he would be nearest to Suseela, but I didn't want to trade on my status to get there. Ramana had his own right of access. I was acting as if I had a plan. Did I have a plan? I had a sort of plan. But if it was a plan, it wasn't a plan to cure Suseela, extend her life or even improve its quality. I only wanted to improve the quality of her death.

My compassion was gross and mundane, no more than an animal's pang. Detachment is the goal. Detachment must be the goal. If pain is religiously insignificant, something that happens to the body merely, why is it important to relieve other people's? If indifference to our own pain is a good thing, why is indifference to others such a bad one? And yet we know it is. This is the deepest part of religion, this is the part that is deeper than religion.

Anyone who 'submits' to 'fate' is doing something presumptuous, not humble. They may be recognizing that the Cosmic Mind is fixed on an outcome, but they are also claiming to be privy to it. How do they know what is meant to happen? Who was I to say, with Suseela dying, that I had been cast as someone from whom no effort was required?

Sadasivam was rocking back and forth on his feet, with his sons next to him, not much more responsive to outer events than his dying wife. Everyone was crowding round Suseela, making it that much harder for her to catch her breath. Even if they hadn't been working themselves up so much, just by being so close they would have been pumping out carbon dioxide just where her failing lungs needed to gather their oxygen. I took Suseela's hand, in which there was no pulse to be felt. Then I put my hand on her erratic heart. It was fibrillating, it was a trembling sparrow fallen from the nest. A lady near me flinched at the impropriety of my touch.

I had to get them to move back before anything else. I could do that myself—'Stand back! Give the poor woman some air!'—but after that, to say anything more contentious, I would need an interpreter. Spoken Tamil is a maze of palatals and dentals which no outsider can smoothly negotiate. Your tongue must become an acrobat in the gymnasium of your mouth. Normally my little mistakes with consonants that seemed to overlap were forgiven me, all those accidental puns, but when you're speaking out of turn you need every possible form of back-up.

I needed to borrow the language skills of a native speaker, and Ramana wouldn't quite do. He was shy, he was sometimes tongue-tied, and he was still regarded as close to an idiot by some elements of village and family. I needed his liveliest uncle, the one I first met as a chatty boy outside a temple, his fingers getting into everything, a regular spider monkey. I needed Arumugam. The name means six sides. A spiritual cube that only a god could see in all its facets.

What sides has this six-sided man shown me? The hyperactive boy, a sort of joyous kleptomaniac who never actually took anything but needed to hold treasures in his hands, has given way to a sad and infinitely sexy young man, who doesn't fully realize the seductive effect he has on people, with his strong facial bones and his out-of-focus eyes. But there's also a dreamer there, and an invalid who was given the wrong drugs for his TB. He came to me for help when his eyesight started to fail, wanting me to sort it out. And who knows what side he'll show us next—husband and father, maybe? But that day he showed he could also be an interpreter, making a connection between two very different ways of doing things.

It made sense to speak through a Tamil middleman, and it also made sense to accommodate myself to the solemnity of the occasion by standing up. I asked Ramana to put the brakes on the wheelchair and I edged myself forward until I could take my weight with the crutch and the cane.

Arumugam had been wailing with the best of them, but he was quiet when Ramana brought him across. Then Ramana went right back to his grandfather, not wanting to leave him alone.

I said to Arumugam, 'Will you be my voice? There's something we need to do for Suseela.' And he said Yes. 'Don't you want to know what it is?' I asked, but he didn't need to know, as long as I did. I felt quite light-headed, on top of all my other emotions and sensations, from the intoxication of his trust. It was a few hours since I'd eaten, and my body likes regularity on that level.

Alien spores of initiative were drifting through a converted cow shed in southern India. I spoke up in English as clearly as I could. I'm not shy. Shyness belongs to people who have a realistic chance of escaping notice. It's their strategy, but it can't be mine. Over time in Ukay I've learned to speak out of turn, on the principle that speaking out of turn, loudly and clearly, is the closest to having a turn I'm likely to get. And I've been a teacher part-time, my voice carries. My arms can't do much to dramatize my text, but I can make little pounding movements that turn my words into italics. All public speakers draw on the same small range of techniques. But Arumugam was my secret weapon, in this quaint and amorous culture; someone who didn't even need to try to make them pay attention, Rumi the universal heart-throb who didn't even notice the women hanging around him till I pointed them out. Delicious all his life, Tamil catnip, and not to know that these attentions were out of the ordinary.

I needed the wailers to stop their lamentations, above all to stop beating their breasts. Often you hear of people dropping dead at deathbeds and funerals, and it's always offered as proof of devotion, in this very devotion-minded culture, but I can't help knowing that if Suseela's heart disease is congenital, and the village is genetically pretty homogenous, then the women in this cow shed are getting themselves worked up, putting their hearts in a tizzy, and then striking themselves on the very ribs behind which their weakened hearts are cowering. So it's not surprising that one death should trigger another, is it? Life expectancy in India isn't so long that people can afford to throw years away in the grief of the moment. 'If it was you...' I said to Arumugam, and he broadcast the phrase in Tamil until the noise had died down just a little. 'If it was you instead of Suseela...'

But there was more to it than protecting the mourners from the dangers of their lamentation. In Hinduism there's a special status to the last moments of a life. This is life in its molten state. Here and now it receives an impression which will carry over into the next body and the next consciousness. What hope for a life begun in the echo of shrieking? Western science compounds the worry with the revelation that hearing is the most stubbornly surviving of the senses. We continue to take in through the ears a world that our dying eyes are blind to.

'If it was you instead of Suseela, would you want to listen to screams and weeping?' As he took in the implications of what I was saying, the challenge to tradition that I had put in his mouth, he almost stumbled, but he went on loyally repeating in Tamil what I murmured in English. 'Or would you rather listen to the wind and the birds?'

Silence didn't come all at once. And in fact I'm a little vague about the order of events. I was wholly present, paying full attention, but even full attention is a sort of lattice, and the air moves freely through it.

'She can't see, but she can still hear. These moments are important.' I know what I meant to say but I don't know if I actually said it. Perhaps it's like concert violinists—brain scans show that they're not actually listening to the sound they make. That area of the brain is quiet, though there are lights on in lots of other places. The soloist and the music are in a rapture of mutual ownership, and yet listening isn't a part of it, particularly. At some stage Arumugam must have put his hands on my shoulders, but by the time I'd noticed their warmth was well established.

Finally a lady said, 'If this is true, then we should be quiet,' with growing confidence, and there was a turning of the tide. As the noise died down, except for the odd gasp and bit of shuffling, we could hear the faint racket of Suseela's breathing. Not being deafened by shrieks gave her a little room for manoeuvre in her dying. Her brain was harvesting all the energy remaining, and there was just enough for one action to be completed. Slowly but very meaningfully she reached out her arms. Someone near me asked, bafflingly, 'Is she dead now?', as if all the rules had been suspended for this occasion, and corpses might move about.

Suseela wanted to hold her husband. Her gesture wasn't directed precisely at Sadasivam, but it was clear what she wanted. He hung back, clutching his grandson, not knowing how to respond.

I had wanted to help Suseela be at the centre of her life at the moment it ended, but I had done something else as well without knowing it. I had taken away from Sadasivam the assurance that he knew what to do, and now unprecedented demands were being made on him. By clothing Suseela in silence I had stripped him naked in front of his people. He looked at me, in something like terror, for guidance that I was unqualified to give. But I nodded, and he left Ramana's arms and moved over to his wife.

She put her arms around him, then she tried to do the same with her legs. She wanted to grip him with both arms and legs. Everyone in the village knew that this marriage had been a lively fountain, knew how much they had liked their loving, before she was ill. She was blind, but her mouth knew how to move towards its kiss. I tried to give her what she wanted and needed. I told Arumugam to translate, 'She wants you to get into bed with her, Naina,' but that was too much. Even if he had passed it on, the taboo on man and woman together in front of the village would have prevented it from happening.

Then I let myself sit down in the wheelchair, and asked Arumugam to move me back a bit. I wanted the scene to play itself out without getting in the way any more.

She gripped her husband as best she could. People die upwards, and her feet were already dead. But perhaps she thought she had managed to wrap them round her husband. And then she died all the way up. A minute went by, and then another, but nobody moved. It was so peaceful. But after all my interfering, it was inevitable perhaps that the whole bereaved village would look to me to announce that this time there was no mistake. I hoped the peace would stay. In my own workable Tamil, without benefit of translator, I told them what was obvious: 'No doubt about it. She's been dead for about ten minutes.' Instantly the wailing came back, doubled and redoubled, as if everyone needed to blot out that unique and beautiful silence. Sadasivam stayed where he was for another minute or so, and then tried to disengage himself. The dead grip was powerful, it wasn't possible to leave his wife's embrace with dignity or tenderness.

Suseela died at about two o'clock on Christmas Day. She was fifty-eight, perhaps. She had been ill for almost a fifth of her life. She was washed the next morning and buried at four that afternoon. According to Hinduism, the body is no more than an old coat. We shrug it off. There's a limit to how much you can bewail the discarding of an old coat, even in a society in which nothing is willingly thrown away.

The washing of a body isn't a reverent business here. Suseela was laid on a wooden bench, and then buckets of water were thrown roughly over her. Perhaps as many as fifteen. Roughly they shook her head and limbs for the final bath. Her old coat of a body was washed the way we might rinse out a gutted fish.

Lives that have known so little privacy, and have disliked the little they had, don't end with the enclosure of a coffin, just a ramshackle palanquin, no more than a stretcher. Suseela was dressed in a red sari. Her arms were tied by her sides, garlands hung round her neck. Her mouth stuffed with green leaves.

Alien spores of initiative had drifted through a repopulated cow shed in southern India, but they found no propagating medium to receive them. Custom is resilient. Rites of passage are rooted deep as teeth. The soil here just isn't receptive to innovation. Every day Ramana will ask me how many chapattis he should cook, as if past experience offered no guide. As if one day I might say 'one' or 'a hundred' quite arbitrarily. Every day I pretend to be thinking aloud, saying, 'Let's see, there'll be three of us, say three each and one for luck, why not do ten altogether?' But he will never feel able to try the maths on his own, he will never stop asking day by day, not because he doesn't understand numbers but because a little brother goes by what his big brother says. And the day when he feels able to do chapatti multiplication by himself is quite close to the day he decides that he has better things to do than prepare a flannel with water not hot and not cold, and to wash inside the ears of a Big Brother to whom he isn't related, to help me scratch all the so many itches I can't reach myself. That day is one I'm in no hurry to see. I know better than to saw off the branch that I'm sitting on, even if I've never handled a saw or climbed a tree.

I tried to change the rules, and I was lucky to achieve as much as I did, an exception. There was gossip about my daring to touch Suseela's chest to feel her heart, but I never heard gossip about the silence. Of course the wailers at Suseela's deathbed fell silent because I asked them to, not because they agreed with what I had said, and because Sadasivam was too traumatized by sorrow to overrule me. They stopped shrieking because I was Jarn Doctor of Doctors, and it seemed like medical advice, which it partly was.

I was immune to criticism, but then I was immune to a lot of things. Hadn't I put known poison on my tongue? Hadn't I kissed a cobra and come to no harm? Even my strangest suggestion had a certain amount of authority, a special status. But no one else in Tamil Nadu, while the culture holds, will share the quiet of Suseela's death, and the clarity of her last moments, while the next life was being moulded.

People took photographs of the body, with no sense of trespass. Photography in this culture has no power of profanation. It's quite usual for people to display photographs of their relatives' bodies. Dead faces with their look of a secret.

Suseela's death made the family taboo for two weeks—a fortnight in which they couldn't circulate, and would have to depend on food and supplies brought in.

There was music, there were drums, there were fireworks. A swami sang a song, not of mourning exactly. We bury an old coat, that's all. The body is a banana leaf on which delicious food has been served, to be thrown away matter-of-factly after the meal. Yet there is a certain amount of poignant ritual, symbolizing the contrary sense that something irreparable has happened. A cracked pot of water is carried round the grave three times, leaking as it goes, and then is broken. People put mementoes in the grave before it's filled in. My contribution was some mantra beads and a little sample bottle of perfume that I had picked up in Robert Sayle's in Cambridge. Suseela loved foreign things. She loved the exotic, duff and pills that work, the scientifically credible placebos of the West.

She loved to hear me talk about department stores in Ukay. She who had never been to a city, Madras being 120 miles away, and had no experience of anything the West would call a shop. Still she loved to imagine a shop that had other shops inside it, a shop like a city, to the extent that she could imagine a city. She'd have been proud to share her grave with the little sample bottle of Noir.

Funeral rites are elemental—fire, water, earth, air, India gives them all their due. Not really surprising, though, that a caste of farmers should make their pact with earth.

After all was sung and done, Suseela's daughter, Mani Megalai, came over to me and said something extraordinary. On that famous earlier occasion she had been sent by her father to test the reliability of my sexual remoteness from women, her kneading hands really part of Sadasivam and his need to know, but now she is here on her own account, with her own message. Her hands are not here to investigate, but to caress. She speaks for herself. She smells of tuberoses, the flowers that the family grows for the perfume industry and for the pious adornment of ladies. Mani Megalai takes my hand, which looks small and pale and clenched between hers, but then I'm used to that. Her hands are warm and cool. She says, 'Jarn... From this day. From this day you are my mother.' □

GRANTA

JOHNNY
John McGahern

BARRY LEWIS/NETWORK PHOTOGRAPHERS

The Ruttledges saw Johnny resting in the shade of the alder tree at the gate, leaning heavily on the girl's bicycle, looking exhausted after the steep climb from the lake. He did not see them though they were only a few yards away. When he straightened, passing his hand over the hair flattened across his forehead, they went towards him. 'You're welcome home, Johnny.'

'It's great to be home. Great to see yous all and to see yous all so well.'

His suit was worsted blue. He wore a red tie with a white shirt. The bottoms of his trousers were gathered neatly in with bicycle clips. His shoes were polished but dimmed with a light coating of dust from the dry road. He leaned the bicycle against the wall of the porch and paused on his way into the house to look up at the shed.

'It's been a big year for you, Johnny,' Ruttledge said as he got out the bottle of rum and found the blackcurrant cordial far back in a cupboard of the press, while Johnny lit a cigarette, striking a match expertly on the sole of his shoe.

'A big year. Ford gave me the golden handshake. Yet it all worked out in the end more or less alphabetical. Jamesie and Mary across the lake were as good as gold as was Jim in Dublin. They all did their level best to get me to throw up England altogether and come home for good. I was tempted,' he said, tapping the ash of the cigarette on a small saucer Kate put on the arm of the chair. The Ruttledges listened in disbelief. Jamesie and Mary had been terrified when Johnny wrote. That he planned to come home and live with them again—his brother and sister-in-law. They wouldn't take him in but they couldn't be seen to turn him away. Ruttledge had written the letter for them which Mary copied and sent. The blow had been softened in the writing but the refusal made clear.

'I was tempted at first but the more I thought about it the more I saw it wouldn't work out. People get set in their ways. They can't manage to fit in together any more. Once you get used to London, a place like the lake gets very backward. You are too far from everything. Jamesie and Mary, God bless them, came to see it that way as well. Without a car it would have been all hopeless. You'd be stuck there in front of the alders on Moroney's hill facing the small river and the bog. It was a great thing to know all the same that in a tight corner you were still wanted by your own. Who else can you turn to in the end but your own flesh and blood?'

He was moving in his blindness, as if he was speaking for multitudes.

'Then Mister Singh got to know and from then on I was more or less on the pig's back. I have as much in my back pocket now at the end of the week than even in the best days when I was on the line at Ford's.'

In other summers he also talked of 'Murphy's Fusiliers'. They had rooms in the house and worked in tunnels around the airports. From work they went straight to the pub and from there to bed until Murphy's bus collected them again the next morning. He spoke of them with tolerant disapproval. Their lives moved at the edge of death and violence.

'Do you miss your old room or the Fusiliers at all?' Ruttledge asked.

'Not the Fusiliers. Though me and them got on the best. The poor fellas are their own worst enemy,' he said. 'I missed the Prince of Wales a sight at first. I found a little old pub in off the High Street in Leytonstone that's very quiet during the day. You can go over the racing pages in peace in the Heathcote.'

'Did you find a new darts team or do you still go back to play for the Prince?'

'They wanted me but it's too far.'

Kate made a plate of sandwiches. Johnny said he would prefer tea to another rum and black and they all had mugs of tea poured from the big red teapot.

'What is your new place like?'

'It'd be far too posh for the Fusiliers,' he smiled. It was a row of old Victorian mansions facing Epping Forest that his old landlord, Mister Singh, had bought and turned into flats. 'They are nearly all professional people in the flats—technicians from the hospital, business people, secretaries, men and women, you don't ask questions. They come and they go. In the basement I have my own entrance, central heating, bathroom, phone, TV, everything laid on.'

'Do you have much to do?'

'You'd like to have more. A Paki woman comes in three times

a week to hoover and mop the stairs and the landings. There are some old fruit trees in the gardens at the back that I prune and I mow the grass. I keep the car park tidy. Otherwise I'm just on call.'

'What sort of call?'

'To see that nobody gets into the flats that don't belong. Clever and all as these people are some don't know how to change a light bulb or a fuse. You name it. They do it. Most things that go wrong I can fix. If it's something serious I call Mister Singh.

'Days I go for a bit of a walk in the Forest. You'd miss having a dog. There's a pond at Snaresbrook where you can watch the ducks and the swans. They're pure tame. At night I go down to the Hitchcock Hotel. A Mike Furlong from Mayo, who made his money in the building game, owns the Hitchcock. We get on the best. Mike often puts up a drink for me in the Hitchcock. Mister Singh has me do all the short lets. I haven't made a mistake yet. Touch wood. Mister Singh drives a Bentley now. Before I left he gave me a rise and said how hard it is to find anybody steady and reliable these days.'

'It sounds as if everything has worked out well,' Ruttledge said.

'It's completely alphabetical.'

In the long pause a finch appeared outside the wide window and with darting mechanical movements started to pick at the wild strawberries on the bank.

'We were putting the trailer on the car when you came,' Ruttledge said. 'I have to run in for a few things before the town closes. Would you be interested in the jaunt?'

'I wouldn't mind. It'd put round a few hours. What about the bicycle?'

'We can hop it in the trailer.'

'That's great. I was puffed after the cycle round the shore.'

They drove in silence, Johnny folded back into the comfort of the car seat. He did not look around, not at the reeds along the shore, the summer breezes rippling the surface of the lake-like shoals, the green brilliance of the leaves of the wild cherry amid the common foliage; not the wild fowl or the few swans or the heron flapping out of the reeds to lead them out before swinging loftily aside and then wheeling lazily around. He was folded back into himself as into tiredness or night.

At the gate he barely protested when Ruttledge jumped from the car, lifted the bicycle from the trailer and placed it behind one of the round stone piers.

'I should have done that,' Johnny said.

When they left the narrow tarred lanes, the car picked up speed and Johnny sat up in the seat: he knew the names of all the houses they passed.

'You know more about the houses and people than I do.'

'I was old when I left. Half strangers sometimes know more about a place than the people who live there.'

'Do you regret having left?'

'Many times over. The whole of Ireland was leaving then and I passed no heed. I didn't even have to leave like most of the rest. You don't get reruns in life like you do in a play. There's no turning back now anyhow,' he said.

There were so many cars outside the healer's house that they had to stop to allow a truck to pass.

'Seventh son of a seventh son. At least he's doing great business. Do you think the cure works?' Johnny asked.

'Many are cancer patients who have tried doctors and hospitals and have nowhere else to turn. He blesses them and tells them what they want to hear. Maybe that in itself does good. The mind is a strange place. Who knows?'

Johnny nodded tiredly but wasn't interested further. He didn't look up as they passed the cattle mart or at the two detectives in the alleyway across from Jimmy Joe McKiernan's IRA Bar. At the creamery he sat smoking in the car while Ruttledge loaded the trailer with bags of meal and fertilizer.

'Would you like to go to Luke Henry's? We could have a drink and it'd be a comfortable place to wait while I get the rest of the things before the shops close.'

'No better place. No decenter man than Luke. It was the one call we didn't make on the way from the train. I'd like to see Luke again.'

They found a place to park across the street from the bar. The bar itself was empty, Luke sitting on a high stool behind the counter, his back turned to the door, looking at the television high in the corner. It took him a long time to recognize Johnny, with help of the clues Ruttledge provided, but when he did he reached his hand across the counter.

'Welcome home, Johnny. Welcome as the flowers in June.'

'Great to be home, Luke. Great to see everybody so well.'

They ordered rum with blackcurrant and a glass of stout but Luke pushed the banknote away that Johnny proffered. 'It's on the house. Welcome home, Johnny. Welcome home from England.'

'I have a few things to get around the town. I won't be long,' Ruttledge explained, intending to leave Johnny chatting comfortably with Luke. To his surprise, Johnny followed him out into the evening street.

'Are you leaving Luke alone? Wouldn't you be more comfortable in at the bar?'

'I'd sooner tag along. We'll come back together.'

The shops would soon be closing. The street was quick with last-minute bustle. In the first shop Johnny stood glued to Ruttledge. No one recognized him or spoke. Silently, he waited at the checkout until the basket was checked through. On the longer walk to the next shop he suddenly started falling behind. Several times they had to pause and stop.

'A bit out of puff,' he apologized, wiping his forehead with his sleeve. The colour of his face had drained to leave an ugly tinge of blue in the paleness.

'Are you sure you're all right?'

'Just that small bit out of puff. It won't take a minute.'

'Wouldn't you be more comfortable sitting across in Luke's than rushing around the town?'

'There's no chance you'd leave me here, Joe? You wouldn't forget to come back and collect me?' he asked in a childlike voice.

'Lord bless us, Johnny. I have never left anybody in the town yet.' Ruttledge was so amazed that he instinctively reached out and put his arm round his shoulders and drew him towards him in reassurance. 'You'll be far happier in Luke's. What put it into your head that I could leave you in the town? I'll come back when the shopping is done and we'll have a quiet drink together before heading for home. We can even have several drinks if we feel like them. It's not every week of the year we get you home.'

John McGahern

They put the purchases in the car and crossed to Luke's. Though the phrasing of the fear was wild, there was no mistaking the anxiety in the eyes, the terror of being abandoned in what had suddenly become a strange place. Because of the suddenness of their exit Luke looked up enquiringly as they entered but he was too good a barman to show surprise. He just moved their two glasses solicitously closer on the counter. There was now a number of drinkers in the bar and three shop assistants were playing a game of darts in the far corner, keeping the scores in chalk on the small blackboard. Sitting at the counter, Johnny seemed to revive and recover his ease after a few sips of rum. Ruttledge ordered another round. He decided to put off the remaining purchases to another time.

'You wouldn't mind, lads, if I had a throw?' Johnny asked the dart players when they came to the counter for drinks during a break in the game.

'Not at all. Fire away. We've just been fooling around,' they said, and gave him a set of darts with red plastic fins.

'I'll probably hit nothing. One of the summers I was home I took up the gun again. I could hit nothing.'

He flexed his wrists as he felt the weight and balance of the darts and took a few very casual practice throws before taking his place on the mat. Because he was a stranger, the whole bar went silent with attention as he threw. Magically, easily, each dart flew true. There was polite applause. Pleased and a little flustered, Johnny gathered the darts and offered them back to the boys but they insisted he throw again. For several minutes he threw and each throw went home. Only a single throw was missed and that by no more than the thickness of a wire. When he finally handed back the darts and took his place beside Ruttledge at the counter there was warm applause around the bar.

'It was the best I ever saw,' Luke seized his hand.

'It's as good as on TV,' the players affirmed.

Johnny insisted on buying another round and they drank in the glow of his success.

'I don't understand it. I don't think I ever threw as well playing for the Prince of Wales. I was sure I'd hit nothing. I haven't lifted a dart in months.'

'It couldn't have come back if it wasn't already there,' Luke reassured him.

'It's a mystery. I doubt if I could throw that well again to save my life.'

It was time to leave. By now the whole bar had come to trace who Johnny was and where he came from and something of his history.

'I'll not say goodbye since I'll expect to be in again before I head back across the pond,' Johnny said to Luke.

'You'll have to come and play a proper game though you'll shame us all,' one of the darts players said. 'If you were staying and we had you on the team we'd be able to beat the rest of the town good-looking.'

'The next time I might hit nothing,' he replied modestly.

'Thanks, Luke.'

'Thanks yerselves,' Luke said as he gathered in their glasses, and they were followed out by a chorus of 'Good luck!' and 'Safe journey!' and 'Don't take to the hedges!'

Johnny was completely revived and needed no guiding to the car and trailer. Except for the bars the town was closed and had the same sense of closure and emptiness as beaches and public gardens at the end of the day.

'Your uncle is still going good?' Johnny enquired politely as they drove out of town.

'Still the same. Dines in the Central.'

'He must be a very rich man now.'

'He has more now than he needs. There's only so much you can do with the day.'

'It may be the whole show,' Johnny agreed. 'Yourself and Kate got on the best as well. When you first got back from London they were saying you'd never last out. Now you are near enough the same as everyone around the place.'

'Your brother gave us great help,' Ruttledge said.

They had left the main road and entered the green lanes, whitethorns brushing the windscreen and filtering down the light. Because of the narrowness, they drove slowly and blew the horn loudly at every turn.

'Patrick Ryan will be sure to be around when he hears you are home. Maybe we could all go into Luke's together some evening and make a night of it,' Ruttledge said.

'That'd be great. Where's Patrick this weather?'

'Last I heard he was building for the Reynoldses who own all the dozers and diggers. He could be gone from here already. Patrick tires of people quickly.' Johnny and Patrick had been great friends and starred together in the local plays, before Johnny fell in love with a girl and followed her to England.

'That's Patrick,' Johnny smiled in recognition. 'He always had to have his own way in everything.'

After the green enclosures of the lanes, the lake met them with space and light. A red sun was low in the sky.

'All I have to do is hop the bike on the trailer and run you up to the house,' Ruttledge said when they reached the gate.

'No. They'd think I was going soft,' Johnny said firmly. 'I'll just get the bicycle from behind the pier and dawdle up at my ease. I have the whole evening.'

They both got out of the car. The engine was left running.

'Are you certain now?' Ruttledge enquired a last time as Johnny took the bicycle.

'No,' he said adamantly. 'We had a most wonderful evening. It helped put round the whole day. It's all A-one. Everything now is completely alphabetical.'

While Ruttledge was unloading the trailer he looked from time to time across the lake. Johnny was climbing the hill slowly, pausing many times, a small dark figure on the pale pass shadowed by the whitethorns. When at last he reached the brow of the hill, he stood for a long time leaning on the bicycle. All he had to do from there was freewheel down to the house. Behind him on Moroney's Hill there shivered a pure sky that was turning pale as ash as the sun went down.

Within the house, Ruttledge told of Johnny's fear of being abandoned in the town and then his triumph in Luke's as each arrow flew true.

'I found the visit disturbing,' Kate said.

'Because of his confusion?'

'That and because he doesn't look well.'

'What I'd like this evening is some wine,' Ruttledge said.

Johnny

The table was laid, a single candle lit, the curtains not drawn. As they ate and drank and talked, the huge shapes of the trees around the house gradually entered the room in the flickering half-light, and the room went out, as if in a dream, to include the trees and the fields and the glowing deep light of the sky. In this soft light the room seemed to grow enormous and everything to fill with repose.

A wild battering on the doors and windows, as if a storm had sprung up on the lake, woke them out of deep sleep. The house was shaking. They looked at one another in alarm and then heard a voice shouting out through all the pounding and battering. Pulling on clothes, Ruttledge ran towards the noise. Outside the glass porch Jamesie stood clear as day in the full moon above the lake. His huge hand was open and beating flatly on the glass while his other hand was shaking the locked door. The glass shook in the heavy frames as if about to shatter.

'Johnny's dead. Johnny's dead. Johnny's dead,' he was calling out. 'Johnny's dead,' he continued calling out when Ruttledge opened the door.

'He can't be. I left him at the lake gate this afternoon...'

'Dead. Had the priest and the doctor. Dead.'

'I can hardly believe. I'm sorry.'

'Dead before nine. Me and Mary were down in the bog. She left his tea ready but saw him come in on the street with the bicycle and went up from the bog to make his tea. She said he was in topping form and spoke of yourself and Kate and the great time he had in the town. When she left him he was watching Mickey Mouse on the TV. He was a sight for them cartoons. Twice we saw him come out on the street when we were in the bog. He stood as if he was looking across at the alders on Moroney's Hill. Mary was the first to leave the bog and heard a sort of a moan when she got near the house and found him slumped sideways. When he didn't answer she shouted down to the bog. When I got to the house he was still able to talk but it was all ravelled. The priest said he wasn't fully gone at the time he was anointed. The doctor said the heart just gave out and it could have happened at any time.'

Jamesie spoke very quickly and his disarray and shock over the death of his brother were obvious but there was a finished feel to

227

the account, as if it had been given a number of times already.

'I'm very sorry. I can hardly believe it,' Ruttledge offered his hand and winced at the fierceness of the clasp. 'I wanted to leave him all the way up to the house but he wouldn't hear. He insisted on walking.'

'I know. He told it all to Mary when she was getting his tea. He had a great appetite after the town and lately he's only been picking at his plate.'

'I'm sorry, Jamesie.' Kate joined them in the porch. 'Will you come in and take something?'

'No. No. We have several houses to call to yet,' and it was only then Ruttledge noticed the small car waiting discreetly beyond the alder at the gate.

'Is there anything we can do to help?'

'Not a thing. Nothing. We can't find Patrick Ryan anywhere. Nobody seems to know where he's been working or gone. Some even said he could be gone to Dublin to do work for the Reynoldses that have houses there.'

'We'll be over as soon as we get dressed. Is there anything we can bring?'

'No. No. Everything's got. Take your time. There's plenty with Mary already.'

The moon was so bright, the night so clear, that the headlights of the small car showed weakly in the spaces between the trees as it crawled out around the shore.

They decided to walk. Wildfowl took fright as soon as they turned round the shore and clattered out towards where flocks of birds were clustered like dark fruit in the middle of the lake. The trees stood like huge sentinels along the shore, casting long shadows back on the moonlit grass. Here and there a barely perceptible night breeze stirred the still water and stretches appeared like furrows of beaten silver under the moon. The heron had been disturbed by the car and did not rise until they were far out along the shore, and was ghostly as it lifted lazily towards the moon before turning back the way they had come.

'The last thing he said to me was here,' Ruttledge spoke when they reached the open gate. '"Everything is now completely alphabetical."'

'It almost was. Somewhere between Y and Z,' Kate answered.

The small street was filled with cars. Beyond the netting wire the iron posts of the empty hay shed stood out in the moonlight as did the whitewashed outhouses. The hen house was closed. Rectangles of light lay on the street from the small window and the open door. The living room was full of people. All the clocks had been stopped. The long inner room was open and several cardboard boxes rested on the oval table. The chairs had been taken from the room and filled the small living room. The door to the lower room was closed.

'Poor Johnny,' Mary clasped their hands. Her face was filled with a strange serenity, as if she had been transported by the excitement of the death to a more spiritual place.

As they shook hands and took their place among the mourners, the muted voices all around them were agreeing: 'I know it's sad but when you think about it maybe it was all for the better. He wasn't old. No family. What had he to head back to? Nobody related next or near. Sad as it is, when you think about it, it could not have happened any better if it had been planned. Of course it would have been better if it had never happened—but sooner or later none of us can escape that—God help us all,' and there was a palpable sense of satisfaction that they stood safely and solidly outside all that their words agreed.

The small car that had waited outside the gate beyond the alder tree returned with Jamesie. He was very agitated. The muted voices stopped as he went up to Ruttledge.

'We sent out word far and wide and can find no trace of Patrick. Nobody appears to know where he's gone.'

'Why is it so necessary to find Patrick?'

'He always lays the body out!'

Jamesie looked anxiously around. The house was full and though it was now well after midnight people were still coming to the house. The cardboard boxes on the oval table were full of food and drink. By custom, nothing could be offered until the corpse was laid out and viewed.

'I'll lay Johnny out,' Ruttledge offered.

'Will you be able?' Jamesie searched his face. The house went silent.

'I worked in hospitals when I was a student,' Ruttledge tried to hide his own anxiety.

'Do you think...?' Jamesie was uncertain.

'I'm sure, especially if I can get any help.'

'I'll help,' a man volunteered readily, Tom Kelly, a neighbour Ruttledge knew slightly. He worked as a hairdresser in Dublin, was home visiting his mother, and had accompanied her to the house.

'You'll need a glass first,' Jamesie said, and poured each man a glass of whiskey and waited until they drank it down as if it was essential for facing into such a task. He handed Ruttledge the flat cardboard box he had been given by the undertaker.

Mary poured a basin of steaming water. She had towels, scissors, a sponge, a razor, a pair of white starched sheets, a pillowslip. She and Jamesie led the two men down into the closed lower room. Johnny lay on the bed in his shirt and trousers. His feet were bare.

'Poor Johnny,' Mary said dreamily before moving to leave the room. Jamesie stood by her shoulder but did not speak. He was strained and taut.

'If there's anything you want, just knock hard on the door and Jamesie will come down,' Mary said.

'Is there cotton wool?' Ruttledge asked.

The flat box contained a large bag of cotton wool, a white habit, rosary beads, a bar of soap, a disposable razor.

Jamesie closed the door firmly as he and Mary left the room.

'We'll have to get off the clothes.'

For a moment, as he held the still warm flesh in his hand, he thought of themselves in the busy evening street of a few hours ago. It did not take an ambush to bring about such quick and irrecoverable change.

By lifting the hips, the trousers were pulled free. There was a wallet, coins, a penknife, a comb, betting slips, rosary beads in a small worn purse. With more difficulty they drew the strong thick arms out of the shirtsleeves and pulled the shirt loose. The long cotton undershirt was going to be more difficult still. The body was heavy and surprisingly loose.

'Cut it off.'

'Wouldn't it be better to do like the shirt?'

'It's too tight.' Ruttledge handed Tom Kelly the pair of scissors and when he looked doubtful added, 'He won't need it any more.'

'There's no earthly edge on these scissors. You can never get scissors with an edge in the country. They use them for everything,' Tom Kelly complained.

When at last he got the incision made, the cotton tore easily. They did likewise with the underpants. The only thing that remained on the body was a large silver digital watch, the red numerals pulsing out the seconds like a mechanical heart eerily alive in the stillness.

'He won't need that any more either.' The hairdresser removed the watch, but it continued to pulse in the glass ashtray until it distracted Ruttledge, and he turned it face down. He then noticed and removed his hearing aid.

They closed the ears and the nostrils with the cotton wool, and when they turned him over to close the rectum, dentures fell from his mouth. The rectum absorbed almost all the cotton wool. The act was as intimate and warm as the act of sex. The innate sacredness of each single life stood out more starkly in death than in the whole of its natural life. To see him naked was also to know what his character and clothes had disguised—the wonderful physical specimen he had been. That perfect coordination of hand and eye that had caused so many wildfowl to fall like stones from the air had been no accident. That hand, too, had now fallen.

'We'd be better to lift him down to the floor.'

'Are you sure?'

'We'll have more room and we have to make the bed.'

In the sheet they lifted him from the bed. Tom Kelly shaved him with quick firm professional strokes and nicked the line of the sideburns level with the closed eyes while Ruttledge washed and dried the body.

'Does he need a quick trim?'

'Whatever you think.'

Taking a comb and complaining all the time about the scissors, Tom Kelly trimmed and combed the hair. When they were almost finished, the door burst open. By throwing himself against the door Ruttledge managed to shut it again before it swung wide. Profuse apologies then came from the other side of the door. They noticed a large old-fashioned key in the lock and turned the key.

'It would have been terrible if he was seen like this on the floor.'

'We should have noticed the key in the first place.'

'It's locked now anyhow.'

They changed the sheet and the pillowslip. Very carefully they lifted the great weight back on to the bed. They arranged his feet and took the habit. It was a glowing white, a cloth breastplate with long sleeves, four white ribbons. The cuffs and breastplate were embroidered with gold thread. They eased the hands and arms into the sleeves, lifted the back to secure the breastplate by tying the ribbons.

'They skimp on everything these days,' Tom Kelly complained. 'There was a time when every dead person was given a full habit.'

'It makes it easier for us. Nobody will know the difference. What'll we do about the beads?'

'We'll give him his own beads.'

Tom Kelly took the beads from the small purse and twined them through his fingers before arranging his hands on the breastplate. They then drew up the sheet and placed the hands on the fold. One eye had opened and was closed gently again.

'We are almost through.'

'All we have to do is get the mouth right.'

Tom Kelly fixed the dentures in place. With cotton wool he moulded the mouth and face into shape slowly and with meticulous care.

'It looks perfect,' Ruttledge said, but as he spoke a final press caused the dentures to fall loose. This occurred a number of times: all would look in place and then come undone through striving for too much perfection.

'I can hear people getting restless.'

'Mark you well my words,' Tom Kelly answered. 'Everything we have done will be remarked upon. Everything we have done will be well gone over.'

The whole slow process began again. There was no doubting the growing impatience and restlessness beyond the door for the wake to begin.

'If you don't get it done this time I'm taking over,' Ruttledge said.

Possibly because of this extra pressure the face became undone more quickly than at any other time.

'Don't you worry,' Tom Kelly said angrily as he gave up his place. 'We will all have our critics. We will have our critics.'

By using more cotton wool and striving for less, Ruttledge got the dentures in place and the mouth to hold shape.

'I had it far better than that several times.'

'I know.'

'The cheeks bulge.'

'They'll have to do. Can't you hear?'

'You may not know it but mark my words our work will be well gone over. We will have our critics. We could be the talk of the country yet,' Tom Kelly said.

'I'll take the blame. You'll be in Dublin.'

'Whether we like it or not we could be scourged,' Tom Kelly said so anxiously that Ruttledge pressed his shoulder in reassurance.

'You did great. We did our best. We couldn't keep at it forever.'

'Maybe it isn't too bad, then. We could still pass muster,' he replied doubtfully.

The clothes and waste were stuffed in a plastic bag and hid in the wardrobe with the flat cardboard box. The door was unlocked, the basin of water removed. Jamesie and Mary came down to the room. They stood in silence for a long time looking at the face.

'He's beautiful,' Mary said and reached across to touch the pale forehead.

'He's perfect. Patrick couldn't have done it a whit better,' Jamesie said emotionally.

'I had no idea he was such a fine figure of a man,' Ruttledge said.

'Stronger than me, stronger than my father, far stronger than me the best day ever I was,' Jamesie said.

A row of chairs was arranged around the walls of the room. A bedside table was draped with a white cloth and two candles were placed in brass candlesticks and lit. A huge vase of flowers was set in the window sill.

One by one each person came and took their leave and stood or knelt. Old men and women sat on the chairs along the wall. The Rosary was said, a woman leading the prayers, the swelling responses given back as one voice.

Huge platters of sandwiches were handed around, whiskey, beer, stout, sherry, port, lemonade. Tea was poured from the large aluminium kettle. The murmurs of speech grew louder and more confident. At first all the talk was of the dead man but then it wandered to their own interests and cares. Some who smoked dropped their cigarette ends down the necks of empty beer or stout bottles, where they hissed like trapped wasps. People wandered out into the night and the moonlight. Jokes began and laughter.

'If we couldn't have a laugh or two we might as well go and lie down ourselves.'

Morning was beginning to thin the moonlight on the street when Patrick Ryan appeared in the doorway without warning, and stood there, a silent dark-suited apparition. The white shirt shone, the black tie neatly knotted; he was clean-shaven, the thick silver hair brushed.

'I'm sorry. Sorry.'

'We know, Patrick. We know. We were looking for you everywhere.'

'I heard. Word was brought. I had to dress.'

With the same slow steps he went down to the room, made the sign of the cross, stood for a long time gazing at the dead man before touching the hands and the forehead in a slow, stern leave-taking.

The loud talk and the laughter his entrance had quelled rose again. Patrick made an impatient movement when he returned from the room but the talk and noise could not be stilled a second time. When offered sandwiches, he made a dismissive gesture, as if what had happened was too momentous to be bartered for the small coinages of food and drink, but he accepted the large whiskey Jamesie poured as if he was absent and the hand that gripped the glass was not his own.

'Who laid him out?' he demanded.

'I did,' Ruttledge said.

'I might have known.'

'I told you,' Tom Kelly whispered. 'Our critics have landed.'

'I couldn't care less.'

With a peremptory wave of the hand, Patrick Ryan indicated that he wished to see Ruttledge alone outside the house. They stood by the lighted window and could see through the bowl of flowers to the lighted candles and the white stillness of the bed.

'Why didn't you wait for me, lad? Were you that greedy to get stuck in?'

'Nobody could find you,' Ruttledge said patiently. 'They looked everywhere. They couldn't wait any longer.'

'They might have known that important word would have always got to me,' he said.

'They didn't know. Someone said you could even be working in Dublin. They thought the funeral would be over before you got word.'

'I suppose it was that molly of a hairdresser who helped you botch the job.'

'Tom Kelly gave great help. Any faults were mine,' Ruttledge said.

'It was some face to give a poor man leaving the world,' he complained bitterly. 'Some face to give him for his appearance in the next.'

'People seem pleased enough.'

'People know nothing, lad. All they want is to be riding and filling their gullets. But there are people who know. The trades know. I know. Anyhow it's matterless now, lad. It's done,' he said as if growing impatient of his own thought.

People were no longer coming to the house and many were beginning to leave. Only those intending to keep watch into the day remained. Kate indicated that she was ready to leave. They took their leave of the dead man. With the watchers on the chairs around the walls and the whiteness of the linen and the flowers and the candles, the small room looked beautiful in the stillness of the ceremony. Ruttledge looked at the face carefully and did not think, in spite of all that Patrick said, that it could have been greatly improved.

Jamesie and Mary insisted on walking them all the way to the lake. After the warmth of the house their own tiredness met them in the coldness of the morning breeze from the lake. The moon had paled and the grey light was now on everything. □

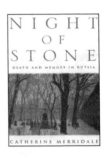
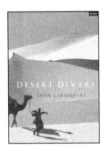

THE SEA HORSE AND THE ALMOND

Paul Broks

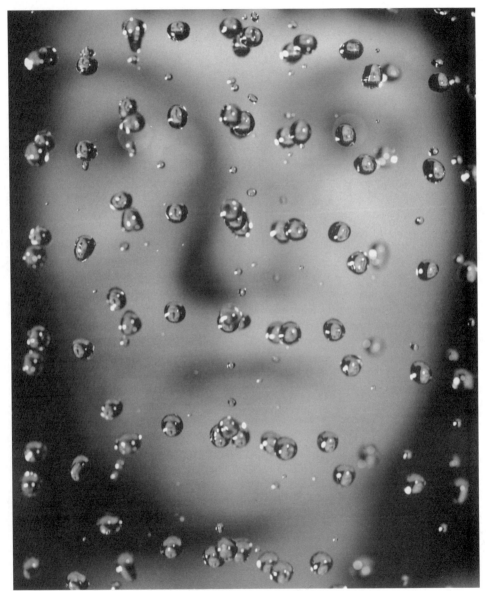

'The Observer and the Observed, #11' by Susan Derges, 1991

Whisky, on top of the wine, was a mistake. This morning it has left me feeling fractionally too *embodied*; too aware of the weight and movement of my head, the bulk of my tongue. I woke late, breaking from a thick crust of sleep and mediocre dreams not much before eight. Now, half an hour later, I'm walking to work, without hurry but still keeping pace with the traffic. It's a couple of miles. It will do me good. Down past the parade of shops and the odd juxtaposition of casino and funeral parlour, past terraced houses and the fringe of the park and on up the other side of the urban valley to the drab monolith on the brow of the hill, visible from most of the city: the District General Hospital. Today it is framed by a sky the colour of cement.

Deep inside this place lies Naomi. It is her nineteenth birthday and she is on a hospital bed which is being pushed by a porter along shiny floors, into lifts and out across more shiny floors. Naomi is tired. She has been awake since the break of day, well before the neurophysiology technicians came to glue the electrodes to her scalp, leaving her with a Medusa's head of angry serpents.

Arriving at nine, I go straight to the angiography suite where preparations are in hand for Naomi's ordeal. The central chamber is small, about the size of a suburban living room, brightly lit and crammed with X-ray equipment, monitors and control panels. The centrepiece is the narrow bed upon which the patient, when she arrives, will be laid. The way it tapers at one end reminds me of an ironing board. In the corner a quiet man from Medical Illustrations is setting up his video camera ready for the show. EEG technicians in white and radiographers in blue filter in and look busy. What we are about to do is anaesthetize one half of Naomi's brain in order to expose the workings of the other. With a bolus of sodium amytal delivered to each cerebral hemisphere via the internal carotid artery, a fast-acting sedative direct to the brain, we are going to isolate and interrogate one side of her head and then the other. This procedure is known as a Wada test. Strictly speaking, 'anaesthetize' is incorrect since the brain has no sensory receptors of any kind. It is always in a state of anaesthesia; numb and dark as a tomb.

Marcus, the radiologist, appears. *Do we have a patient?* We do. Naomi is sitting up in her mobile bed, which has been parked just down the corridor, nowhere in particular. It has arrived as if by time-lapse photography moving from one indeterminate station to the next, and now here she is. She looks lonely, so I go and chat with her a while. I wish her Happy Birthday.

I like Naomi. I've got to know her quite well these past few months as she has negotiated the hoops and hurdles of the obstacle course of clinical investigations that will lead finally, she hopes, to the neurosurgeon's list, to the operating theatre and to the carving away of a small streak of scarred brain tissue, the source of her debilitating epilepsy. Naomi has hopes and ambitions, and she has a boyfriend. Her hopes go without saying. She has faith in the doctors and surgeons and is full of expectation that they will, in the end, solve her problems, despite the signal failures of medical science in this regard up to now. Her ambitions, not unrealistic if the fits die down, are to go to university to study history and, should she accomplish the statutory twelve months free of seizures, to apply for a driver's licence. I've forgotten the boyfriend's name. He seemed pleasant enough when I met him; hopeful, too, but appropriately troubled by the prospect of major surgery on his sweetheart's sweet head. And by the possibility of failure; the possibility that the operation, the last resort, will not work. You're *such* a pessimist, Naomi told him when I saw them both in the clinic. I like Naomi. My problem with her, if it is a problem, is her incorrigible optimism. Naomi, you are *such* an optimist. Be troubled. We are going to do difficult things which may not work, bear this in mind. The surgeon, if he gets his hands on you, is going to open your head and take a piece of you away, an important piece, not a little finger nail or even a little finger. How important? Well, to be honest, Naomi, we don't really know. And still the fits might resist and prevail. Too much hope and faith can be counterproductive. I think these things but, of course, this is hardly the time to voice my concerns. This is a time for platitudinous reassurance; it's not my strongest suit, but is a necessary part of the repertoire and well practised.

Meanwhile, Marcus is sifting through his tray of paraphernalia and realizes something is missing. *Do we have any amytal?* No, not yet. Our batch of the stuff looked suspiciously cloudy and was thought to be contaminated. But, no problem, a phone call to

Pharmacy and I am assured that a supply of the drug is already on its way from the Radcliffe Infirmary. Why it has to come all the way from Oxford I've no idea. I don't enquire.

This morning's Wada test is the final hurdle. If Naomi passes the test she can go on the surgeon's list. She is prepared. She will know what to expect. Yesterday she rehearsed the procedure with Rachel, one of my colleagues from the Neuropsychology Unit, who got her to lie on her back, raise both arms to the vertical, count up to twenty, imagine (at around ten) that the left arm has become limp, and let it drop to her side. This will be the consequence of the drug perfusing the right side of the brain. Then they went through the motions of testing basic speech comprehension and limb control by having Naomi perform a series of simple actions (*touch your nose, close your eyes, blow*). Next, she was asked to recite the days of the week, then count backwards from ten. A picture was produced, busy, full of detail and action, and Naomi was asked to describe the scene (*a man up a ladder, a boy with a ball, a girl, a kite, a dog and a cat, a pond, some ducks*): childish, playschool images. She also had to name a series of objects, read a word, a sentence, and do some simple arithmetic. Sodium amytal is fast-acting but its effects are short-lived. In the test proper the injected hemisphere will sleep for just two or three minutes and this is all the time we have to conduct our business with the other hemisphere, its wakeful twin, so the instructions and the questions come thick and fast. The rehearsal, though, would have been a breeze. Naomi is bright and articulate and, for now, has the benefit of a whole brain.

Rachel arrives carrying a clipboard, a stopwatch and two black ring binders, one large, one small. On her way into the angio suite she exchanges smiles and words with Naomi whose bed has now been pushed even closer to the main door. Rachel has a smile for me too. She already knows about the delay with the amytal and suggests there's time for a coffee. It's not caffeine she needs, it's nicotine, so I get the coffee and biscuits while she lights one of her needle-thin roll-ups in the smoking room. Then, after the cigarette, the coffee and the snacks, Rachel and I sit next to the machine that spills out the X-ray negatives and we flip through Naomi's case notes.

The history is unremarkable. It all started with a fever when she was a small child. She'd been off-colour for a couple of days but seemed to pick up. Her mother wasn't sure, but in the end dropped Naomi off at nursery school on her way to work. Midway through the morning she fell asleep in the sandpit, or so the teachers thought, but when she wouldn't be roused they sent for an ambulance. She went shaky before she fell asleep, the other children said. The doctor said it was probably a febrile convulsion: not to worry, a lot of kids are prone to fits if their temperature climbs too high. They mostly grow out of it. And so, it seemed, she did. There were no more fever fits and although she still had a tendency to get high temperatures her mother was vigilant, dosed her with Calpol and sponged her with cool water until her bones shivered and the temperature dropped.

But the fits returned at the dawn of puberty, on the first tides of menstruation. They were shadowy figures with a pungent smell of electricity. That's how Naomi experienced them. A sense of presence, but no one there; a strange smell. Indescribable. Electricity came closest. Odd, she now thinks, that something that doesn't really have any odour should best describe the smell of a seizure. But then she has read up on her condition and thinks it is apt to see epilepsy so often described as an electrical storm in the brain. She knew all along it was something electrical.

The shadowy presence hovering at the visual periphery and the electrical smell are components of the epileptic aura, a state of altered awareness that serves as a forewarning of the approaching seizure. Another feature of Naomi's aura is also quite typical of this form of epilepsy: it's called a rising epigastric sensation. She describes it as being like a little sparrow fluttering its wings in the pit of her stomach, ascending to her throat where it becomes trapped and struggles to escape, choking her and provoking nausea. Up to this point, under the gathering gloom of the brainstorm, in the company of the empty shadows and the sparrow, she remains fully aware of what is happening to her, and can articulate her experiences. Then the storm breaks and the seizure moves into a phase which takes her beyond the bounds of conscious reflection and subsequent recall. Now her eyes are glazed and empty. She tugs at her clothes, she smacks her lips and wipes her nose repeatedly with the back of her hand. I've seen her in this state. The vacuum of the shadowy presence has sucked Naomi away. She is an unconscious automaton, acting out a purposeless, robotic routine.

After the tone poem of the aura—the unformed images, the unnameable scents—and after the rhythmic automatisms, there sometimes follows a third, catastrophic, movement. About one in five of her attacks develops into a full-blown, 'tonic-clonic', generalized seizure, what would once have been called a *grand mal*. There are two distinct phases. First, the tonic phase: her muscles suddenly contract and she falls to the ground, sometimes spurting blood as her jaw clamps shut and her teeth sink into her tongue. She stops breathing and, unconscious, she urinates. Then comes the swing into the clonic phase: demonic and discordant, convulsive, limbs jerking mechanically for several minutes, followed by release into a deep sleep. Despite inventive cocktails of anti-epileptic medication with dosages almost to toxic levels, Naomi's seizures have steadily increased in frequency to the extent that the visitations are an almost daily occurrence, worse still in the pre-menstrual phase. She is, you will understand, desperate for a cure and willing to take risks.

I notice that Naomi has brought her mascot with her, a soft toy, a ragged little giraffe. For reasons of hygiene this is as far as he will be allowed to go. Where's the Dostoevsky? I ask. The giraffe and a copy of Dostoevsky's *The Idiot* lay side by side on Naomi's hospital bed when she first came in for investigation. Strange bedfellows, I'd said, or some such. It's about epilepsy, she said. Dostoevsksy had epilepsy. I should read it. I'll get around to it one day, I told her. I doubt that I shall.

Naomi's planned operation has an ungainly name: amygdalohippocampectomy, so called because it involves removal of the amygdala (from the Greek for almond) and part of the adjacent structure, the hippocampus (sea horse). There is an almond and a sea horse in each hemisphere of the brain. The purpose of the Wada procedure is to clear a way for the operation. We know that it is the right side of Naomi's brain which bears the scar tissue and drives the seizures because we've seen the brain scans and we've logged the clinical signs. But we are also making an assumption, possibly unwarranted, that her left hemisphere, which looks normal, is also functioning normally. This Wada test will help determine whether the supposedly healthy side of her brain is indeed healthy and performing as it should. (It is 'Wada', by the way, not 'WADA' as I've just been reading in the case notes; a common error. The procedure is named for Juhn Wada, the Japanese-Canadian neurologist who first proposed its use. It must be disappointing to be elevated to the status of an eponym only to be continually mistaken for an acronym.) We need to be as sure as we can be that there is no 'silent lesion' on that healthy side; in other words, a malfunction that has not declared itself on any of the brain scans. Appearances can be deceptive. Brain tissue can look clean and plump and healthy but, without putting it to the test, you can't be sure of its functional capacity.

One of the targets of surgery, the hippocampus, is a vital component of the brain's memory circuitry, essential for laying down new traces. We need to know, above all, whether the left hemisphere of Naomi's brain is up to the task of sustaining basic memory functions. To the extent that each of us is the sum of our memories, the hippocampus is the instrument by means of which we assemble ourselves. Everything accessible to conscious recall has been registered and recorded through the channels of the hippocampus. Think. What were you doing ten minutes ago? Who was the last person you spoke to? What did you have for breakfast? What did you do yesterday, last weekend? When was the last time you wept, and why? Conjure an image of your first school, the name of your teacher, your best friend, your first kiss. And then, stretching to the mental horizon, rising through the storms and sunshine of personal experience, picture the towering stacks of information in the public domain, the raw materials of culture, the stuff that gives you common currency with others in your society. What does the word *democracy* mean (or *word*, or *the*, or *mean*)? How do you use a telephone? Who is the president of the United States? At what temperature does water freeze? Who wrote *King Lear*? What is the function of the liver? All this information, personal and public, finds its way into the metropolis of memory by way of the hippocampus. As an aid to recall, medieval scholars developed elaborate, architectural systems of mental imagery—'Theatres of Memory', 'Memory Palaces'—through which they would take purposeful, imaginal strolls depositing or retrieving nuggets of information at strategic locations as they went. I like the idea that the keeper of the gates of the Memory Palace should take the name of so ambiguous and fragile a creature as the sea horse. All it would take is a twist or a slip of the surgeon's knife to finish off this delicate creature and close the gates for good. The flow of information would stop. If, as planned, the surgeon were to remove the right hippocampus but it turned out that Naomi had no spare capacity in the left, the operation would, in a sense, cause Naomi herself to stop. She would form no new memories of events or facts beyond her present age of nineteen. It would not prevent her from growing old, but her ageing body would forever house the mind of a nineteen-year-old girl.

In the early days of epilepsy surgery, the 1950s, there were some catastrophes of this sort. As a result of surgery to both sides of their brains a handful of people, most famously a young mechanic known as patient 'HM', ended up with a dense and irreversible amnesia, unable to retain new information for more than a few minutes at a time, and so unable to establish new memories. You could visit HM every day for a year and each time he would greet you as a stranger. Leave the room for ten minutes on any one of these visits and when you returned he would have not the slightest idea who you were. Since those early days the surgeons have restricted their interventions to just one side of the brain but, even so, there have been some similar disasters in cases where, prior to surgery, it had not been established that the other side was in good working order. Wada testing will provide an assurance that Naomi can proceed to surgery without significant risk of a devastating post-operative amnesia like HM's (or not, as the case may be). That's the reason we're here today, I remind myself, going through these arcane rituals. We want Naomi to continue in mind as well as body.

What of the amygdala, neighbour to the hippocampus and the other target of surgery? We understand less about this little structure, but if the hippocampus is the gateway to memory then think of the amygdala as housing the levers of emotion. Through its numerous interconnections it links the information-processing activities of the higher, cortical areas of the brain (the machineries of language, perception and rational thought) to deeper, older, structures involved in the regulation of emotion and motivation. In short, it tells us how to feel about what we are thinking and perceiving, and how to act on those feelings. Patients with damage to the amygdala on both sides of the brain inhabit a world devoid of natural emotional contour and colour. Diminished insight into their own feelings and behaviour is mirrored by a distorted perception of the emotional lives of others, too, doubling the damage to social competence. Suffice to say that the stakes are high for Naomi: memory and emotion. We need to get this right.

The amytal arrives, delivered to Main Reception by a motorcycle courier. He hands over a Jiffy bag which a nurse opens to find two phials containing a plain liquid, the stuff that will shortly work its spell on Naomi's brain. Our patient is now stretched out on the special bed, at the centre of things, waiting, her head resting on a small, square cushion at the tapering end. She is covered to the neck with a green surgical sheet except for an exposed patch around her groin, where, having administered a local anaesthetic, and made a small incision, Marcus is working to gain access to the femoral artery. The young woman's face at the top of the sheet and this framed expanse of pale flesh and pubic hair (and now blood from the cut) seem quite unrelated. Many people are surprised to learn that the most feasible route to the brain for these purposes is by way of the groin.

The catheter, a length of ultra-fine plastic tubing, is inserted and Marcus pushes it, inch by inch, along the femoral artery, up through the abdomen and into the chest. Its journey is visible, magnified grainily in spectral shades of grey, on the X-ray monitors. I watch as it finds its way to Naomi's heart and from there to the junction with the internal carotid. She, too, is watching. She can see her insides on the monitors suspended just above and in front of Marcus which, with exquisite integration of hand and eye, he uses to find his way from groin to gut to heart to brain. Next, a radio-opaque dye is pumped through the newly installed plastic piping to flood the blood vessels of the brain, enabling Marcus to take a few X-ray snaps. In this way we confirm that we have reached our intended destination on the cerebrovascular map and that there is no significant seepage of fluid from one side of the brain to the other. Stationed at her middle, Marcus offers Naomi an occasional word of reassurance, glances now and then in her direction, means well, but the exchanges between them are perfunctory. Naomi, for her part, is being a good patient. Her body is passive, receptive, the face betraying no trace of emotion. Almost no trace. A nurse goes over and squeezes her hand, brushes a strand of hair from her forehead, and her eyes moisten.

We have here Naomi the body, Naomi the mind and Naomi the person. These, at least, are the differences of emphasis across the professional divisions of labour. Marcus works in the realm of the flesh. He knows the intricacies of the vascular system and is on good terms with the ghosts of his X-ray machine. I, the neuropsychologist, will shortly signal a pharmacological invasion and deconstruction of Naomi's mind, which, for a few minutes, will enforce a radically different and quite unnatural configuration. The nurse, for now, is with Naomi the person. Did I imagine a tear in her eye too? This procedure, the Wada test, is an event of considerable significance for all three Naomis. Passing the test opens the door to surgical treatment of the root cause of her epilepsy and with it the possibility of relief from the random physical assaults of seizure. It would, with luck, also allow the cessation of long-term, insidiously damaging, anti-epileptic drugs. Surgery, though, is surgery, entailing the loss of a portion of brain, no more than the size of a thumb perhaps, but part of the engine of the soul.

We're all set to start when a drilling sound breaks in rudely from the floor above. Then the noise subsides. We wait. Do we dispatch someone to find the driller, or do we take a chance and proceed? We wait some minutes more. Silence. So we continue. Naomi has her arms raised and she begins to count. I look to Rachel standing opposite with her black folders, stopwatch and clipboard, ready to assist with the test materials and to record responses. The neurophysiologists are a few feet back monitoring every squiggle of brainwave activity being siphoned through the long bridal veil of multicoloured leads attached to Naomi's head. After a nod from me, Marcus starts to inject the amytal.

The drug takes effect within a few seconds and I grab Naomi's arm as it swoons, guiding it to rest at her side. At that moment of collapse, the catching of the lifeless arm, something collapses inside me too and I catch myself thinking, *I have no desire to be here.* I am thinking that maybe I would prefer a different sort of job. And, if not quite *anything* else, then *something* else, well away from this mind-meddling. But here before me now lies Naomi, and I have work to do and, after all, better to be doing this to a relative stranger than to someone you love. That would be unbearable. She looks remarkably calm and ordinary given that her right cerebral hemisphere, half her brain, is now temporarily defunct. How *ordinary* she looks. How deceptive.

What are we doing to this young woman? A Wada test: a routine pre-operative test procedure that serves a clear medical purpose. But my question has a different thrust. It has more to do with the primitive illusions of vitality that fill the space behind the face. I'm curious to know what is happening, behind those pale eyes, to 'Naomi the person', a question entirely peripheral to the immediate medical concerns. Our procedure is pharmacological, not surgical, the effects are transient and reversible, but for those few minutes that the drug works its suppressive effects on the injected hemisphere we are, effectively, amputating one side of the brain. I wonder if the forced asymmetry of cerebral capacity also enforces an asymmetry of self? By engaging with just one half of Naomi's brain are we doing business with just one half of Naomi?

I first heard of Wada testing as an undergraduate. There was a great deal of interest in the duality of the brain, in the idea that, for some purposes, the left and the right sides perform distinct, though complementary, functions: left hemisphere for language, right for spatial awareness; left for rhythm, right for melody; rationality/ intuition; analysis/synthesis, and so on. There was some good science, but much wild speculation. At the centre of attention at that time, scientifically and imaginatively, were the so-called 'split-brain' studies. Split-brain surgery was a radical method of treating people who suffered from certain severe and intractable forms of epilepsy (of a different sort, incidentally, than Naomi's). The idea was that by cutting the corpus callosum, the main band of nerve fibres connecting the two hemispheres, it should be possible to confine the abnormal electrical activity to one side of the brain and so prevent the development of major seizures. I was not much concerned with the clinical aspects of the operation, having by then developed no great interest in epilepsy.

What intrigued me was that these people, the split-brain patients, were *thought experiments made flesh*. They fell into the category of philosophical conundrum that also includes the 'brain in the vat', the 'brain transplant' and a whole bundle of Star Trek fantasies about teleportation and mind duplication. Thought experiments are 'Imagine if…' scenarios designed to challenge our ordinary intuitions. In the seventeenth century John Locke explored the concept of personal identity by imagining an exchange of brains between a prince and a cobbler. It's psychological continuity that counts, he concluded. The prince 'goes with' his brain and now finds 'himself' in the body of the cobbler (and vice versa). More recent variations on the theme, some inspired directly by the split-brain cases, are less straightforward. What if someone's cerebral hemispheres are divided and transferred separately (memories, character traits and all) to the heads of two different people? Similarly, what if you were to swap a hemisphere with your best friend, or your worst enemy? Which of you is which? There would be some continuity in these cases, but not unity. And where does that leave the idea of personal identity?

The split-brain cases were for real. Real people with a real and irreversible surgical division of the brain. Inevitably they provoked as much philosophical interest as scientific. Like many people who took an interest, my own imagination was captured by the suggestion that, in dividing the brain, the surgeon's knife was also dividing consciousness, dividing the person. The very idea of bisecting the living, conscious brain clean down the middle was bizarre and absurd. It had a touch of the macabre, a whiff of the chamber of horrors. There are many weird creatures in the menagerie of neurological disorder but the split-brain patients were of the purest strangeness. I was drawn in. 'Strange cases', closely observed and well described, have an important place in the neurological literature. Alexander Romanovich Luria, an important figure in the history of neuropsychology, was an acknowledged master of case description and a persuasive advocate of the value of 'romantic science'. 'When done properly,' he said, 'observation accomplishes the classical aim of explaining facts, while not losing sight of the romantic aim of preserving the manifold richness of the subject.' I don't hesitate to recommend the popular writings of Luria, Oliver Sacks and others to students as a way of introducing them to the field. But I recognize that part of the appeal, part of that 'manifold richness of the subject', has little to do with science or philosophy. It has more to do with the intrinsic fascination of the aberrant and the bizarre. *Morbid fascination* would not be too wide of the mark.

In this light, neurological case histories have a certain Gothic appeal. Replace the dark forests, the craggy mountains, the ruined abbeys, and the elemental storms of the traditional Gothic tale with a desolate urban landscape. Let a dilapidated modern hospital stand for the crumbling medieval castle with its labyrinthine passages, gloomy dungeons and torture chambers. The white-coated mad scientist in his cobwebbed laboratory, surrounded by Van de Graaff generators, lightning conductors and the paraphernalia of alchemy, becomes the green-gowned surgeon in the sterile gleam of a hi-tech operating theatre, knife in hand, ready to rework the slimy fabric of the cerebrum. At the centre of things is the monster, waiting for the life force from the heavens to jolt its dead limbs, and the patient, brain naked to the air waiting for the blade.

And here I am now, in the shadow of Dr Frankenstein, having pharmacologically separated one half of Naomi's brain from the other, about to engage in a dialogue with...with what? A person? A half-person? Half a brain? It's difficult to say.

I find that Naomi seems to have cheered up a little. She is garrulous, chirpy and chatty, and she answers my questions obligingly. She passes my little tests with hardly a moment's hesitation. Those vital three minutes fly by. You've done very well, I tell her. Now just rest quietly for a few minutes.

We wait ten minutes. The effect of the drug wears off: the left arm has regained full sensorimotor function and the EEG trace has returned to normal. Her eyes are closed and Naomi looks as if she's asleep. We know she isn't from the rhythms of the EEG—her brain is idling in a comfortable alpha rhythm, indicating relaxed wakefulness. It's time for the next part of the procedure; to see whether she has any memory for the test material she was presented with during the amytal phase. For Naomi, this element of the ritual is critical. Failure here would outweigh success at any other stage. If she is to proceed to surgery she must pass these simple memory tests. First, I will challenge her with a series of recall tasks ('I asked you to remember a phrase; what was it?' 'I showed you a picture; what was going on in the picture?' 'You saw some objects; what were they?'). Should she fail at any stage she will be presented with the materials in a forced-choice recognition format. That is, she will be invited to select target items from sets of alternative possibilities. Recall carries greater weight than recognition and there is a simple formula for deriving an overall score.

We are meant to keep reasonably quiet between the different phases of testing so as not to cause undue distraction for the patient but now, just as I am about to begin testing Naomi's memory, there is a commotion outside in the corridor, someone in a blind rage shouting, *No! No! NO! This is NOT acceptable!* I catch a glimpse of one of the consultants strutting past, bellowing straight ahead at some miserable junior trailing several paces behind, *This is not acceptable!* He is tall, red-faced, straight-backed, full of explosive menace. That drilling noise has also started up again, though more distant and muffled. Will someone tell that man to shut up, says Marcus. No one does, but he falls silent anyway, quite suddenly, as if the driller drilled him. The drilling continues for a few seconds then stops.

She's not doing so well. Come on, Naomi, come *on*, I'm thinking. The picture, Naomi, what can you remember? Perplexity, then a burst of information—*A man on a ladder, a dog chasing a cat, a pond with some ducks on it, a girl with a kite, a boy with a ball.* All of this, unfortunately, is from the picture she was shown at yesterday's rehearsal. She recalls some of the single objects, though, and some words, and picks up points in the recognition tasks.

Formal testing completed, we customarily ask the patient about their experience of the whole process of injection and testing. Partly, this is to determine if there were any special perceptual difficulties we need to take into account in interpreting the results—were they experiencing visual or auditory disturbances, for example? It is also useful to get some feeling for the patient's insight into their own performance. Naomi's response is fairly characteristic of someone whose right hemisphere has just been closed down, giving the left free rein: No problem; what's all the fuss about? She was not aware of any special difficulties. It was a breeze, just like the rehearsal. The articulate left hemisphere is the eternal optimist.

It'll be an hour before we repeat the procedure with the injection of the left hemisphere. The lifts are temporarily out of action so I take the stairs ten floors up to my office and there, waiting for me, is a young woman. This is Katrina, the new trainee psychologist. I realize immediately who she is, and that I'm two hours late for our appointment. I'd forgotten all about her. Your secretary let me in, she says. I went straight to the angio suite, I tell her, as if this is an acceptable explanation. You've been here all this time, since eight-thirty? I'm breathless from the climb. I've loosened my tie and I feel sweaty and dishevelled. My new trainee looks cool and immaculate. Most of them do. She has spent the time productively, reading a textbook. No thanks, she won't have a coffee but she delves into her rucksack and produces a selection of herbal teas. Sit down and get your breath back, she advises me. I drink coffee, she drinks camomile and honey and accepts my invitation to observe the rest of the Wada.

D isturbance, or complete loss, of speech is the usual response to injection of the left hemisphere, but in other ways the effects are less predictable. Some patients appear confused and disoriented, some become agitated, some disinhibited. Others, like Naomi now, just look desolate. Her head is still but her eyes flash left and right. She will not respond to my simple commands: *Touch your nose, Naomi, touch your nose*. Nothing. When we get to Days of the Week she is clearly trying very hard, but all we get is, *fa-fa-fa-fa-fa*. On Counting Back from Ten she approximates the number words but gets locked in a perseverative loop: *tem, nipe, ape, ape, ape ape...* She looks at the busy picture and has an urge to point at things, *da, da*, she says. For a while she seems to be warming to the task, appears engaged, but her concentration suddenly fades. At one point she looks me in the eye and chuckles wickedly. But then another wave of emotion moves her in a different direction. Her eyes start darting left and right again. She looks terrified; she looks *feral*. Fine, Naomi, just fine, I say as we complete the routine. Relax, we're nearly there now.

We retire to a side room leaving Naomi to rest and recover from the amytal. The conversation turns to epileptic auras. I explain to

Katrina that some people experience more complex hallucinations than Naomi's in the lead-up to a seizure and, occasionally, they're quite bizarre. I recall a neurologist once telling me about one of his patients whose aura would begin with a strong smell of celery, which was followed by an impression of a vivid green field. White railings appeared. It was a racecourse and, next, the horses and jockeys entered the scene. The jockeys were always nursery rhyme characters and the race was invariably won by Humpty Dumpty. It was always the same, like rerunning a silly, surrealist film; surreal but relatively benign. Other people have more intimidating experiences. One of my own patients would feel a sense of apprehension, rising to terror and culminating in the appearance, through the wall, of a medieval knight brandishing a bloody sword. Full-blown hallucinations of this sort are unusual but feelings of unfocused terror are not. There is a name for this, *ictal fear*. It is the handiwork of the diseased amygdala. I heard another strange example recently at a clinical case presentation. This was a boy whose seizures were prefigured by hallucinations of a hippopotamus and a monk he would often see sitting on the stairs, face hidden by the shadow of his cowl. It was one of those pygmy hippos the size of a small pig and it would scuttle by without a sound. The monk just sat. The woman sitting next to me in the lecture theatre, one of the junior doctors, had been on the verge of nodding off to sleep but lifted her head from her hands and sat up to take notice at the mention of the hippo and the monk. She began to scribble something on her notepad. Leaning across, I could see it was a rhyme: 'There's a boy who hallucinates hippos/And a monk who sits on the stair/And once a cadaverous dragon/Making love to a silvery bear'. And by an odd coincidence, later that day, on the way to the supermarket, I saw someone dressed as a monk. Katrina is not sure whether to believe any of this, though it's all true. It's also true that I bought some monkfish medallions at the supermarket. But I withhold this snippet. Katrina would think it ridiculous. She is not yet comfortable with the absurd.

The speech disturbance confirms for us that Naomi's language control centres are located primarily in the left hemisphere. This is relevant for the surgeon to know, giving him greater licence for excursions into the right temporal cortex should this be necessary, with minimal risk of disrupting language functions. And when it comes to memory testing, there are no surprises. Her almost total failure to recall any of the test items confirms that we have just been placing unreasonable demands on her damaged right hippocampus: taunting the crippled sea horse. The one exception is her accurate recall of the mental arithmetic task. Under the drug she had stared at the sum printed on one of Rachel's cards and said, *Sebber, seffen, fife, fife, five.* Now, correctly, she recalls, *Four plus five equals nine.* I've seen this several times before. Somehow, I think, the numerical information must gain back door access to the left hemisphere in a way that the verbal information cannot.

Recall of the experience of left hemisphere suppression is, again, less predictable than for shutting down the right hemisphere. Different patients show different degrees of insight. Some have no recollection of events at all, at least nothing available for verbal articulation. Others have at least partial insight into the frustrations of their temporary loss of speech. Some, as Naomi is doing, just tell tales. Oh, it was OK, she says. Well, perhaps she did have some slight problems with her speech at first, but after that she was fine. Well, maybe, it was a bit different than first time around, but not much, not really. No, it wasn't too bad. Quite enjoyable. This is the left hemisphere confabulating again, filling the gap. It does this all the time, for all of us, every waking moment. It edits our conscious experiences, makes them comprehensible and palatable, puts a gloss on things, justifies our every action or inaction. The brain's spin doctor.

Two things disturb me during the night. One is the hoarse, sotto voce bark of an urban fox, receding in triplets down the street. The other is a fragment of dream, sharp enough to wake me. I stagger, giddy from being spun in a large machine they called an Accellotron. It has made me invisible, temporarily. I see my daughter sitting out in the garden and approach her. I speak. She looks towards me but her eyes continue searching. I have, truly, become invisible. There's no way I can reassure her. I touch her hand and she becomes terrified. I become terrified.

The Sea Horse and the Almond

Next day, first thing, I'm sitting in my office with Rachel, watching the video of Naomi's Wada test. It's easy to miss important points of detail in the patient's responses so we always check the video. There *was* something I failed to catch, as it happens. It comes during the time that Naomi's left hemisphere is suppressed and the origins of her fragmented, mumbling speech are uncertain. Is this the incoherent stammering of the left hemisphere running on empty, or is it emanating from the right side of the brain? For a moment, her confusion seems to subside and there is a look of accusation in her eyes. *Watafamadooneer*, she seems to be saying, *Watafamadooneer*. I listen closely a second and third time and realize it's a question, *Watafamadooneer?* The penny drops. *What the fuck am I doing here?*

☐

NOTES ON CONTRIBUTORS

Paul Broks is a neuropsychologist and clinical lecturer based at the University of Plymouth. He has written for *Prospect* magazine. His book, *Into the Silent Land*, will be published by Atlantic Books.

Anne Enright's most recent novel, *What Are You Like?* (Vintage/Atlantic Monthly Press) won the Encore award and was shortlisted for the Whitbread Novel Award in 2000.

James Hamilton-Paterson's most recent novel, *Loving Monsters*, is published by Granta Books. He lives in Italy and the Philippines.

Jackie Kay's short-story collection, *Why Don't You Stop Talking?* will be published next year by Picador. Her novel, *Trumpet,* won the *Guardian* Fiction Prize in 1998. She is a poet and lives in Manchester.

Norman Lewis is the author of thirteen novels and fourteen books of travel and memoir. 'An Amateur Spy in Arabia' is adapted from his fifteenth, *A Voyage by Dhow*, which will be published by Jonathan Cape this year.

Alex Majoli was born in Ravenna, Italy, in 1971. He became a full member of Magnum Photos this year. His previous projects include *Leros* (Berlin Press Westzone) about an asylum for the insane in Greece.

Adam Mars-Jones's books include *Lantern Lecture* and *The Waters of Thirst*. He was one of Granta's Best of Young British Novelists in both 1983 and 1993.

John McGahern lives on a farm in County Leitrim, Ireland. 'Johnny' will form part of his forthcoming novel, *That They May Face the Rising Sun*, which will be published by Faber in the UK and Knopf in the US in Spring 2002.

Michael Mewshaw is the author of eight novels and five books of non-fiction. His memoir, *A Writer's Account*, will be published next year.

Richard Murphy was born in the west of Ireland in 1927. An autobiography, *The Kick*, will be published by Granta Books in 2002. His *Collected Poems 1952–2000* are published by the Gallery Press in Ireland and Wake Forest University Press in America. He lives in Dublin and Durban, South Africa.

Alexander Stille is a freelance writer based in New York. His book on new technologies and old cultures, *The Future of the Past*, will be published in Spring 2002 by Picador in the UK and Farrar, Straus & Giroux in the US.

Paul Theroux's most recent novel, *Hotel Honolulu*, is published by Hamish Hamilton in the UK and Houghton Mifflin in the US. 'At the Villa Moro' is drawn from a work in progress.

Susan Derges—photograph on page 238—has a new permanent exhibition at the Museum of the History of Science, University of Oxford, which opens on October 11, 2001.